D1320040

W·J·CASH:
Southern Prophet

W·J·CASH:
Southern Prophet

A BIOGRAPHY AND READER

BY *Joseph·L·Morrison*

19   67

Alfred·A·Knopf NEW YORK

Library of Congress Catalog Card Number: 67–18611

THIS IS A BORZOI BOOK
PUBLISHED BY ALFRED A. KNOPF, INC.

Manufactured in the United States of America.

FIRST EDITION

The photograph used on the frontispiece was taken by
Alfred A. Knopf in 1939.

For Lucy and Peter

PREFACE

I saw W. J. Cash once, and at that time he was talking his heart out about editorial integrity to a group of starry-eyed high-school journalists. The time was May 3, 1941, and the place was the campus of the University of North Carolina at Chapel Hill. I was a recent graduate who was doing some tentative college teaching while awaiting a military call-up, and I looked upon the prestigious speaker with as much envy as admiration. He was then the associate editor of the Charlotte *News,* had recently written the much-admired book *The Mind of the South,* and had just been awarded a Guggenheim fellowship, which he and his wife were about to enjoy in Mexico. The largish, bald, bespectacled man impressed me deeply—as did his book, when I eventually got around to reading it after doffing a World War II uniform.

Cash's suicide a scant two months after I saw him led me, in the years that followed, to ponder his bitter fate and to pick up random biographical data that later became the nucleus of a systematic search. So it was that I finally came to publish my preliminary findings in an article, "The Obsessive 'Mind' of W. J. Cash" (*Virginia Quarterly Review,* Spring 1965), which sufficiently interested Cash's original publisher, Mr. Alfred A. Knopf, so that he proposed that I write the present book. The completed work includes a Reader portion, which is intended to supplement the biographical study and to satisfy those who want to read more written by Cash.

To confer upon Cash the title of prophet is simply to recognize the truly prophetic nature of his role, that of analytical interpreter. Perhaps often "a prophet is not without honour, save in his own country, and in his own house," but Cash's prestige is not so restricted, for the South of 1941 did honor him. However, he was honored for comfortable, and therefore wrong, reasons. Discerning critics praised his insights in interpreting the Southern past, but they failed to appreciate his relevance to the future. They preferred not to inquire too closely into the brooding and foreboding note on which Cash ended his book. Without spelling out the future in explicit detail—nobody could in 1940, the year in which Cash completed his manuscript—Cash looked grimly upon a Second World War from which America could not remain detached, and upon a postwar South in which the shibboleths of the past would no longer serve. His life's experience had taught him the South's infinite capacity for self-deception, and he concluded as if to say: "My fellow Southerners, I love you but you have fooled yourselves. You have been misled by your own myths and the time is short; you cannot secede from the twentieth century."

Early in my study I found that Cash had disliked writing letters and hence had left all too few. This circumstance now deepens my gratitude to the manuscript repositories that were able to contribute to this study. The largest single hoard of W. J. Cash letters reposes in the office files of Alfred A. Knopf, Inc. The firm kindly opened these to my inspection and photoduplicated all letters, both to and from the late author, for my use. Mr. Knopf also allowed me to use his personal correspondence with Cash during 1941; these letters are in the Manuscript Department of the New York

Public Library. Other manuscript repositories to which I acknowledge my debt are: the Library of Congress, for the Josephus Daniels Papers; the Southern Historical Collection, Chapel Hill, North Carolina, for the Howard Odum and Jonathan Daniels Papers; the University of Florida Library, for the Lillian Smith and Paula Snelling Papers; the Joint University Libraries, Nashville, Tennessee, for the Edwin Mims Papers; the Margaret Mitchell Marsh Estate, Atlanta, Georgia, for the Margaret Mitchell Marsh Papers; and the Z. Smith Reynolds Library of Wake Forest College, for the Thurman D. Kitchin Papers. Mr. R. P. Harriss of Baltimore, Maryland, made available several Cash letters in his possession.

I am also in debt to Hoyt P. Galvin, director of the Public Libraries of Charlotte and Mecklenburg County, who arranged to ship here for photoduplicating under my direction some four hundred pounds of bound volumes of the Charlotte *News*. The articles and editorials by Cash that appeared in this newspaper are the main source of the Reader portion of this book. I acknowledge too the help of the University of North Carolina at Chapel Hill, which, through its Research Council, provided a grant for secretarial assistance.

My greatest debt of all is to Cash's widow, Mary Cash Maury of Silver Spring, Maryland. She even ventured beyond personal interviewing to exchange with me a series of draft narratives—hers based on personal recollections and mine on research into documents—on Cash's last months of life. Our efforts could have been published as a coauthored article, but it was thought preferable for Mrs. Maury's first-person account to appear independently (*Red Clay Reader*, IV, 1967). Several narrative passages in my Chapter v were derived from Mrs. Maury's authoritative account; necessarily so, for she was the only eyewitness to the last episode of Cash's tragic story. In sum, as a biographer I am greatly indebted to my subject's widow, who, as his literary executrix, has permitted me full and uncensored use of her late husband's writings.

After Cash's death his widow gave all his personal papers to his sister, Mrs. Bertie Cash Elkins of Winston-Salem, North Carolina. I am greatly indebted to Mrs. Elkins, who operated above and beyond the call of duty in submitting to interviews and made freely available the family scrapbooks, letters to and from Cash, phonograph records of his "Lost Speech" at the University of Texas commencement of 1941, and—best of all—the original and two variant versions of the manuscript of *The Mind of the South,* bearing the author's personal corrections. Mrs. Elkins has also kindly granted permission to publish three hitherto unpublished works: the letter from W. J. Cash to his father, the "Report From Mexico," and the University of Texas Commencement Address of 1941, here titled "The South in a Changing World." I also had the kind cooperation, in the matter of interviews, of Cash's two brothers, Henry B. Cash and Dr. Allan H. Cash, both of Charlotte.

To this list of indebtedness must be added the host of Cash's contemporaries who gave me important aid at critical junctures. Space permits mention of only a few who were particularly helpful. Among Cash's schoolmates at Wake Forest these include Edwin Holman, Atlanta, Georgia; the late A. M. Burns, Jr., Roxboro, North Carolina; and Forrest W. Clonts, Winston-Salem, North Carolina. Among Cash's newspaper friends these include Katherine Grantham Rogers, Washington, D. C.; and John A. Daly, Brodie S. Griffith, and C. A. McKnight, all of Charlotte, North Carolina. I must not fail to mention Cash's personal physician and friend, the late Dr. Claude B. Squires, Charlotte, North Carolina, nor his literary friends the late Lillian Smith and Paula Snelling, with whom I spent one memorable afternoon atop Old Screamer Mountain at Clayton, Georgia. Miss Snelling has kindly granted permission to reprint the book review of Francis Griswold's *A Sea Island Lady* from *North Georgia Review* (later *South Today*), Spring 1940.

My University colleague Dr. George B. Tindall of the Department of History, whose special field is the history of the South, read and criticized not only the present manuscript but my preliminary article. In coping with Cash's ultimately inexplicable suicide, I had important help in shaping my thoughts at three stages of my study. At the outset, I was guided to the psychiatric literature and invited to test some tentative conclusions by Dr. Lawrence Bryskin, then resident in psychiatry at the Duke University Medical Center. As my study progressed, I was given further reading suggestions and some apt insights by Dr. Seymour Baxter, a psychiatrist engaged in private practice in Detroit, Michigan. At the last, I benefited greatly from consultation with Dr. John A. Ewing, chairman of the Department of Psychiatry at the University of North Carolinia School of Medicine. His readiness to trade common-sense questions and to read and criticize my key Chapter VI place me in his special debt.

In acknowledging help from the foregoing, I do not, of course, seek to burden them with my errors. I readily accept that responsibility myself.

JOSEPH L. MORRISON

University of North Carolina
Chapel Hill, N. C.
December 1966

CONTENTS

xiii

W·J·CASH:
Southern Prophet

CHAPTER 1

The Making
of an Iconoclast

When Wilbur Joseph Cash, an obscure North Carolina newspaperman, came forward with his original and important book *The Mind of the South* in 1941, he achieved no more than a mild *succès d'estime* that was swallowed up by his own death and by World War II. At the war's end, with a new generation of American whites and Negroes confronting one another, Cash's prophetic work gradually came into its own as obligatory reading. During this second half of the twentieth century, it has been accepted by virtually everyone that studies of the South—and, by extension, of the Negro revolution—must begin where Cash left off.

It is small wonder that the almost unknown author has won, is still winning, admiring readers, for *The Mind of the South* is an audacious tour de force that, on the whole, comes off brilliantly. In hard-burnished rhythmical prose its author undertook what no historian would dare, an interpretation of the Southern "mind" in its totality. Cash dealt masterfully with the imponderables and intangibles of the Southern experience. He developed the ingenious literary device of the plain white man, "the man at the center," who could experience all these phenomena. The book is not the product of conventional scholarship—though its author was sensitive, intelligent, and well read—but Cash nevertheless has managed to overshadow the Southern historians. Over the years his book has held up remarkably well, despite its occasional flaws, because it is both readable and profound.

Cash was ashamed—for he was no hypocrite—at the way the local Negroes idolized him as their champion when his book came out. He knew only too well that he was no activist; more than that, he was thoroughly pessimistic about chances for racial progress in the then-current atmosphere of adamant and unyielding white supremacy. Walter White, then secretary of the National Association for the Advancement of Colored People, thanked Cash for the book in the name of his organization—and what had the author done to deserve it? He had simply concluded that Southern white men, rich and poor, had always remained yoked together in their common and enforced ascendancy over the Negro, first in the days of slavery and then later in legal and extralegal white supremacy. Cash referred to this brotherhood of white men by the high-flown expression "proto-Dorian convention" (in which the common white was elevated into a position comparable to the Doric knight of ancient Sparta), but this did not in the least becloud his point that the rich white man often paid off his poorer brother in white-supremacy status instead of coin of the realm.

Union organizers wrote to thank Cash for his explanation of their failure to organize Southern workmen, which failure each had thought his own personal one—and what had the author done to deserve their thanks? He had simply popularized the findings of Professor Broadus Mitchell in showing that the Southern gentry had founded the cotton-mill industry not only in expectation of profit, but surprisingly often to provide employment for the post-Civil War surplus of white labor. Consequently—and here Cash supplied the emphasis—grateful white labor "loyally" and "patriotically" resisted labor unions. The author enlightened the union organizers still further by his discussion of the Southern "savage ideal" (violent intolerance of dissent), which, because it existed side by side with an extreme individualism in nonessentials, was often lost in the smoke screen set up by the latter. Indeed, just how strait a conformity could be enjoined in the older South was newly demonstrated during the 1950's after the school-desegregation decision of the U. S. Supreme Court, when the White Citizens Councils took over.

At the publication of *The Mind of the South*, one of the wealthiest of the textile barons, a group especially belabored in the book, came forward to thank Cash for a work that was "a cool breeze blowing through our land." The author had indeed coolly and methodically demolished the myths of Old South and New South by which twentieth-century Southerners were fooling themselves, yet his dissent was met not with savage intolerance but with respectful—even prideful—attention. Cash's immunity to bodily assault was due partly to the fact that Kluxers and their kind do not read books. More than that, however, Cash's *Mind* was so obviously foreign to the belittling and denigrating Yankee dig, so incisively accurate, that the native Southerner felt quite naked reading it. The book was obviously written, as one Southern reviewer put it, "in bitter truthfulness and love."

The Mind of the South must be understood as the fruit of a lifetime's search by a sensitive soul who strove to "understand" his native South. There is not an interval in Cash's entire adult life during which he was not either reading, writing, questioning, probing, or pondering the South's infinite variety, and especially its wrongheaded mythmaking. His book came upon the South like a sobering dash of cold water, for it was a distillation of Cash's own educative process, in which he had, in order to remain true to himself, painfully to unlearn during each new phase of growth what he had been taught during the previous one. Because his book was written in love, and because Cash was so obviously bone of the bone with the generality of Southerners, they listened thoughtfully while he lashed them with his truths: that the Old South with its vaunted aristocracy was a fairy tale; that the New South and its ideal of Progress was all too often a pretext for exploitation; that the "savage ideal" continued in effect because public opinion and the "best people" gave tacit approval to what the lynchers and Kluxers were doing; that the "proto-Dorian convention" was perpetuating racial injustice of a kind to provoke the wrath to come. Then, having had his say, and a scant five months after the publication of his book, Cash committed suicide.

One must walk softly in the presence of a mind brilliant enough to conceive such a book and seemingly imperious enough to command self-destruction. It is altogether too tempting to jump to the conclusion that Cash could no longer bear to live with the contradictions he had uncovered so close to home. That would perhaps be making too much "sense" out of so radically irrational an act. If there is, however, some kernel of truth in that hasty conjecture, one would do well to seek it in the total process by which that unusual man arrived at his conclusions, in the total context of his brief sojourn here on earth.

As a child of the New South, which he was later to probe so incisively, Cash was born in the rather drab cotton-mill town of Gaffney, South Carolina, on May 2, 1900. He was christened Joseph Wilbur—the Joseph for his maternal grandfather and the Wilbur for an admired preacher—but he grew to dislike both given names. First he reversed their order (so as to differentiate himself from his father's initials, also J. W.) and then he took to the plain reversed initials, but nobody ever called him W.J. To his family he was Wilbur, to his newspaper friends he was Jack, and to his schoolmates he was Sleepy. The "Sleepy" was acquired during high school, when he showed up one day with a bruise on his face and his schoolmates got him to explain. He had read himself to sleep on the porch one Sunday morning, and the next thing he knew he had tumbled—chair, book, and all—into the yard.

Gaffney was an inconsequential if typical mill town in the Piedmont industrial crescent that was the fruit and flowering of Henry W. Grady's New South. Nearly all of Cash's ancestors, since the early eighteenth century, had lived in the Piedmont Carolina foothills south and east of Kings Mountain, where Patrick Ferguson's redcoats had been wiped out in a turning-point battle of the Revolution. Now, in the wake of the Cotton Mill Crusade of the 1880's, Gaffney stood ringed about by a few cotton mills in which the marginal white farmers of the hills, with their wives and children, gladly sought steady employment for wages.

Gaffney's own cotton-mill crusade was a direct offshoot of the precedent set at Clifton, just outside Spartanburg twenty miles away. There the mixed motives of profit and benevolence operated on D. E. Converse, who, with business associates, bought the land and built the mills known from 1880 as Clifton Nos. 1, 2, and 3. Converse's philanthropy extended, beyond finding work for white hands, to the endowment of Converse College in Spartanburg. Gaffney's first cotton mill, the Gaffney Manufacturing Company (1893), was a prime example of community endeavor pushed mainly by one man but with the banker and other citizens subscribing to stock. The town then contained only two or three stores, two bars, and an eating place. After exerting much persuasion, the Gaffney men finally lured into their enterprise the former superintendent of the large mill at Clifton, Edward Rufus Cash. This was Wilbur Cash's Uncle Ed.

Uncle Ed later helped build and operate Limestone Mills in Gaffney, where Wilbur's father (Ed's youngest brother) was manager of the company store. Wilbur's family lived on

Railroad Avenue (Wilbur once pulled his baby sister off the tracks and stood there shaking) about midway between the mill and the rows of identical cottages that sheltered the factory hands. There the Cash house stood isolated in a little stream-split valley, where Wilbur had few playmates and where from a little black nursemaid he absorbed "preposterous notions, particularly in regard to sex." As the grown man recalled his childhood to H. L. Mencken:

> I literally played with the wind and ran with Pan, spending whole days in the tops of maple trees, and sometimes leaping down to flee in incomprehensible terror before the rustling of the leaves and the rippling of the brook beneath. The keening of the five-o'clock whistles in the morning drilled me in sorrow. And for years, under the influence of the Baptist preacher's too-graphic account of the Second Coming, I watched the West take fire from the sunset with a sort of ecstatic dread.

As manager of the company store, the boy's father was the instrument of the millowner's paternalistic concern to "carry" (for a price) the "spendthrift" millhands from one payday to the next. John William Cash came of plain enough people, as did the boss himself and virtually all the self-styled "aristocrats," and John differed only in his devoutness. In fact, he met his bride at Gaffney's Baptist Church, where, in 1896, he sang in the choir and Miss Nannie Hamrick played the organ. John was then clerking in another company store, and Nannie was newly arrived from her nearby ancestral village of Boiling Springs, North Carolina, to teach music in the public school. Nannie and the smitten John were rooming in the same house—that of Uncle Ed Cash—but John knew nothing about it until he inquired about the pleasingly plump new organist. The young people were married in Boiling Springs by the Rev. Mr. G. P. Hamrick, who, like the bride, was one of the innumerable Hamricks who clustered so thickly in that sector of the Piedmont.

John William Cash was of medium height and of the spareness of frame that conduces to longevity—he died in his ninety-second year, a quarter century after the death of his son Wilbur. Father Cash was a Baptist of straitest sect, puritanical, often opinionated, who went to church every time the church bell rang and became a charter member of the Cherokee Avenue Baptist Church in Gaffney. Nannie Lutitia Cash was his forthright and outspoken mate, quite as devout but more tolerant and possessed of more humor than he. Mother Cash understood her children better than her husband did (although Wilbur was no easy one to fathom), and it was she who taught them their ethical values. She called her husband Daddy and he called her Mamma, and they lived contentedly enough in the orthodox and fundamentalist atmosphere of a homogeneous society. These decent people were plain and unassuming enough, and their ancestry was the same.

Because of the ineradicable misnomer "Scotch-Irish," meaning simply those Protestant Scotch who were settled in Ulster, in Catholic Ireland, W. J. Cash liked to dwell on his "Irishness" to the point where some of his friends found evidence in him of "Irish mysticism." His fellow reporter Cameron Shipp gleefully recalled Jack in a moment of happy lubricity rising from his bleacher seat at a Wake Forest football game, announcing himself a descendant of the red Irish kings, and challenging the world to mortal combat. To H. L. Mencken, Cash later confided of his ancestors:

> In religion, they were mainly Calvinists—Baptists and Presbyterians—but I never heard of a Methodist among them or a minister of any sect. One of them, a waggish old fellow with a notable reputation as a connoisseur of the liquors to be had in the back country, was a militant atheist, much given to spouting Tom Paine and to dramatic expositions of his convictions.

"In the Old South," Cash wrote to Alfred Knopf, "we were never rich or aristocratic, certainly, but good upcountry farmers with land and niggers in proportion to most of our neighbors." Indeed, the Old Irishman who figures in *The Mind of the South* (p. 15, Vintage Paperback edn.) is based on the author's great-great-grandfather. Around the year 1800 this ancestor was a robust young man of humble origin and no particular education. He cleared an upcountry farm, became a prosperous planter of upland cotton, and came to be styled a "gentleman of the old school" in the years just before the Civil War. The author amusedly disclaimed direct kinship with the family of the more aristocratic Cashes, whose notable member, Colonel E. B. C. Cash, reverted to the code duello and killed his man. W. J. Cash was forever being queried about his kinship to other Cashes by people who had seen the tombstone of the dueling colonel near Cheraw, South Carolina, or by those who knew the many Cashes of Kentucky and Tennessee. All he ever knew was that he came of plain people.

The Civil War found the author's grandfather James Henry Cash and great-grandfather Sidney Cash working at the Confederate munitions plant at Hurricane Shoals (later the site of the Clifton Cotton Mills No. 1) on the Pacolet River. This antebellum mill (besides rolling iron and manufacturing nails, it now cast bolts, shot, and shell) was part of the South Carolina Manufacturing Company, which owned more than twenty-five thousand acres of land lying between the Pacolet and Broad rivers. The principal fuel at Hurricane Shoals was charcoal, and the company's tramway, on which cordwood was hauled, was operated by the Cashes with about a dozen flatcars. After the war a Spartanburg lawyer, the Hon. Simpson Bobo, bought up about a thousand acres, including the future cotton-mill site, where the power source had remained intact. Lawyer Bobo employed James Henry Cash, who operated a family farm nearby, to help build and operate a sawmill there during the 1870's. After the later sale of the site to the cotton-mill interests, the old rollers and other iron and steel components were sold to companies "up North," and James Henry Cash helped to load and move the remains of the former Confederate munitions plant.

The post-Civil War hard times had caught up with James Henry Cash, a circumstance that made both John William Cash and his older brother Ed poor boys in a family of ten children. Ed was little more than a boy when he helped haul the bricks that built the pioneer cotton mill at Clifton. He stayed on as an apprentice machinist and advanced quickly to master mechanic and eventually to superintendent. When he was invited to manage the new mill in Gaffney (after a spell in Charlotte with the pioneer textile-machinery firm of D. A. Tompkins), Ed Cash was followed by John, nine years younger, who was running away from the harsh rule of an unloved stepmother. Brother Ed was by this time a substantial family man, and he made room in his house for young John and wangled him a job clerking in his company's store.

On the Hamrick side of the family, although by now it contained a goodly admixture of "Scotch-Irish" also, the original Hamrick strain was German. To this day Nannie Hamrick's home county, Cleveland County, North Carolina, contains more Hamricks than people of any other name, all ultimately traceable to one Hans Georg Hamerick. He arrived in Philadelphia in 1731, a poor German Protestant farmer fleeing the religious persecution of the French, who had devastated the lower Rhine Valley. Seven years before the American Revolution, Charles, Benjamin, and George, sons of Hans Georg Hamerick, migrated to what is today Cleveland County. Soon their name became Hamrick, or in some cases Hambrick, and the hard-working farmers set about earning their bread and following the biblical injunction to replenish the earth. So W. J. Cash's own family history bore out his later formulation about the origins of the plain white man, and the history of his native section already bore out his later formulation of a cotton-textile industry founded partly on philanthropy and maintained in an atmosphere of paternalistic white supremacy.

More than that, Cash's later criticism of the South's romantic self-delusion grew directly out of his own background. The boy Wilbur was reared an intense sentimentalist about the South; his favorite boyhood dream was to re-fight the Civil War with himself leading the charge on the cannon's mouth and bearing aloft the Confederate battle flag. As an adult he admitted not only that his blood leaped to the band's playing of "Dixie"—understandably, for it is a rousing tune—but also to such flourishing rhetoric as "the sword of Lee." In later years he had to laugh at himself because, before militantly sentimental ladies of the United Daughters of the Confederacy, he consistently stood sheepish and dumb. He recalled:

All of us who grew up in the first two decades of the 1900's—in that south with its heroic rhetoric, its gyneolatry, its continual flourishing of the word noble, and its constant glorification of the past—were foreordained to the thing [romanticism]. All of us learned to read on "The Three Little Confederates," all of us framed our hero-ideal on Stuart and Pickett and Forrest—on the dragoon and the lancer—ten thousand times, in our dreams, rammed home the flag in the cannon's mouth after the manner of the heroes of the Rev. Tom Dixon, ten thousand times stepped into the breach at the critical moment on that reeking slope at Gettysburg, and with our tremendous swords, and in defiance of chronology, then and there won the Civil War; all of us learned to choke for "The Conquered Banner" and southern womanhood—to think of women in terms of some enhaloed vision compounded out of the fair-haired Helen, the lily-white maid of Astolat, and the hunting goddess of the Boeotian hill; all of us, in a word, lived absolutely under the sway of what Cabell calls "Domnei," of glory, and of patriotic worship of the idea of the south.

Those "heroes of the Rev. Tom Dixon" were not so easily laughed to scorn in the Gaffney of young Wilbur Cash. The boy heard often enough that Thomas Dixon, a native of Shelby, North Carolina (in Mother Cash's home county), was the highest exemplar of Southern patriotism in print and had made even the Yankees pay him heed. Dixon was a fiery orator and preacher, successful even in ungodly New York City, who had turned novelist to nationwide acclaim. His "Trilogy of Reconstruction," of which *The Clansman* (1905) was best known, formed the basis for the later motion-picture classic (with David Wark Griffith) *The Birth of a Nation*, a pictorial rendering of Dixon's racist ideas. In later years Cash wrote amusedly enough about his "watching the Rev. Tom Dixon's Ku Kluckers do execution of uppity coons and low-down carpetbaggers, and alternately bawling hysterically and shouting my fool head off." He was bearing witness to the fact that his self-education, in college and after, was devoted to unlearning virtually every tenet of "Southern patriotism" that had been taught him in those early days of the century.

Just what were Thomas Dixon's notions of "Southern patriotism"? He started with the imperialistic premise, popularized during the Spanish-American War, of the peculiar superiority of the Anglo-Saxon and his rightful duty to rule the lesser breeds. From this point of departure, shared in varying degrees by such respectable advocates as Beveridge, Lodge, and Theodore Roosevelt, Dixon moved on to a dramatic description of the stereotypes that one could develop by oversimplifying the so-called Dunning school of Reconstruction history. Here was Abraham Lincoln talking like a Southern planter, Thaddeus Stevens personally imposing Negro equality in "Piedmont, South Carolina," the illiterate and newly enfranchised blacks lording it over white ladies and gentlemen—and all proceeding from Dixon's explicit belief in the Negro's inherent and inevitable inferiority to the white man. Dixon's marriage of Southern white supremacy to the nationalist Anglo-Saxon doctrine of superiority, in addition to his flair for self-advertisement and his lavish application of melodrama, helped to account for the emergence of his novels as best sellers even outside the South. Inside the South—inside the Cash household in Gaffney, South Carolina—Thomas Dixon was not only a best-selling author but a local hero whom one's children might hope to emulate.

Furthermore, the homogeneous society of Cash's South Carolina boyhood was as firmly attached to the legally sanctioned white supremacy of "Pitchfork Ben" Tillman as it was to Tom Dixon's ideological counterpart. As the architect of South Carolina's white-supremacy apparatus, including Negro disfranchisement, Tillman had personally given to Dixon the story that led to the writing of *The Clansman*. First Tillman and then Cole Blease came upon the South Carolina scene as paladins of white-supremacy politics, which meant nothing more or less than winning political place by shouting "nigger" louder than one's opponent. Tillman succeeded with the rural wool-hat boys generally, but Blease got to be governor in 1910 by appealing to just the sort of millhands who were carried on the book in Father Cash's company store. These sovereign electors, who were again and again to be persuaded to vote their prejudices instead of their pocketbooks, were cynically exploited by "Coley" Blease, who advertised himself as friend of the poor but never delivered. Father Cash was as regular a Democrat as a Baptist, and it never occurred to him that his political captains were not great men. His son Wilbur came to know better, and as an editorialist in the New Deal days he found that such South Carolina politicoes as "Cotton Ed" Smith and

Olin D. Johnston—one against and the other for the New Deal—were still competing to see who could yell "nigger" louder. Editorialist Cash did not hesitate to say so.

Still, neither the theory nor the practice of white-supremacy doctrine could impinge much on the experience of a boy growing up to savor and delight in life's new mysteries as they unfolded before him. First came the love of books, which was born in Wilbur on exactly the day he ignored his mother's call to come and fetch in the stovewood and hid himself under the porch in shivering delight over *Jack the Giant Killer.* He was six years old, had learned to read at five, and thereafter began reading indiscriminately everything he could lay hands on. With his first book, he remembered, he shared "the fate of Jack of the terrible sword and the seven-league boots, looked in the oven while the j'int fee-fawed concerning the delicious blood of Englishmen." After that came Alger, Henty, Mayne Reid, Clark Russell, Scott, Dickens, Hugo, Milton, Bunyan, Law's *Serious Call*, all read with even-handed impartiality. It goes almost without saying that despite his father's displeasure, the boy read the most lurid weeklies on the sly, and loved them.

The little boy who learned to read before he went to school—who "read, read, read, and ruined his eyes reading"—grew up a solitary sort. He would play a little yard ball, first with his younger brother, then with a second brother, but he got bored and out of patience with organized sports. He was noncombative and generally a good obedient boy around the house except when concealing himself under the porch with a book and rendering himself incommunicado to those calling him to his chores. There was many a morning he should have been in public school, when:

> I used to play sick so that I might devote myself to the pleasant business of building Indian tents out of cottonseed hull sacks, and swing in the top of a tall maple tree which

grew in the meadow below the house. Even in that time my mother used to shake her head sadly and fear that I would come to no good end.

While other youngsters were caught up in the spirit of Christmas and glorying in the prospect of the gifts the holiday would bring, Wilbur would be dismantling an alarm clock or peering up the chimney and trying to ascertain the mechanics of Santa's arrival. The boy became ambidextrous, the result of his parents' training him away from left-handedness, and in later life he thought that the imposed change had had an adverse effect on his nervous system.

Long vacations from public school would bring frequent visits to the tall old house of Grandfather Hamrick in Boiling Springs, North Carolina, only thirteen miles away. Wilbur's mother would turn in to her girlhood home from the yellow road in front, a long yellow road that ran away to the blue hills crouched on the horizon. The boy loved to scamper on the other side of that road through the wide sweet orchard that was full of the heady winy smell of slow-rotting apples. As the grown man could remember, behind the house were barns and the gabble of ducks and the honking of guinea fowl—and the red fields and the blue wood shimmering in the hazy summer sun. A half-dozen Negro 'cropper families, unobtrusively dependent, lived there and farmed Grandfather's land with him.

In the cool dark parlor of the Hamrick house, crayoned family portraits looking down from the walls, the nine-year-old Wilbur became fascinated with a book that lay on the table in a place usually reserved for the family Bible. This book was bound in white leather, splendid with gilt wreaths and curliques, and bore the elaborately worked-out title *Barrack-Room Ballads*, by some outlander with the improbable name of Rudyard Kipling. Without knowing the meaning either of barrack-room or ballad, the boy then and there felt himself caught up in the mood of those verses: He saw the red-coated soldiers, heard the solemn drumroll, caught the sense of "splendid things and far places" that could be conveyed through the power of words. Not that the Bible was in any way slighted, for Father Cash had purchased a Student's Bible when Wilbur was seven years old—though Wilbur quickly grew disillusioned with orthodox organized religion, he kept that volume by his side the rest of his life. The King James Version, because rehearsed and reread, constituted a ponderable influence and made an incalculable impression upon the style and imagination of that generation. The maturing Wilbur came to grow attached to that worldly-wise Hebrew preacher Koheleth, who, as Ecclesiastes, spoke in the accustomed Shakespearian accents fashioned by King James's translators: "To every thing there is a season."

Grandfather D. J. Hamrick and Wilbur's father differed in politics. The old stonemason, Boiling Springs' first mayor, was a rip-snorting upcountry Republican, and his son-in-law was a Southern Democrat to the core. So they tacitly avoided talking politics and talked business instead. Hamrick's proposal, quickly accepted by John Cash, was of a partnership in a new general store in Boiling Springs along with help in building a new house for the transplanted Cashes. The Cashes remained for a time in Gaffney while across the state line their new house was going up, and on its completion in 1912 they moved in next door to the Hamricks. Wilbur was the eldest of the Cash children at twelve; his brother Henry was two years younger, brother Allan seven years younger, and sister Bertie just two years old.

Boiling Springs, in North Carolina's Cleveland County, offered an unexpectedly good educational opportunity to young Wilbur Cash, for it boasted an academy recently established by the Baptists, the Boiling Springs High School (since grown into Gardner-Webb Junior College). North

Carolina was still in the throes of the Educational Awakening set in motion by its first white-supremacy governor, Charles B. Aycock (1901–5), who during his term zealously built "a schoolhouse a day." Aycock's conversion of Negro disfranchisement to the purposes of literacy and universal education was statesmanlike, to be sure, but too long-range to be of immediate help to Wilbur Cash entering high school in 1913. The academy at Boiling Springs was easily superior to any accessible public high school. So Wilbur was enrolled as a day student in the boarding academy, which was patronized by country boys and girls whom he preferred to remember as somewhat older than himself. At all odds, the academy had a good library and, for a boy who could not remember the time when he did not intend to be a writer, that was enough. Local tradition has it that Wilbur Cash proceeded to read every book in that school library, with the result that he was soon better read than most of his teachers.

The village of Boiling Springs got its name from a phenomenon located on the school campus, springs that sent water into the air almost waist-high. As the "boiling" water shot up it took some sand along with it, which heightened the likeness to boiling water. Aside from this bit of local color and the existence of the Baptist-run high school, Boiling Springs was an unexceptional and homogeneous Piedmont country village. The town charter, granted the year before the Cashes moved there, reflected the conventional puritanism, prohibiting, among other things, the sale of cigarettes and the appearance of carnival shows lest the high-schoolers be exposed to undue temptation.

In high school Wilbur's nickname of "Sleepy" came to stick, probably because of the heavy-eyed look partly the result of increasingly poor vision. The preoccupied boy would walk down the street, his narrow-eyed look fixed ahead of him, and not see the people who spoke to him. Some mistakenly thought him egotistical, but more took it for the absent-minded absorption that it really was. In any case he was remembered as something of an odd fish, never talkative or aggressive, and still quite likable when mates went out of their way to approach him. Always sensitive in a personal way, he would be moody or cheerful by turns. Otherwise he fitted in well enough: a gum-chewing boy who never openly carried a book, something of a whiz at geometry, a generally carefree youngster who was also a better-than-average school debater.

Life in peaceful Boiling Springs gave Cash a lifelong nostalgia and feeling for the country life of the South that was never beclouded by his impatience over the Southern penchant for self-delusion. He even came to take on the rolling gait of his Grandfather Hamrick, whose farm he could see, feel, even smell, as an adult. Wilbur worked on that farm in the summer, hating the work heartily because it deprived him of reading time, but in later years he remembered it vividly and affectionately. He recalled to a friend:

> Riding home from the fields in a wagon after dark and seeing the new grounds burn red against the dark woods, I am sure I was more quietly happy than I ever have been since or will be again. And do you remember how the sand followed the felloes around, hissing, and the breathing in the pines when you awoke at night and the wind was about to rise but had not quite begun?

One day Wilbur ran out of the academy to the shelter of his home when one of the "professors" was about to whip him for some infraction. Mother Cash knew that "Wilbur is not the type to be whipped," as she firmly informed his teacher, and she made both of them sit down and talk out the difficulty in her presence. Nannie Hamrick Cash knew that her Wilbur was more sensitive than most boys, a great sentimentalist in looking after every stray cat or dog, and already an easy mark for every hard-luck story. Besides, both parents remained anxious for the state of his soul while they waited for Wilbur to come forward voluntarily for baptism. He had wanted to join the church as a little boy, but his parents had preferred to wait until he matured enough to consider his action, and now he kept them in suspense until he finally took his decision for baptism in high school.

When he was fourteen, the guns of August 1914 boomed out in some impossibly far-off Europe, but Cash had no ears for them. He then regretted only that the Civil War had come before his time and that he could never bleed and die for Dixie. He, his parents, his teachers—indeed, the South generally—lived in innocent isolation from the pressures of any world balance of power, and they cheered the Southern-born Woodrow Wilson as he quickly proclaimed the nation's official neutrality. Southerners would hasten to answer, as they always did, their country's call to arms, but for the time being it was pleasant to reflect on a war-born agricultural prosperity in a quiet land free of the exacerbations of mass European immigration and with the Negro question "solved."

At fourteen, too, Cash discovered the girls "and so abandoned the Harvard Classics somewhere in the middle." As he recalled to Alfred Knopf, he "spent the next fifteen years contemplating them—the girls, not the Classics—often painfully." The boy was incurably shy, and as he later confessed to Mencken, at the high school "the principal business in hand was the making of love."

> Inevitably, I myself promptly fell into the tender state, but the charmers laughed at me as an infant, and so, for two years, I suffered horribly. A bit later, after I had shot up to my growth, and had developed a deep voice and some capacity as a debater, I had better luck.

More, he became a brilliant student as a high-school senior. By the testimony of his old high-school teacher, Wilbur Cash never quit being an avaricious reader, and now he wrote classroom themes on subjects much beyond the range of his fellows. He was, moreover, a close observer with a tenacious memory. As historian for the graduating class of eight boys and eight girls, he gave a commencement speech—which was, however, understandably blurred as prophecy. The date was April 18, 1917, and on April 7 the United States had entered the war.

During the year that followed, Wilbur worked and drifted between shipyards and cantonments all the way from Sparrows Point, Maryland, to Jacksonville, Florida, spending most of the time with his father at South Carolina's Camp Wadsworth, an Army cantonment located at Spartanburg. He served in such modest capacities as tally clerk, time-keeper, and carpenter's helper, and at one stage he almost succeeded in enlisting in the Navy. His first exploration beyond the South brought him the chance, which he seized without question, of bravely asserting the white supremacy on which he had been raised. The encounter came on a rail-road coach. A Negro ventured to sit down next to him, whereupon the intruder got the then-conventional Southern warning to find another seat because Wilbur Cash was not about to "sit with a nigger." As long as he lived he was not to "sit with a nigger," but only a year or two later, when Wilbur returned from college speaking up for Negro education and predicting a new era in race relations someday, a few of the home folks grimly muttered "nigger lover." In the course of working outdoors at Spartanburg during the terrible wartime winter of 1917–18, Wilbur suffered frostbite to the extent that his eyelids became affected. They contracted into narrow slits, making the schoolboy nickname "Sleepy" all the more appropriate. At this time Father Cash embarked on a profitable business of providing transportation for the soldiers commuting between camp and town, hiring civilian drivers for a small fleet of cars that he managed. Wilbur wanted to drive a car and help look after the business, but his father would not hear of it.

John William Cash had attended only the Gaffney Male and Female Academy, and that as an adult. He cherished the experience so much that he always kept the manuscript of a school debate speech he had written favoring higher education for women. How much more, then, did he favor higher education for his eldest son! Wilbur was interested, to be sure, in going to college—eventually—but his father made him see that the present moment of high prosperity was the time to go. Even so, all Wilbur's pre-adult experience, specifically his overexposure to his father's brand of religion, rebelled against his father's choice of Wofford College, a Methodist institution in Spartanburg. In Spartanburg, moreover, the father would be peering over the son's shoulder at every turn. But Father Cash was paying his board bills, and the Army would pay his tuition through his enrollment in the Student Army Training Corps, so in September 1918 Wilbur Cash was enrolled as a Wofford freshman.

By the time of the Armistice three months later, Cash had gotten to be a corporal. At Wofford, where he lived for a time on as well as off campus, he smoked a pipe, was a member of the Pipe Dreamers Club, and wrote literary pieces and poetry. A classmate who sat with him in "Uncle Gus" Gamewell's Cicero class remembered him for a fair and ruddy skin, a broad mouth, an interesting and intelligent face. "He didn't have too much to say," this classmate recalled, "but there seemed something more back of his live expression than he uttered." Despite the high adventure connoted by an inscription written by some classmate in Wilbur's yearbook—" 'Sleepy hum,' 'member the night at the ——. Well, you know!"—despite such intimations of collegiate derring-do, Wilbur and Wofford never got along. Coming upon him just at the stage when he most wanted to test his wings away from home influences, the Wofford experience confined him in what he hated as a narrow, fresh-water preserve of provincialism.

That summer of 1919 Wilbur pleaded to be allowed to go to school "up North," to Valparaiso University in northern Indiana. He had been impressed by one of his contemporaries who was planning to attend Valparaiso, and by the school's reputation as the "poor man's Harvard." Before World War I the school had boasted an enrollment of six thousand, but wartime conditions and the death of its galvanic president Henry Baker Brown had seriously hampered it by the time Wilbur considered attending. He obviously was attracted by the promise of a people's university, without entrance or terminal examinations, "where theory squares with practice," and where thousands had been educated at not much more than a hundred dollars a year for tuition, room, and board. During the early 1920's the debt-burdened Valparaiso was to get international notoriety as the proposed Ku Klux Klan University, and it was eventually purchased by the Lutherans. In September 1919, however, Cash went off to Valparaiso with another boy, ambitiously enrolling in American Literature, Latin, Emerson, Physics, French, and Latin Composition. He could tolerate it only until Christmas, whether for reasons not given or because, as John Cash recalled it, "the winds howled around his dormitory." Wilbur was remembered as being "cold-natured" as a child, and it is possible that in the winds sweeping down from Lake Michigan and perhaps also in the campus atmosphere he "about froze to death," as John Cash put it.

Wilbur apparently struck his colors. He pleaded with his father to be allowed to come home; he would now accede to his father's wishes and go to Wake Forest College in North Carolina. Much as Wilbur hated the idea of attending still another "preacher school"—for Wake Forest was supported by the Baptist State Convention—it was a college at a sufficient remove from Boiling Springs to allow considerable independence. And so early in 1920, Cash stepped off the Seaboard train at the dusty little Wake County village fifteen miles north of Raleigh.

Wake Forest College, slumbering beneath its magnolias, was nevertheless to awaken Sleepy Cash. If the school was the alma mater of Baptists like Thomas Dixon, it served in the same capacity for Gerald Johnson, the perceptive editor and writer admired by Mencken. It was at Wake Forest that Sleepy Cash was to unlearn and discard the excess intellectual baggage of his boyhood. It was there that he began to probe and analyze the mind of the South.

CHAPTER 2

Those Terrible Twenties

*C*ollegians in the South identified much more, generally, than other Southerners with the revolution in manners and moral standards that swept America after 1918. At Wake Forest the boys had long delighted in flouting the rules simply because those rules were there. There were rules against fraternities, but the *sub rosa* Greeks at Wake Forest went so far as to boast about their faculty advisers; there were rules again hazing, but they were regularly and enthusiastically violated; there was, especially, the North Carolina prohibition law, passed in 1908, and that prewar outlet for collegiate rebellion now took on added glamour. After the wartime excitement came the national manifestation of "flaming youth," in which Wake Forest modestly shared. Now that national prohibition made social drinking fashionable, the boys carried their hip flasks with newfound style; now that the automobile extended the frontier of lovemaking, the boys became less inhibited Don Juans than ever.

Granted that the standards of the fathers were falling fast, Don Juans like Wilbur Cash were fortunate in having chosen Wake Forest to help cushion the shock. It was a small Baptist college but had much of the liberal outlook and intellectual integrity of a great university. Whenever the "preacher bloc" of the parent Baptist State Convention threatened to overwhelm the college with a dictated form of hillbilly fundamentalism, Dr. William Louis Poteat and his faculty serenely fought them off. "Dr. Billy"—a biologist, not a clergyman—manifested a personal piety that rendered him immune to fundamentalist bigotry and a personal integrity that made him a hero to his students. Later he was to earn his state's gratitude for leading the successful counterattack against an effort to pass the same kind of anti-evolution "monkey" law that in 1925 made Dayton, Tennessee, a laughingstock.

As a member of Wake Forest's coterie of angry young men of the time, Cash, Class of '22, rallied around Dr. Poteat whenever he needed support in withstanding the onslaughts of the orthodox. Cash's first chance to defend him came at home, because Cleveland County's most celebrated Wake Forest alumnus, the Rev. Dr. A. C. Dixon, came all the way from London to attack Dr. Poteat at the college commencement of 1920. A. C. Dixon—brother of the racist Thomas Dixon—was an even greater orator than his brother and was pastor of the great Metropolitan Tabernacle in London. Dr. Poteat had to sit in his college chapel and hear himself denounced by A. C. Dixon for teaching the "atheistic" doctrine of evolution. On that occasion the *Biblical Recorder*, organ of the Baptist State Convention, did publish Dr. Poteat's rejoinder and then judged that his teachings were not really dangerous; *i.e.*, that one need not accept the Genesis account of Creation at face value. But the fundamentalists had tasted blood, and now they lusted for more.

There was no question that in reviling the fundamentalists, Wilbur was in part acting out his rebellion against John Cash and his puritanical code. The same was true of his "independence" in the matters of smoking cigarettes (he had abandoned the genteel pipe of Wofford days), of drinking

(Cash could get drunk on one belt of the particularly vicious corn whisky to which he was exposed), even of joining in an occasional foray into Raleigh's notorious vice district. He held in deepest contempt the orthodox among the students at Wake Forest, which then was pushing toward an enrollment of five hundred. These orthodox consisted of about a hundred older men who had come to the campus as Baptist preachers and were dubbed "skies" in consequence. Cash would hang out the dormitory window and regale passers-by, especially the "skies," with—delicious scandal of a Baptist campus—marathon quotations from the archagnostic Colonel Robert G. Ingersoll.

Wake Forest classrooms harbored considerable freedom of speech and exchange of ideas, invited and stimulated by the professors, who followed Dr. Poteat's lead. Outside the classrooms there flourished bull sessions, under the magnolias or indoors, almost any hour of day or night. At the all-night bull sessions he frequented, Cash held forth with great eloquence, but never more so than in speaking of something he called "the mind of the South." Or he might use that expression under a magnolia where the company was congenial, even trying it out on passing professors who happened on the bull session and joined in the fun. In any case, Cash used the expression "the mind of the South" well before Vernon L. Parrington, who used it to open Volume II of *Main Currents in American Thought*, specifically *The Romantic Revolution in America, 1800–1860* (1926).

Cash was one of the bright ones tapped by his history professor, Dr. C. C. Pearson, to join the Political Science Club. The club met monthly in the lean professor's bachelor quarters to listen to a student-written research paper. Cash would never work quite as hard as Dr. Pearson and his other teachers urged, so his grades were acceptable rather than brilliant. He was, however, stimulated to dip into a prodigious variety of books. Naturally taciturn, looking rather like a bespectacled owl, Cash would finally utter a remark, and his mates would find that it had been worth waiting for.

Dr. Pearson was a Yale-educated Virginian who liked to compare, say, "the mind of a Virginian" with "the mind of a North Carolinian" (always to the latter's disadvantage) and never failed to arouse a rejoinder from Cash. The student and the professor enjoyed a great admiration for each other. Dr. Pearson never laughed outright at the young man's sallies but responded with a contagiously delighted snicker. Egged on, Cash would spout out the whole torrent of new ideas and systems of ideas with which he was being overwhelmed and with many of which he was, in truth, not yet ready to cope.

Aside from his regularly assigned reading, Cash was forever breaking off to read someone off the beaten track: W. C. Brann (*The Iconoclast*), or that supposedly "erotic" Virginian James Branch Cabell, or that troublemaker par excellence H. L. Mencken. A complete edition of Brann's writings had been published in 1919, and one of its admirers was Dr. Poteat's son Hubert, professor of Latin and faculty adviser for the college paper that Cash wrote for, the *Old Gold and Black*. Dr. Hubert W. Poteat often read Brann aloud to the student editors in admiration of his brilliant writing style, and he somehow gave the impression that Brann's anathematizing of the fundamentalists of eastern Texas had a wider application.

Cash read Cabell's scandalously successful *Jurgen*, of course, but paid even more attention to the Virginian's non-fiction credo, *Beyond Life* (1919). There he learned something vital about universal romanticizing and mythmaking (like "domnei" or woman worship), which he was later to apply so incisively to his study of the South. Cash also gasped with delight at the audacious picture of the benighted South, "Sahara of the Bozart," which he found in the second series of Mencken's *Prejudices* (1920). Mencken's Dutch-

28

uncle hectoring was just what was needed to help bring on the Southern literary renascence of the twenties, and the college boy—not the Babbitt, who broke his teeth gnashing them at Mencken—perceived it at once. Mencken's *Prejudices* and his brilliant book reviews for *Smart Set* added new stars to the constellation by which Cash steered.

To be sure, Mencken heaped ridicule on democracy, and many an admirer like Cash had to overlook the Baltimorean's apparent preference for the Junker ideal. Nevertheless, disillusion with professed war aims had set in after America's awkward repudiation of the Peace Treaty and its League of Nations. Outraged ridicule was all that the college generation could feel for "normalcy" in the Harding manner. Moreover, Cash, enthusiastically shocked, could agree with the prime objects of Mencken's ridicule: ignorance, cant, prohibition, prudery, and organized religion. To the idealistic young man (Mencken also detested idealism, but never mind) the devastating catalogue of boobery summed up virtually every tenet that his father, John Cash, held dear. Mother Cash came to believe that her son Wilbur's "irreligion" came of his disillusion in once rooming with a Wake Forest preacher and observing the holy man abusing his family. It is more likely that the enlightened and easy rein of his Baptist college kept Cash from experiencing an even greater cultural shock than he did.

In the matter of writing, where he shone, Cash probably was most influenced by the erudite Dr. Benjamin Sledd, who had taught such literary craftsmen as Gerald Johnson, Laurence Stallings (co-author of *What Price Glory?*), and the gifted but short-lived Tar Heel poet John Charles McNeill. Cash was welcome as a contributor to the college magazine, *The Wake Forest Student*, although as a member of the wrong clique he was not considered for a staff position. For the *Student*, Cash produced five poems and two short stories. Both stories were in a distinctly gloomy vein, one being entitled "The House of Hate" and the other—selected by the faculty adviser as the best story of the issue—"The Derelict." The latter was a sea story "in which the 'Mollie B.' becomes a drifting rudderless hulk, and carries with it to ruin the happiness and lives of the people to whom it had brought pleasure."

Such literary endeavor, plus a celebrated oration he composed for a desperate fellow student—these and the extracurricular bull sessions were about the only evidence of vigor from Cash. Otherwise he was as indolent a student as was ever seen, unkempt, usually careless of dress, with all the personal habits usually assumed by the nonconformist and bohemian. He recorded for Alfred Knopf: "I hated a laboratory so much that I rarely went—and so was in constant difficulties with the authorities." As for the compulsory two-hour course in personal hygiene, which was a highly interesting affair because taught by the able Dr. Thurman D. Kitchin, Cash sometimes attended for the sake of Kitchin but not for the hygiene. He was, as classmates remember him, crazy for the girls, not even remotely an athlete, a punchless fighting fool when drunk (unable to remember it afterward), and in all ways a long long way from Boiling Springs, North Carolina. On one occasion, while reeling uncertainly in Raleigh's disreputable quarter, Cash ran afoul of the police and was thrust into the lockup until he could be identified as a Wake Forest boy and turned loose.

Only because the campus paper, *Old Gold and Black*, appeared once a week could so haphazard a journeyman as Cash have served as one of its mainstays. Yet for the final two years of his foreshortened stay at Wake Forest, he gave the paper more loyal service than his courses, and he found in journalism both the writing outlet and the writing discipline that he needed. Like many another aspiring novelist, Cash looked upon newspaper work as a welcome haven from which to launch the occasional flights of higher inspiration that are presumably too elevated for journalistic expression. During 1920–1 he was merely one of four associate editors for the paper; his occasional editorials were buried in anonymity, and his only signed contribution was a letter to the editor. In that missive he stood opposed to an alumni benefaction for grading the athletic field, because the result would be to pre-empt the intramural field for intercollegiate sports. It was a theme, tied in with his editorial dislike for the professionalization of college athletics, to which he would repeatedly return.

Cash came into his journalistic own during his senior year as sole associate editor. His superior was Edwin Holman, who later went on to a career with the Associated Press in Atlanta. President Poteat's son, Dr. Hubert M. Poteat, was the paper's faculty adviser, but it was a rare occasion indeed when the two young editors consulted him. Whenever they did, he was apt to toss their problem right back at them with something like: "Use the rule of reason and you won't be far wrong." Then Dr. Poteat would go on to regale his young visitors by reading aloud the slashing essays of Brann the Iconoclast. Whether or not Dr. Poteat so intended, Cash and Holman interpreted the readings as an invitation to adopt more and more iconoclastic tones in their own editorials. At any rate, the good doctor never demurred.

Holman took the lead, with Cash as right bower, in delightedly baiting the *Biblical Recorder*. The editor of that Baptist organ, the Rev. Dr. Livingston Johnson, had asked for it with an editorial, "Our Dancing President," in which he castigated Warren G. Harding for tolerating "indecent" social dancing in the White House and for thus setting a bad example to the youth of America. The fun was intensified when, early in 1922, a White House staff member sent Editor Johnson an asinine letter taking the criticism seriously. Mrs. Harding would have North Carolina Baptists know that "no modern dancing or 'jazzing' was tolerated at the White

House, and the President has danced once in twelve years."
After siding with the White House and giving Editor Johnson a good tongue-in-cheek spanking, the *Old Gold and
Black* concluded: "As we see it, Mr. Harding has not committed one of the cardinal sins, as Dr. Johnson would have
us believe, but, at the worst, has only perpetrated a doctrinal
error."

The outraged Baptist editor responded with an angry
editorial, "Does This Represent Wake Forest?" Holman and
Cash basked in their notoriety as the state press joined in the
fun. What the boys most enjoyed, perhaps, was the way the
faculty privately egged them on. As for the college president,
Dr. Poteat invited the student editors to his home, read the
contending editorials aloud, quietly observed that good
humor would continue as their most potent weapon, and
then served coffee and cookies. To cap their triumph, the
student editors published a testimonial from an alumnus,
"Laurence Stallings, B.A. '16, Washington, D. C." Stallings,
who was then Sunday editor of the Washington *Times* and
was yet to write *What Price Glory?* with Maxwell Anderson,
wrote: "I think it by far the best college weekly, workman-
like and jam-up, published anywhere."

But Dr. Poteat's administration of Wake Forest was already in trouble in early 1922 by reason of a December
hazing incident in which a student's shorn head was painted
with silver nitrate. The fundamentalist bloc later followed
the lead of the preacher T. T. Martin of Mississippi, a leading figure in the anti-evolution lobby and author of *Hell and
the High Schools*, and launched an open attack on Dr.
Poteat. The April issues of the *Biblical Recorder* were filled
with editorials, articles, and letters for and against the Wake
Forest president. (Editor Johnson now rallied to Dr. Poteat's
defense.) Dr. Poteat had to publish an account reminding
his Baptist brethren that he had been teaching biological
sciences for forty years, that he had published two books on

the relation of science and religion, and that he had nowhere derided the Genesis account.

Cash chimed in with a campus editorial that began: "The forces of intolerance are never asleep" and wound up with an observation about the fundamentalists: "What strange instruments does his Satanic Majesty sometimes choose to carry out his work!" In between, he enthusiastically smote them hip and thigh, heaping ridicule upon "Willie J. Bryan" and happily name-dropping his way through Darwin, Huxley, Haeckel, Emerson, John Wyclif, and Roger Williams. After giving a logically unexceptionable reply to fundamentalist narrowness, Cash went on to gild the lily: "Conceived in the primitive slime of ignorance, it [fundamentalism] seeks to thwart and retard the march of truth and knowledge by playing upon the fears of the credulous and the wilful blindness of the prejudiced." In a companion editorial ("Possibilities," reprinted in this volume), Cash sarcastically proposed as fundamentalist successor to Dr. Poteat either William Jennings Bryan or Wilbur Glenn Voliva—the latter insisted that the earth is flat.

Dr. Poteat rode out the storm that commencement, but Cash almost came a cropper. Early in May, on the heels of his "Possibilities" editorial, Cash and a whole crew of his fellows were suspended from the college for being members of a social fraternity. Cash was, in fact, one of the organizers of this *sub rosa* Greek-letter society, which, like all the others on campus, was well known to the authorities. In this case, however, an overzealous printer displayed to a faculty member an incriminating sample of his handiwork. This sample was the printed program of a social function sponsored by Cash's fraternity, and the faculty member had no recourse but to report the members whose names were thus publicly displayed. Back in Boiling Springs the Cash family was in great alarm at the peril to Wilbur's graduation, but it turned out all right; the boys were not only reinstated but exempted from final examinations. The extra-lenient treatment grew out of the atmosphere in which the college's trustees and administrators were reconciled at the end of that difficult school year.

The senior-class prophecy in the college yearbook, *The Howler*, noted only that "Sleepy's" experience with the product should qualify him for a demonstrator's job with a chewing-tobacco company. Another political enemy wrote the sketch for "Wilbur Joseph Cash . . . Age 22; Height 5′10″; weight 158″ as follows: "While not the friendliest fellow in college, 'Sleepy' is important in the social life of his chums here." But the carefree Cash laughed off being dismissed with such faint praise, for life was generally good. It is doubtful whether he could have ordered a "smooth" dinner or sent flowers with the right nonchalance, but he later admitted that he had settled on Wake Forest precisely because such "country-club" skills would not be required of him there. He had a certain voice for singing, liked to dance, even gave one girl friend his fraternity pin (and walked the floor all day when she wired him some time later that she was getting married). He affected a pompadour in those days when he had hair, and he was generally attractive to the girls. On a romantic expedition one vacation, while driving his father's Jordan touring car, the wool-gathering "Sleepy" ran it into a cow on the road.

Father Cash could afford an automobile now that he had become superintendent of Boiling Springs' new hosiery mill, an absentee operation owned in partnership by three prosperous physicians of the area. In the flurry of new postwar economic activity John Cash invested his savings in a few machines that he could operate at the mill independently. The hosiery mill gave Boiling Springs its first electric lights, generating electricity from its operation, and the Cashes got the first electric lights in town. Uncle Ed Cash was now superintendent of a cotton mill at Rockingham, North Carolina, having overextended himself by organizing two new mills and going bankrupt in the same postwar business flurry that worked out so well for his younger brother.

Home during college vacations, Wilbur spelled his father during the night shift at the mill. There were times when Wilbur fired the boiler because the regular Negro fireman was drunk, and there were times when he tended a machine, but he worked those summers at the prevailing twenty cents an hour. Wilbur came into the mill all in favor of putting down strikes with the bayonet, but his contact with actual mill conditions and palpable social wrongs made him uneasy. He saw child labor in its pristine form, more or less, and during the long nights he noted how many of the tired and sleepy workers were mothers of young children. At summer's end he would be free of the mill, but not they.

In the fall of 1922 Cash entered the Wake Forest Law School, not really for any vocational reason but because he had no other haven. There at least he could continue with Dr. Pearson's Political Science Club and could attend the celebrated course on Blackstone given by Dr. N. Y. Gulley, a particularly magnetic teacher. By this time Cash was already suffering from the hyperthyroid condition that was to plague him throughout his adult life. Even in high school he had been known to suffer from spasms of choking that suggested hyperthyroidism, but at Wake Forest he had to wear his collar open because of an incipient goiter. Cash was more touchy now, more emotional, more a trial to his few friends, apt on occasion to burst into tears. Out of his physical difficulty arose a fear that also plagued him throughout his adult life and that he voiced that year to a college mate: that he was becoming sexually impotent.

Giving short shrift to his formal studies of law and no longer on the staff of the *Old Gold and Black*, Cash addressed his literary muse. "At twenty-three," he reported in a later Guggenheim fellowship application, "I attempted a novel in the manner of Joseph Conrad's 'Lord Jim,' but concluded dismally at the halfway mark that Conrad somehow knew more of life and the English language that I knew, and burned it." As it happened, Cash was known as a terrible storyteller, and this trait may have its importance for his ambition to write fiction. Even so, he remained insistent in his ambition to "understand" his native South so well that he would one day write a book about it. He told enough people about this ambition so that it became an accepted tradition at Wake Forest.

Of course Cash was as yet in no position, psychologically, to write a "mind of the South." He clearly perceived the romanticizing and sentimentalizing that beset his native region, but he was nevertheless overwhelmingly sentimental himself. He would speak in gushing tones of his childhood, excessively romanticizing his family, being overcome at times with waves of self-pity at how "poor" he was. Nevertheless, when it came to select a writing model, Cash abandoned the sentimentally gentle personal essays of Isaac Erwin Avery, the old city editor of the Charlotte *Observer*, and adhered with new force to the astringent H. L. Mencken, whose plans to launch *The American Mercury* were the talk of the literary world.

At the end of his "wasted" postgraduate year, Wilbur made it all up to his father by applying for the position of instructor in English at Georgetown College (Baptist), in Georgetown, Kentucky. "I don't want to be a lawyer—you have to lie too much," John Cash remembered as his son's explanation of his altered course. Wilbur got the teaching post, thanks to a recommendation by his old English professor, whose cautious praise of him as "not a brilliant student but a good one" made the adult author laugh at the recollection. The idea of "Sleepy" Cash as a plugger in college was too much, he later recalled, "after all those years of industrious loafing." At any rate, with the Georgetown job secured and his health temporarily improved, the young man got a summer reporting job on the Charlotte *Observer* and headed for the Queen City, some fifty miles from his home.

Because it is the custom for men of all crafts to curse their callings and warn away newcomers, Cash got a baleful picture of his journalistic future from his city editor. The latter took the cub reporter out to coffee on his first day in a newspaper shop, but later gave him the best kind of eye-opening assignment—covering a forlorn little textile strike in town. Reporter Cash attended the strikers' meeting in the union hall over a drugstore in North Charlotte and listened to the promises of support from the millhands at Hunters-ville and from several railroad union men. He interviewed the mill superintendent, who did not choose the benevolent paternalism of Cash's own father and who explained quite candidly that he gave workers their jobs a day at a time and their rented homes a week at a time. He had already hired workers to replace the strikers, and eviction proceedings against them would become effective on the weekend. The strikers adopted a resolution protesting against the regime of intimidation under which they had to live, but having made their sad little protest, they resignedly called off the strike. Just as he now hated sham peddlers in matters religious, Cash harbored a deep-rooted anger—precisely because he was born and raised in cotton-mill country—against injustice in Southern mill villages.

Within a month after covering that strike in Charlotte, Mr. Cash—as was styled in a manner befitting a faculty member—took his place as fledgling instructor in English at Georgetown College for the school year 1923-4. As he wrote Mencken of his teaching experience in Kentucky: "There I lost such illusions as had survived college, suffered an incipient nervous breakdown, and discovered that I had no business in a sectarian institution." More humorously he later recorded: "I remember with terror to this day the warnings issuing from the elder members of the faculty when I once upon a time briefly and ingloriously set up for a college instructor." Still, the Kentucky experience was not pure loss, for Mr. Cash there met the pretty little Peggy Ann he pursued—or whose idealized image he pursued—for the next dozen years.

She was a freshman beauty who dreamed of someday pursuing a stage career, and she would have had no time for the poor and socially awkward young instructor except that he *was* her teacher and was so charmingly smitten. In later years Cash answered his own question "Why Write?" with a good-natured reference to his youthful passion:

> I suspect that nearly every jack caught in the thing [the writing mania] is there ultimately because in his moon-calf youth some creature in skirts sicked him into it on the ground that it was necessary if he was to be considered available husband material, kept him there until it was too late for him to retreat, and then, having demonstrated her capacity as a Helen and done her duty to literature, quite reasonably married the nearest wholesale grocer or barber.

It may be that Peggy Ann was the Helen who launched Cash on his attempt to write a realistic novel in the manner of Theodore Dreiser (it was so bad that he burned it), but in any case she was the only consoling element for him in what he later termed that "jerkwater" college. She seems to have provided him with some intellectual stimulus, too, in introducing him to the current wave of revisionist historians of World War I who were questioning the official war-guilt line. In any case, for Peggy Ann's sweet sake Mr. Cash was prepared to plunge into the thicket of graduate studies and emerge solidly *Philosophiae Doctor* as Dr. Cash.

The "incipient nervous breakdown" of which he wrote Mencken would seem related to an instance of sexual frustration he experienced with Peggy Ann. He confessed this humiliation to a friend in after years just as he had confided to a Wake Forest schoolmate his fear of becoming sexually impotent. And the girl never made the grade as a professional actress, settling for the role of housewife until she lost her life in a tragic shipboard fire a decade after Cash's death. At all events the young instructor was now quits with Georgetown College. He obtained a teaching post for the following school year near his home, at the Hendersonville School for Boys in Hendersonville, North Carolina.

At that school, beyond possibly trying a novel in the manner of Dostoevsky, he merely confirmed his already low opinion of contemporary Southern education. To the sociologist Howard Odum he wrote: "Two years as a teacher have led me to believe that the average Southern high school graduate is about as well informed as an inferior grammar school product should be, that he can't think, and that, worse, incompetent teachers have made it pretty certain that he never will think." Further, his contact with Southern college students, he said, "makes me think that only a handful have any genuine interest in the ideas that begin to circulate in some of them, and that the great mass is satisfied with football, rah-rah, and Commerce A."

Disillusioned with teaching, and as critical of his native South at twenty-five as he was uncritical at fifteen, Cash left both teaching and the South. Although he had been intimidated by the wintry blasts at Valparaiso University, he headed for nearby Chicago, then in the heyday of its literary and journalistic glitter, and got a reporting job on the old Chicago *Post*. Unfortunately, this starveling sheet could muster a circulation of some 48,000 at a time when its leading competitor in the evening field, the *Daily News*, claimed 400,000. Cash made little headway on the moribund *Post*, which was destined to perish in the first days of the Depression, and the impecunious reporter remembered little of his experience except amusedly observing the courtships of some monkeys in a pet-shop window.

He was back in North Carolina in 1926 on the staff of the Charlotte *News*, and he was successively reporter, assistant to the city editor, and state news editor. He introduced himself as Jack Cash and was at once at home in the tiny city newsroom. His contempt for the *status quo*, his impatience with "right thinking," never turned him sour on the human level. Jack Cash is remembered as warm, sympathetic, generous, listening more than talking (slumped in a chair with his balding head propped against a wall), but a brilliant conversationalist when aroused. He was already expressing scorn of the growing reputation of the group of Nashville poets who had founded *The Fugitive* (1922–5). He rejected their "posing" as he was to reject the later Agrarian thesis some of them published in 1930 as the symposium *I'll Take My Stand.* As always Cash kept reading everything he could lay hands on: Mencken, of course; but of the older writers Voltaire was his particular god, and his other favorites included Montaigne, Villon, Verlaine, Heine, Rabelais, and Eckermann. He had, of course, grown up with Gibbon, Hazlitt, Keats, Pepys, Jeremy Taylor, and Shakespeare.

Cash roomed with his editor of college days, Edwin Holman, who was working for the opposition Charlotte *Observer*, and in November 1926, when Holman married, Cash had to be dispossessed. Cash was one of those people who take an instant liking, or an instant dislike, to those whom they meet. He was also considered a "problem," and he knew it. Indeed, he warned Holman, when Holman invited him to meet his bride in their new home: "I may be nervous. I have done such things as knocking things off a table. I may be a total flop." But Cash also liked to be kidded and teased, so when Holman's bride sat him down to a table whose cloth she had taped down against his presumed clumsiness, he roared with laughter. They got along famously thereafter.

His plain country upbringing—of which he was proud, because he was not one to "go back on his raising"—nevertheless made him admittedly uncomfortable and self-conscious in the presence of "the country clubbers," as he called them. It was this unease that kept him from meeting the girl he was to marry more than a decade later. Jack feared she might be "snooty." To be sure, most of the people who made him nervous were not his intellectual equals, but his self-consciousness held him in thrall until the spell was broken years later with the publication of *The Mind of the South*. All the more, then, were his hard-bitten mates on the *News* good for him: men like Tom Revelle, the one-armed mountain-bred Republican; the widower Tim Pridgen, from whom Cash often cadged a night's lodging; John Dickson, the courteously wry city editor; and Tom Jimison, the bantam lawyer-preacher-journalist, who later had to bow out of the Gastonia strikers' defense staff when the Communists took over. Old Mr. Warren, a broken-down proofreader who was allowed to salvage his pride by writing a Sunday column, warned Jack against churches and churchgoers. Cash laughingly agreed with the erudite old man that no modern civilized parents would ever send their kids to Sunday school.

During those newspaper days Jack continued his efforts at writing fiction, in a later Guggenheim application recalling "a subjective novel which I destroyed without submitting to any publisher, a blood-and-thunder romance which I disposed of in the same fashion, and two short stories, one of which I submitted to Harper's Magazine, and the other to The American Mercury; both came back very rapidly and very properly." The "blood-and-thunder romance" that Cash later destroyed may well have been a manuscript left in his desk at the *News* after he left the paper in 1928. Katherine Grantham, the paper's book editor and his friend, returned the manuscript; she recalled the plot centering pretentiously on a beautiful young white goddess of a primitive South Sea people. If published, this potboiling novella would scarcely have enhanced Cash's reputation.

Though Jack's glandular trouble with hyperthyroidism had subsided by this time, he recalled in a later Guggenheim application that "it had left behind it a marked nervous erethism [extreme irritability] and made it necessary for me to decline opportunities to join staffs of newspapers in Cleveland and New York." He now consulted a urologist in Charlotte, with whom he came to form a personal friendship, and also began his own investigation of abnormal psychology, an investigation that was, for a layman, quite thorough. The urologist, Dr. Claude B. Squires, found certain malfunctions—expressed in the medicine of that day as "imbalance"—in a variety of his patient's internal secretions, and Cash suffered from the standard symptoms of moodiness and depression. In the summer of 1927, he recalled to Mencken, "threatened with a complete nervous collapse, I went abroad."

Before embarking for Europe in New York City he looked up the lovely Peggy Ann, who was then making her bid for a stage career while supported by a handsome allowance from her banker father. To someone as fiercely proud as Cash, it was galling to see Peggy Ann so expensively dressed and so financially independent of the likes of him. She insisted on their going everywhere by cab and slipped him large-denomination bills to pay their way at the fashionable restaurants and theaters to which she took him. He recalled with humiliation that her entertainment of him cost more than his entire third-class passage to Europe.

Cash spent the summer and fall of 1927 overseas, returning in December with a love for Europe that he cherished ever after. He did send distress cables to his Charlotte *News* friends when he was down and out in Paris and London, but that was his usual improvident way, and somehow it was all made right. He bicycled his way through France, England, Italy, Germany, and Belgium. "Once rode a bicycle," he noted for Alfred Knopf, "from Paris via Tours to Brest and back to Granville in Normandy, and from Lyons to Nîmes. Have tramped the Riviera, and in the Pyrenees and the French and Swiss Alps." His overexposure to the Baptist fundamentalism of his youth was in part redressed at Chartres Cathedral (having devoured Henry Adams, Cash wouldn't have missed it). Katherine Grantham recalled Jack telling her: "As I stood looking at the magnificent blue lancets, and then at the rose window, I found myself crying. I didn't believe a word of the notions that inspired such a masterpiece, but I kept on weeping and damn-near dropped to my knees. At last I blew my nose hard and went out and walked around that massive structure and I started crying again."

Jack observed later about Europe that, unlike in America with its raw newness, "Everywhere you looked you saw the work of man," but like many Americans without enough time to spend in England he found the English cold and unresponsive. It was continental Europe that really earned his love as he tramped and bicycled, rebuilding his health, among people whom he found natural and friendly. At the outbreak of World War II he was reminded of Mainz as he saw it in 1927 and of the contrast in behavior of Germans and French as conquerors. The French finally evacuated the Rhineland in 1930; Hitler's troops marched in in 1936. He recalled:

> The French soldiers sat along the Rhine embankments and played with the German children, they walked through the streets as they might have walked through the streets of a French town, without anything of self-conscious arrogance. And, though I did my best, I could find no hatred for them among the Germans of the town.

In his later certitude that he understood his psychological difficulties, Cash often referred to the Europe of 1927. On one such occasion he wrote:

> It is my vanity to fancy that I know a good deal about myself. I can observe and catalogue and account for my vagaries. But as to why the sight of a not particularly lovely apple tree flinging its arms grotesquely against a red field should invariably move me to rapture—as to why, stepping out into the little square beneath the soaring tower of the great cathedral at Strasbourg, I should suddenly (and though some finer cathedrals had left me cold) have been stricken with a nearly irresistible impulse to burst out bawling—I can't tell you, for all my diligent searching of Freud.

Cash quite simply fell in love with France and its people. Once, after interviewing the sister of Thomas Wolfe, Mrs. Mabel Wolfe Wheaton, he wrote:

> I have seen brown-faced women about Arles, where all the strains of the North and the Mediterranean have met and merged, who reminded me a great deal of Mrs. Wheaton—of Thomas Wolfe. Contemplation and force: these are the qualities in those faces that immediately impress you. The brown eyes look at you with a penetrating directness, give you the impression of extraordinary concentration. And there is something else there, too—a feeling of profound kindness and understanding, an eager will to like and be liked, the absence of the mean little hostility and suspicion, the will to impress, with which most of us encounter strangers.

Enjoying another momentary restoration to health on his return, Cash buoyantly wrote for the *News* the following April a luminous and introspective memoir of a lotus-eater's day on France's Mediterranean coast. The piece is stylistically so different from Cash's *Mind,* so cryptic where the other is elaborate, so dreamlike in tone where the other is coolly analytical, so nearly stream-of-consciousness, in fact, that it must have been an experiment in fictional style. But unlike his French fishing village, where under his window sounded "the slow lap-lap of the Ancient Sea," Charlotte, North Carolina, all too soon meant a return to Cash's precarious near-breakdown state. After a consultation with his urologist, Cash resigned from the *News* and, in his home county, took a job that was supposedly less taxing: editor of the semiweekly *Cleveland Press* in Shelby, North Carolina.

In that summer of 1928 Shelby's brightest political star, O. Max Gardner, was already a sure thing for governor of the one-party state (in local politics), but Cleveland County was girding as for Armageddon with the impending Smith–Hoover election campaign. In Charlotte, which was the headquarters of the anti-Smith propaganda, Cash had already familiarized himself with the elements of the conservative establishment. He discerned a gentleman's agreement involving the Duke Power Company and Duke Endowment, the church leaders, the textile barons, and their organ, the Charlotte *Observer*. The pretense of the drys that it was prohibition and not anti-Catholicism that defeated Smith impressed Cash not at all; he saw too much cynical exploitation of latent anti-Catholic feeling for that. For the Guggenheim Foundation, Jack later recorded:

> The county in which I was located was violently anti-Catholic, and my editorials deriding that sentiment quickly involved me in a bitter fight. The upshot was that, shortly after the end of the campaign, the sheet died, and, on the advice of physicians, I retired to my native village to rest for a few months.

Back in Boiling Springs, Cash set to work organizing all the political notes he had made in Shelby, the county seat. These notes would result in a magazine piece about Senator Furnifold M. Simmons, the state's political little giant, who was against Al Smith; but in the winter of 1928–9 Cash dropped it for a rather frenzied trip by day coach to somewhere in the North Central states to plead his cause before the "only girl" he would ever marry (as he repeatedly insisted)—Peggy Ann. Perhaps he had heard of her marriage, or her impending marriage. Perhaps he was newly hopeful of an independent writing career and thought he could now ask her to marry him. At any rate, her reply was in the nature of a rebuff, and he wept when he told a Charlotte friend the story. He well knew that his "first failure" with her would always stand between them. He should have known, however, that his particular brand of woman worship, in which premarital sex with "decent" women is subconsciously taboo, was the probable cause of that "first failure." Instead, he allowed that memory to haunt him.

Nevertheless, he returned to Boiling Springs determined to succeed as a free-lance writer, to complete his article about political boss Simmons. In May 1929, Cash mailed his manuscript, "Jehovah of the Tar Heels," to his idolized Mencken at *The American Mercury*. The author had little trouble showing that Simmons had really been a covert Republican in a one-party—and only nominally a Democratic-party—state. Cash's own Menckenian tone was equally marked. Simmons's career, he avowed, "is a devastating exposé of the essential sottishness of democracy" (this from a later New Dealer). As for the white-supremacy campaign over which Simmons had presided at the turn of the century (Cash rather mangled the chronology in his account): "The coon shivered at home behind closed shutters. . . . It was in fact the end of the blackamoor as a menace to the ascendancy of the Goth." It was all a Mencken-type pulverization of Simmons, plus a secondhand but generally sound analysis of Tar Heel politics, but most of all a gorgeous and virtuoso writing display.

Later that May, Cash swaggered into the small, incredibly dingy city room on the ground floor rear of the old Charlotte *News* building. He was flourishing a two-hundred-dollar check from Mencken (which he had almost torn up thinking it a subscription letter), plus an encouraging note from the Baltimore Sage, who accepted the first article and wanted more. The middle-aged Mary Pressly, who was then editor of the church and school pages and used to mother Cash in his blue moods, instantly swept her "Bill Joe" into her arms. She and his other friends crowded around to congratulate him, although Mary Pressly, who deplored Cash's inveterate "blasphemy," might not have been so enthusiastic had she known the article would appear in the July *Mercury* as "Jehovah of the Tar Heels."

A short time afterward, Cash again changed his characteristic shuffle into a little swagger to announce another sale to Mencken. In this article, he struck some of the major chords that had sounded in his perceptive being for the last decade: the continuity of the Old South mind with that of the so-called New South, the South's moony sentimentality, its extreme individuality, its harsh Calvinism as the South prepared to become even more of an industrialized Babbitt haven than the North. Cash's language was at this time totally and spectacularly Menckenian, for the Baltimore Sage usually exacted that kind of stylistic uniformity from his contributors. Nevertheless, Mencken was delighted to find a Southerner with an original turn of mind who could crack dull heads along with the master himself, and Mencken had a vastly energizing effect on the young author.

Cash's latest article appeared in *The American Mercury* of October 1929. Its title was "The Mind of the South."

CHAPTER 3

The Loner

*A*s was to be expected from a typically acidulous article in Mencken's *American Mercury*, "The Mind of the South" stirred things up admirably—to the tune of about fifty editorials (all but two from the old Confederacy) and uncounted letters. One of the letters came from a nice old gentleman in Nashville, Tennessee, who was named Cash and now pronounced anathema against Jack and read the traitor out of the family and out of Dixie. *The New York Times*, in its editorial page "Topics," sniffed superiorly as such "callow articles" that set themselves up as the bases of sociological comment. The most charitable editorial was contributed by Grover Hall of the Montgomery *Advertiser*, as Cash remembered with good humor: "Mr. Hall did allow that I wrote well, but for the rest he proceeded to opine at great length that I was unmistakably an idiot." Cash could afford to laugh, for the article showed first-rate promise, and the author himself was quick enough to perceive its occasional flaws of overgeneralization. It is instructive to note, too, that the adverse criticism largely stirred up by the provocative tone of the article (1929) changed to a chorus of almost unmixed praise for the book (1941).

On publication in the *Mercury* of "Mind," Cash showed up in the Charlotte *News* city room flourishing a letter he

had received from Blanche W. Knopf. At that time the
Knopfs shared the same offices with Mencken, and manu-
scripts were thus freely exchanged. Mrs. Knopf had invited
Cash to send his first book—he must be writing a book—to
Knopf, and would he send her an outline of work to be done
plus a sample chapter? An outline wouldn't take long, Jack
airily informed his friends, and in the sample chapter he
planned to attack the Fugitives for their romanticizing of the
Old South, and Dr. Edwin Mims, then head of Vanderbilt's
English department, for doing the same with the New. Like
Mencken, Cash greatly admired Dr. Howard W. Odum of
the University of North Carolina, and in framing the reply
to Mrs. Knopf, Cash now sought the advice of that pioneer
regional sociologist. So Dr. Odum received from one W. J.
Cash of Boiling Springs, North Carolina, a prodigious six-
page single-spaced typewritten letter outlining in detail
ideas for a book to be called *The Mind of the South.*

In the letter the younger man rehearsed virtually every
element of his exploration, but mainly the persistent sentimentality that he found barring a realistic view of the South's
plight. "I want to go into the psychology of the cotton-mill
hand, the baron . . . I'm much interested in the reasons for
the prevalence of Ku Kluckery. And I'm even interested in
the effect that the Negro has had on the thinking of the
white man of the South." Odum encouraged Cash while
warning him against any too pat use of categories and clas-
sifications in discussing the Old South. The younger man
quickly agreed that the Old South was indeed marked by a
relative absence of class lines, and this exchange of views
with Odum evidently led Cash to his literary device of "the
man at the center." He wrote Odum: "I comfort myself with
the hope that my fictions will serve for the getting at of at
least part of the truth, and that is the part which is being
pretty generally ignored."

Meanwhile, the reply to Mrs. Knopf had to wait while

Cash busily prepared another article, this time on the great Gastonia strike of 1929. That spring, union organizers had moved into the mill town of Gastonia, where the Manville–Jenckes Company of Pawtucket, Rhode Island, was "economically" producing yarn for cord tires at the Loray mills. One thousand Loray workers struck on behalf of a twenty-dollar minimum weekly wage, a forty-hour week, an end to the stretch-out system, reduction of utility rates in their company-owned houses, and recognition of the union. The millowners replied that the union organizers were Communists and promptly closed their mills. These organizers were indeed Communists who were exploiting the very real misery of the mill workers, but the militantly anti-union millowners had the identical response to all organizers whether AFL or Primitive Baptist. Governor O. Max Gardner quickly called out the state guard to keep order in Gastonia, where nine of every ten men were now jobless.

As a penetrating observer of the strike at Gastonia, twenty-nine miles from his home in Boiling Springs, Jack Cash needed nobody to tell him that the Communist leaders were exploiting the extreme need of the Loray workers in the interest of a copybook proletarian uprising. Nor did he need anyone to tell him that the mill owners and the business establishment were suspending civil liberties and appealing to mob action as part of their inveterate enmity to collective bargaining, Communists or no. Cash knew that the mob of masked men who destroyed the union headquarters was led by "the best people." Later, when Fred Beal (who was not even present, and who in later years recanted his Communism) was tried for conspiracy to murder Gastonia's police chief, Cash heard his lawyer friend Tom Jimison tell reporters that the trial was a frame-up. Jimison warned them not to be "fooled into believing that this is nothing but a murder trial because it is a Labor Case." Cash then and there learned his lesson about the climate of opinion in which

Southern justice had to operate, and about the make-up of juries that would hear the same "patriotic" arguments to convict Fred Beal, who had shot nobody, as were used to free the sheriff's deputies at Marion, North Carolina, who had indeed shot five men to death and wounded twice as many more.

Cash's article about the Gastonia textile strike was published in *The American Mercury* of February 1930 as "The War in the South" (reprinted in this volume). In it he clearly acknowledged his debt to Dr. Broadus Mitchell on the "philanthropic" origin of many cotton mills, and then went beyond him in positing a precariously employed white man who was grateful for the millowner's philanthropy and thus possessed a built-in resistance to "foreign" unions. The author was appropriately Menckenian in denouncing the stupid Communist leadership of the strike. He reminded his readers that even a legitimate AFL union like the United Textile Workers of America (which had sponsored the sad little strike that reporter Cash covered in North Charlotte in 1923) had unavailingly "tried the introduction of the Brotherhood of Man into that amazing and sulfurous land below the Potomac." He also paid his jeering respects to David Clark of Charlotte, spokesman for the millowners in his *Southern Textile Bulletin* (the "Southern" was dropped a few years later), Clark being the ultraconservative son of an aristocratic radical father, Walter Clark, North Carolina's longtime chief justice.

Despite all, Cash predicted that a new generation would see Southern strikes successful. He wrote: "And the ultimate outcome is as inevitable as the cycle of the sun: the labor union will conquer." But in *The Mind of the South* Cash did not repeat his earlier naïveté, because a full decade of Southern union-busting (fully detailed in his book) had taught him better. The book has stood up so well precisely

because Cash nowhere showed himself an easy mark for
facile optimism.

That March, still fighting off ill health, he sent a carefully
detailed sketch of his book to Mrs. Knopf. He wrote:

> My thesis is that the Southern Mind represents a very definite
> culture, or attitude towards life, a heritage, primarily, from
> the Old South, but greatly modified and extended by con-
> scious and unconscious efforts over the last hundred years to
> protect itself from the encroachments of three hostile factors:
> the Yankee Mind, the Modern Mind, and the Negro. In other
> words, it is a combination of certain orthodoxies and a defense
> mechanism. On that basis, it seems to me that this book ought
> probably to fall into some such division as this: Introduction,
> The Mind of the Old South, The South and the Yankee Mind,
> the South and the Modern Mind, Conclusion.

But the earlier approbation of Dr. Odum, and now that
of Mrs. Knopf, could not prevent the physical collapse that
had been threatening Cash all along. He was forced to enter
a hospital in Charlotte, where he remained for several
months. On his discharge he was ordered by his doctors, as
he recalled it later for the Guggenheim Foundation, "to
refrain completely from writing and study of any kind, and,
indeed, even from reading. For the next two years, these
doctors kept me outdoors—riding a bicycle over the country-
side, walking, swimming, and cutting wood." At home, he
could see a little more of his father now that John Cash's
hosiery mill was kept working only one or two days a week—
mostly out of *noblesse oblige,* to keep the millhands from
utter privation. Against a too strict father, Wilbur Cash acted
as his sister Bertie's champion; she was ten years his junior
and the sort of "tow-headed blonde" who reminded him of
the girls he had seen in Germany. Nevertheless, Wilbur also
harbored a strong Victorian streak, and he was scandalized
at Bertie's desire to spend a summer as a waitress in Washington. He insisted that she become a teacher—not a nurse—

and helped her to apply for certification when the time came.

Cash's skepticism in religious matters was accepted at home, where an occasional clutch of local "missionaries" would disperse after battering in vain against his obduracy. On one such occasion, after a stonily prolonged silence in the face of his proselytizers, he explained: "Well, Mother, they would never understand." But there is evidence that John Cash tried to "understand" his son's unorthodoxy. In Wilbur's Student Bible, the rear flyleaf contains a passage in John Cash's hand taken from Doughty's *Arabia Deserta* (1923 edition), and following on the same page, in Wilbur's hand, are his notes on a reading of Sayce's *The "Higher Criticism" and the Verdict of the Monuments*. The father headed his page of quotes from Doughty "Jeremiah 48:23," happily having found the author's reference to Jeremiah's antique city of basalt, which the archaeologist was confirming as a historically accurate biblical text. On the other hand, Wilbur's notes on Sayce indicate that he was especially interested in the areas of the Bible that the author insists are not, in any case, supposed to be interpreted as historical. It is a truism that fathers and sons do not easily communicate across the time-gap that separates them, but at least Wilbur and John Cash were making an honest effort.

The son confessed to Alfred Knopf:

> Since childhood I have had an unconquerable aversion for parsons because of their cocksure certainty in a world in which nothing is certain but that nothing is certain; because their professions have always seemed mawkish; and because their inquiries after one's soul has always struck me as indecent: a man's soul, if he has one, ought obviously to be his own private concern. Yet I know a few parsons who have my respect and liking.

One of those few parsons was a man he knew in Boiling Springs. At the time of his physical and psychical low point,

Cash formed an attachment for a certain "Preacher" Honeycutt, with whom he exchanged evening visits that sometimes
lasted into the wee hours, discussing the most intimate problems of life and destiny. Preacher Honeycutt was a Baptist
clergyman who had never been able to hold a congregation.
He was too unorthodox for fundamentalist tastes but a brilliant and genuinely pious man who was well read enough to
stimulate Cash. He and Preacher Honeycutt would talk of
man and God, of the human soul and immortality, often
disagreeing but always urbane and mutually respectful. On
leaving the Honeycutts' place, Cash would often smile at the
other's sons and say: "You dad is just a mystic."

To Alfred Knopf he elaborated further:

> I have developed a great interest in the sciences. Yet, for
> all my belief and confidence here, the universe seems to me
> to be ultimately an impenetrable mystery. And though I have
> no time for creeds or theological constructions of any kind,
> I sympathize fully with the awe which is perhaps the pri-
> mary source of religion. . . . I think La Rochefoucauld and
> not Karl Marx laid his hand on the true primary key to human
> action—that vanity and not economic interest prevails. But
> even that is only a half-truth.

If Preacher Honeycutt served as catalyst to Cash's religious development, his political education was largely
guided by Everett Houser, a newspaperman and Superior
Court clerk at the county seat. In the days when Cash was
not building bookshelves for his father's house or bicycling
the fifty miles to Charlotte, he would hitch a ride out to
Houser's home and inspect the town's only copy of *The
Nation* magazine. With Houser he would share his enthusiasm for Don Marquis, his indifference to the great success
scored by the first novel of Thomas Wolfe, and his tastes in
literature, which at that time ran to the esoteric, like Lafcadio Hearn. To Houser, Cash would confide his distaste for

the establishment that then ran North Carolina with startling openness—the consortium formed by owners of power companies and textile mills. Instead of accepting such domination as a fact of life, as Houser did, Wilbur seethed inwardly, particularly at the white-supremacy hypocrisy he discerned in the state's political leadership. In fact, the one magazine article he could turn out in this difficult period was about another Red Shirt leader like "Jehovah" Furnifold Simmons: Senator Cameron Morrison, a Charlotte prohibitionist and former governor.

In *The American Mercury* for October 1931, Cash wrought destruction on Morrison. Editor Mencken hated nothing with such malevolent joy as the Noble Experiment, and the piece obviously was attuned to him, because Cash inserted another of Mencken's pet hates: "Walter Hines Page [of North Carolina], gentleman-in-waiting to His Majesty, King George V." This article, like the one about the Gastonia strike, was the offshoot of many hours of talk with Everett Houser, talk during which Cash's words could not quite keep up with his overstimulated thoughts. Poor Cameron Morrison had to take his lumps by comparison, as the author saw it, with such cynical showmen as Tom Heflin and Cole Blease. Wrote Cash: "Our hero, on the other hand, has no more showmanship in him than that innocent minimum which naturally inheres in any true protagonist of an essentially histrionic land."

Even in the wake of an unbroken series of acceptances by Editor Mencken, even with the avowed interest of the Knopfs in his writing career, Cash could not follow through because of his health difficulties, physical and mental. Like many neurotics this man with the brilliant but brittle mind thought that a physical change of scene would work a change in him personally; that going to sea, as he went to Europe in 1927, would somehow straighten him out. Accordingly he wrote away for, and obtained, a seaman's berth on a merchant ship sailing from New York. Then he hurried off to New York, but he became ill in his hotel before shipping out. The house doctor had to send for John Cash, who came up from Boiling Springs to take his son home. As a result of that experience, and on referral by his urologist in Charlotte, Cash started the year 1932 by going off to the Johns Hopkins Hospital in Baltimore. Raising the money was exceedingly difficult, for many bank failures had already hit the Carolinas, but Everett Houser helped out with a loan.

In a Guggenheim application written later in 1932, Cash set it down: "Early this year I consulted specialists at the Johns Hopkins Hospital, in Baltimore, and was assured that my health was now quite good." In fact, as the Charlotte specialist recalled, there were brilliant results from Cash's urology treatment at Baltimore, and so far as his recurrent fear of impotence was concerned, the author was assured that he was physically quite sound. What he needed, but did not get because it was not then available to him, was the kind of psychiatric help that could have spared him. But at that time the connection between endocrine and psychological disorders was not yet generally understood. A quarter century after the author's death, his urologist, Dr. Squires, stated flatly that had Cash been in the hands of the right psychiatrist during the 1930's, when he suffered intermittent spells of depression, he would have survived into ripe old age.

Cash thought he understood his difficulty, thought he could live with it. He recorded for Knopf in 1936: "Five years ago I was a complete neurasthenic, but I have since largely cured myself." To author Lillian Smith he reported in 1936 that he had first been visited by "neurasthenia in 1929, and threw away five years industriously nursing it." But his condition persisted, for he again noted to Knopf, this time in 1940: "A big fellow, I am a confirmed neurasthenic, habitually expect the worst." And to the Guggenheim

Foundation later that same year he wrote: "The illness [of the early 1930's] was mainly neurasthenic rather than physical, but it was some years before I got any insight into that and began to pull myself out of it, haltingly."

Pronounced fit at Johns Hopkins, Cash took himself off to New York, where he looked in at Blanche Knopf's office to see if the latchstring was still out for him and his *The Mind of the South*. Mrs. Knopf scolded him for being lazy like all authors, but had to admit a continuing interest in his book, whereupon the relieved author laughingly took his leave. With his Charlotte *News* friend Katherine Grantham, who was now working in the New York area, he went window-shopping on Fifth Avenue and then entered St. Thomas Episcopal Church, where Katherine used to take off her shoes and otherwise relax her spirit in that gem of Gothic architecture. "As we made our way to a pew in the dimly lit rear," she recalled, "the afternoon sun was striking the beautiful windows over the nave, and a boy's choir was singing 'Jesu, Joy of Man's Desiring.' As we listened to those lovely soprano voices and looked at the radiant windows, Jack began crying, then so did I." Being low in pocket they bought the cheapest seats in the steepest gallery of the old Metropolitan Opera House. "Early in the first act," Katherine Grantham recalled about Cash, "I managed to grab him as he started to fall, and somehow got him out to safety, a bench, and a drink of water in the upper hall. About thirty minutes after he took a pill, we began hearing the opera again from that bench."

Despite this frightening episode Jack was determined to resume his free-lance writing career back home. The Depression in Boiling Springs, North Carolina, meant cardboard shoe soles and patches in Cash's shiny pants. Both his jobless brothers had come home to join Cash's parents and his younger sister, for home at least afforded all of them a roof and fairly regular eating. There were no office buildings where Cash could work in peace, but he got the use of the musty "office" behind a partition in the tiny post office that his Aunt Bertha operated as postmistress. He set up his clangorous Underwood and went to work as best he could in the frigid room, his old overcoat pulled up around his ears. The only artificial light available was from a single drop-cord electric light bulb on the post-office side of the partition, so like the old slave he worked between "kin-see and cain't." It was no quiet retreat, Cash's goldfish bowl, because it exposed him to contemptuous comments about a fellow who hadn't the manhood to shoot him a few squirrels for the family table. One of the lads who tormented Cash, Jay Jenkins by name, became a journalist in his turn and did penance for his youthful sins by recording:

> We haunted him. We would slink up to the window, stick out our tongues and leer at him. Failing to get attention in that manner, we pecked tantalizingly on the glass with our fingers. In our devilish way we thought the sight of Cash standing in the door of that room, defaming our ancestry, was the funniest sight in the world. Then Cash departed for Durham to utilize the library there for research material. The story got back that he thumbed and had to walk 40 miles. We thought that was funny, too, which proves our minds were no larger than our small bodies.

One way or another, work in the Boiling Springs goldfish bowl went forward. It went forward despite a certain defeatism that understandably now took hold of Cash. It went forward, more uncertainly, in the face of real qualms about his responsibility, as a young man able to place his writings in influential publications, not to appear a traitor to the South, not to "go back on his raising." He later formulated his dilemma this way:

> To support the status quo in its entirety, to speak not at all or but with exceeding softness against what seemed to me to be crying evils, unforgivable stupidity, on the theory that the

bad that is, is the necessary concomitant of the good that is, and that to arouse sentiment against the one is inevitably to arouse it against the other—or to strike down the whole fabric and possibly to call into existence unknown and greater evils?

He simply was not sure, and, with other things, it kept him in a state of chronic indecision that was disastrous for his writing plans.

Still, by October 1932 he was informing the Guggenheim Foundation that he had completed some sixty thousand words of his work and was hoping to put a completed manuscript in the publisher's hands early next year. Speaking of the same manuscript to the Foundation four years later, Cash wrote, however:

> But I tried to write too rapidly. I discovered that I knew a great deal less about the South than I thought I knew, and above all I grew to dislike the attitude with which I had begun. When it was complete, I looked at it and found that, while it seemed to me to contain some excellent ideas and some passages of good writing, it was neither reasonably fair nor organized into a continuous piece. And so I deliberately destroyed it, without sending it to the publisher at all.

In any case, as he wrote Alfred Knopf when the book was finally and miraculously completed in 1940: "When I first undertook it I was in too much of an emotional stew to do anything which required extended attention."

At that time, however, Cash had talked himself clear of *The Mind of the South* (which was supposed to be completed by early 1933) and was asking the Guggenheim Foundation to underwrite his project to trail Lafcadio Hearn through New Orleans, Ireland, Wales, "increasing my somewhat sketchy acquaintance with London; then to take up residence in Paris, the capital of literary romanticism." To be sure, Hearn as a true romantic—not a precious exotic—was well worth extended study, the man who was born on the Greek island of Leucadia and died on the Japanese island of

Honshu after a fascinating life's journey. But it was an impossibly ambitious undertaking for Cash. Yet he wrote the Foundation:

> I propose an analytical biography of Lafcadio Hearn, to be titled or subtitled, THE ANATOMY OF A ROMANTIC. At any rate, that title is a very good key to what I have in mind. What I intend is not, primarily at least, the gathering and setting forth of new facts about the subject, but the using of the known facts and his letters as a basis for the study of his psychological make-up, and, through him, of the psychological make-up of romantics in general. Further, I plan to study him in connection with the romantic movement in literature, particularly as it has manifested itself in America.

That was the last time anyone heard of Cash's Lafcadio Hearn project.

At the very nadir of the Depression, while President-elect Roosevelt and the New Deal still waited in the wings, Cash let down his personal barriers so far as to write Katherine Grantham, now teaching in a New York academy, for a loan. He was running out of paper, with no money to buy more, and couldn't pay the postage for scholarly books he needed to borrow from the University of North Carolina library at Chapel Hill. After responding with a few dollars and some stationery lifted from her allotment of school supplies, she urged Jack to shelve his research temporarily and write an article for ready money. His next letter was more hopeful, written atop the surge of expectation that mounted during Roosevelt's Hundred Days. And he had indeed written an article for ready money.

The article was about Charlotte, North Carolina, which he depicted with Menckenian brilliance as a den of Babbittry and ancestor worship. "Close View of a Calvinist Lhasa" was published in *The American Mercury* of April 1933 and read with fascinated horror by the whole of Charlotte's literate element, who bought up every copy in town.

True, Cash had worked in Charlotte and would work there again, but he lit into that "citadel of bigotry and obscurantism" with gleeful zest. He pointed out that Charlotte took to Yankee go-getters and Babbittry like a duck to water, and wedded the new order to the old with marvelous efficiency. Cash wrote:

> Do the peons in the mills begin to rise and protest that to work for five dollars a week—as they do work these last bitter days—is too much for human flesh and blood? Then what better answer than the Presbyterian answer that it is all God's will, ordained from the first day?

Cash did detect a few lighter spots on the horizon, including the newfound courage of his old paper, the Charlotte *News* (in defiance of its principal advertisers), in fighting against the Tatum petition that would have removed from the University library at Chapel Hill the works of such troublemakers as Darwin and Freud.

The momentum of "Calvinist Lhasa" enabled Cash to direct an effort at one of Mencken's dearest targets, those "godly" universities established with the proceeds of piratical gain. In "Buck Duke's University," published in *The American Mercury* of September 1933, Cash was as entertaining as ever. The founding tobacco and power magnate, he wrote of Duke, "remained to the end essentially what he was at seventeen, a red-headed, shambling Methodist jake out of Orange County, North Carolina—which is to say, a sort of peasant out of the Eleventh Century, incredibly ignorant, incredibly obtuse, incredibly grasping and picayune." But Cash saw the joke beginning to turn against the late James Buchanan Duke, for Duke's fundamentalist professors were dying off and were being replaced by men of an altogether different stamp. The Babbitt mill that Buck Duke had created was cut out for a different fate, Cash grinned, and "will go over, lock, stock, barrel, hoof and horn, to theory."

Between publication of those two *Mercury* articles, in the summer of 1933, the hard times dictated a family move from Boiling Springs to Shelby. There, in his bedroom on Belvedere Avenue, Cash tried to write while fighting off ill health and the guilty feeling that he was the family drone. John Cash, renting out the big house in Boiling Springs, for a while commuted the ten miles to the hosiery mill, which was steadily losing money. It was not long before he lost his superintendency at the mill, together with some savings. He brought out of the wreckage only a few machines, with which he proceeded to manufacture men's hosiery in Shelby. John Cash turned out, as always, a product of uncompromisingly high quality, and in those days he could occasionally be seen in Charlotte peddling his good cotton socks at two pairs for a nickel.

Wilbur Cash tried his best, but in the light of his still-powerful defeatism it was mostly of no avail. "Sometimes I lost heart altogether," he recalled later, "and did nothing for months on end." To be sure, he wrote an occasional pot-boiling piece for the obscure Southern Newspaper Syndicate. He placed a piece with the Baltimore *Evening Sun* in November 1933, in which he misjudged North Carolina's vote for state prohibition as a repudiation of Roosevelt's policies. Also he sold his only poorly done piece of the *Mercury* series, "Holy Men Muff a Chance," which was published in the issue of January 1934. In it he observed: "The preachers have flatly failed to make anything out of it [the Depression], either for religion or for themselves." This sneer at the "rev. clergy" was accepted and published in the issue following Mencken's own valedictory in *The American Mercury*. The article was downright tiresome, acceptable only to a bored Mencken who himself realized that the old days of high adventure on the *Mercury* were gone.

All this was the unpromising picture that Cash called up to the good people of Shelby: a grown man, and a skeptic at that, sponging on the unremitting toil of his indulgent and Christian parents. Those parents, to their everlasting honor, stoutly defended their son and put every ounce of their credit as God-fearing Baptist pillars behind Wilbur. Mother Cash had, of course, realized that her eldest was an extra-bright boy, and she did so long before her preoccupied husband. It was like John Cash to refrain from teaching Wilbur that he was bright; he would not have done so even if he had been aware of it. John Cash was Leveler enough not to have wanted Wilbur to think himself superior to his neighbors. But, in his ninety-second year, the father thought about it quietly for a few moments and then said, in hushed words: "I never taught Wilbur that he was extra-smart— but he was."

Of Cash's contemporaries in Shelby, only Cameron Shipp fully appreciated him for his intellect. The newly married Shipp was then editor of the semiweekly *Cleveland Star*, which became a triweekly in 1935 and a daily, the Shelby *Daily Star*, the year after that. Shipp enjoyed Cash's wit, which he knew how to stimulate, admired his really awesome store of universal knowledge, and listened fascinatedly as he unfolded his theses of "The Mind of the South." Cam Shipp thus came to be Cash's benefactor and champion, lending the prestige of his editorship to this queer duck who had no regular job to go to in the morning. Cash liked to spend his evenings with people who understood him, and it became a sort of family joke among local wives as to whose husband was bringing Cash home this time. The author had an utter disregard for where his cigarette ashes fell—he rolled his own smokes—and the wives who had to clean up after him muttered rebelliously that he ought to know when it was time to go home.

Another sympathetic listener to the welter of ideas that Cash was trying to subdue into some kind of order was Erma Drum, the *Star*'s women's page or "society" editor.

Her late husband, another of Cash's cronies, had been editor of the *Star* at about the time the Cash family first moved to Shelby. However, Cash did not talk much about himself to Erma Drum, or to Cameron Shipp or other friends. Although most Shelby people in the mid-thirties had little money, Cash obviously had even less; but he would never talk about his poverty. Later, when the Shelby installment of the *Mind* manuscript was being assembled for the Knopfs, Erma Drum would take her typewriter home from the *Star*—not having one of her own—and type Cash's manuscript after putting her children to bed. She recalled: "I don't even remember how it came about that I did the typing chore, except that I was a good typist and he was a friend in sore need of such a skill, and without the money to pay for having it done."

He was Sleepy Cash to adults in Shelby, but Mr. Cash to the high-school youngsters, who would question him with respect. He kept his distance from most people; above all, he kept his dignity. One would see him talking to a high-schooler, gravely trying out some of his ideas on the lad with the same courteous concentration he would give a judge—even more than on a judge, perhaps, for he was known to be out of step with the local political hierarchy. Cameron Shipp used to invite Cash around to the *Star* office, and Cash even wrote a few editorials, including some prescient ones about Hitler as early as 1935, until publisher Lee B. Weathers got wind of his unorthodox editorialist. Unwelcome at the *Star*, Cash would gravitate elsewhere. After one Sunday breakfast, he and Lindsay Dail of the *Star* drove over to Hendersonville and passed the time deciphering the epitaphs on tombstones in an old church graveyard.

Cash often frequented the benches around the courthouse square, but his most familiar station was outside the old Stephenson Drug Store, where he would wait quietly for some human contact. He needed people; he was not self-propelled. Inside Stephenson's he would read the magazines and books. He quietly inveighed against the powers of Shelby, who were then dominant in state politics, for boasting about their municipal payroll while unable, they claimed, to afford a public library. With his friends he would sip beer at a local hangout, and at such times his tongue would become somewhat loosened; or he might go to the movies, which he enjoyed if they were serious enough. Cash was absolutely noiseless in a crowd, as opposed to tête-à-tête, and would drift away if the conversation lagged. Lindsay Dail recalled that Cash let down his reserve with a woman only if she was someone who worked for the *Star* and was regarded as "one of the boys."

Physically he looked quite well, plump but not fat, a big fellow with a comparatively large head, broad forehead, and large compelling brown eyes that were surprisingly soft when he took off his glasses. Mentally alert, he nevertheless appeared always to be thinking of something more profound and more remote than the matter immediately at hand. If approached and drawn out, he would talk freely. To Lindsay Dail he would impart an encyclopedic history of weaponry and express the fear of a new weapon that would some day emerge as too destructive for human control; to Charles Keel of the *Star* he would speculate that the newly developed system of FM radio held great promise; to another he would state that this or that New Deal measure would not solve the unemployment problem; to another he would warn that the people of the South were living with a false pride and were headed for a fall. On one occasion, considering the human condition and speaking in the abstract, he actually avowed to his boyhood friend Dr. E. V. Moore that perhaps the man who committed suicide was wiser than his brother who did not. The real Cash, according to a friend of those days, was rarely cheerful and basically pessimistic.

In the spring of 1935, as he wrote to Alfred Knopf later

that year, Cash again took up the manuscript, most of it written three years earlier, and found that it "was so hopelessly out of line with changes in my ideas and so unsatisfactorily organized that the best thing to do was to scrap it *in toto* and start in again virtually from the beginning." A few years later Cash gave his Charlotte *News* readers a more whimsical explanation of that unsatisfactory manuscript. One of his problems, he recalled,

> resided in the fact that I felt myself bound to try to back up some of my statements with references to facts in the books of other men. Which, I thought, must mean footnotes. So I started cheerfully out to pile them up on almost every page. Here I was writing a tome that was going to look like nothing so much as a doctor's thesis, and calculated to scare off all the cash customers—something I certainly hadn't planned. Wherefore, having gazed at the facts with the long reluctance of a lazy man, I at length heaved all I had done away and started over again.

Cash's health was now somewhat restored, he no longer felt himself balked by those awesome footnotes, he had overcome the self-styled defeatism that had been plaguing him, so in 1935 he once again set to work. He was still very much a perfectionist, throwing away perhaps twenty pages for every one he kept, but the acceptable copy began to mount. The first evidence was the appearance in *The American Mercury* of May 1935 of Cash's "Genesis of the Southern Cracker." Appearing in the magazine after Paul Palmer had acquired it, the article carried one step further the idea of the mill baron and the poor white as "brothers." Cash dropped the spectacular Menckenian language and developed further his own "savage ideal" and, at least embryonically, his "proto-Dorian convention." Moreover, while the pages of the new *Mind of the South* were piling up, Cash turned to that aspect of the "savage ideal" called Negro lynching, a subject that he had pursued with Everett Houser and many another sympathetic listener.

That same May saw the pistol suicide in Tuscaloosa, Alabama, of a kindred spirit who had criticized the "best people's" tacit toleration of lynching. Cash wrote in his *Mind* (p. 334, Vintage edn.):

> . . . Clarence Cason, who taught journalism at Alabama, felt compelled to commit suicide, in part at least because of his fear of the fiercely hostile attitude which he knew that both the school authorities and his fellow faculty members would take toward his criticism of the South in his 90° *in the Shade,* published by the University of North Carolina Press a few days after his death.

Because Clarence Cason's book was so mild a critique and his fear of nonconformity so extreme, Cash found the episode a classic case history of the Southern intolerance of dissent from racism and of the attitude of the "best people" as the basic reason for the persistence of Negro lynching.

That August, author Cash hit the Baltimore *Evening Sun* with "North Carolina Faces the Facts," which, in citing a new enlightenment in the Tar Heel attitude toward lynching, unhesitatingly recorded his conviction that the "best people" were to blame because of their tacit approval of the outrages. In the course of his argument Cash used the following figure: ". . . the masses stand to the master class very much as, say, the veterans of Austerlitz and Marengo stood to Bonaparte and his marshals." In his later *Mind* (p. 114, Vintage edn.), Cash used the same figure, this time to indicate the post–Civil War hegemony that the captains exercised over the plain people of the South. By extension, of course, that leadership would involve Negro lynching to the extent that the captains countenanced or condoned it. Although Cash opposed a federal anti-lynching law because he feared that it would enrage rather than control the mob, he demonstrated quite conclusively that Negro lynching could not have flourished in the face of a public opinion resolutely hostile to such lynching and guided by an enlightened leadership.

At about this time, Cameron Shipp left the *Star* to become book page editor for the Charlotte *News*, and he wangled just enough from the budget to offer Cash a small subsistence payment in return for a weekly book-page article plus a few editorials as needed. On November 17, 1935, Charlotte *News* readers inspected Cash's first contribution and were introduced to the newcomer by Shipp. Shipp wrote:

> A new contributor, also to become a regular, is W. J. Cash, who discovers, directly above this department, that southern realistic writers are haunted, in particular the clinical Mr. William Faulkner. I commend you the Cash lucubrations, which, whether you always find them agreeable to your notions, are always amusing. This Cash is the same who wrote the Mercury articles. He is now in Shelby completing "The Mind of the South," a performance that is certainly far and away above any contribution I know of attempting to explain why we think like we do.

Three days later, Alfred Knopf wrote Cash: "It is a long time since we have exchanged letters, but I hear rumors that your book is definitely nearing completion. I hope it is still your intention to let me see it, for I am still greatly interested in it." Even though the book was incomplete, it had been awaited so long that Knopf waived his usual rule against considering unfinished manuscripts. In January 1936, Cash sent forward 306 pages of manuscript (through p. 161, Vintage edn.), and he promised the rest of Book Two shortly, which he thought would leave something less than 200 pages to write. However, the manuscript was destined to spin out its length through no fewer than 810 pages. With his book

"60 per cent complete," as he mistakenly thought, the author now looked into the matter of employment in the WPA Federal Writers' Project. Fortunately for Cash's writing plans, Edwin A. Bjorkman, director of the North Carolina unit, advised the author against making too strenuous an effort to land the editing job he had applied for. As soon as Cash had mailed off his 306 pages of manuscript, Cameron Shipp delightedly told his readers in the *News*, "Cash immediately went on strike, refusing to do his contribution for this week. But he was collared at the last minute and under severe goading, complaining that he had sprained his typewriter finger, produced his copy on time."

Both Alfred and Blanche Knopf read Cash's manuscript with approval, as did the house readers. H. L. Mencken chimed in on March 2 with a hearty "aye," and the work was accepted that same day. Cash's friends in Shelby got to see one of his rare smiles when he told them he had received the contract, and on March 6 the *Star* broke the news, complete with alleged plans for two more books "by the Shelby author. He said they will likely be a biography and a novel, to be completed sometime within the next two years." After ironing out the details with Mrs. Knopf, Cash agreed to an advance of $250, with $50 at signing and $50 a month for four successive months. He himself inserted the completion date of July 15, 1936, explaining that the advance would make it possible for him to give the manuscript six days a week until its completion. A month after signing, Cash was sending forward promotional material for his forthcoming book, explaining that he had no particular choice in bindings except that he disliked green. "In types," he continued, "I like Bodoni, Garamond, and Caslon, in that order." (He later got Granjon.)

Otherwise, Cash was complaining to Knopf about "the neuritis which has been afflicting me intermittently this Spring [and] has had me out for the last four days." Still, he was promising to furnish a duplicate copy of his manuscript for inspection by a possible English publisher. In August, Knopf did indeed receive a batch of manuscript from Shelby, but it turned out to be merely a revision of the original, "the second copy of the book I am having made for submission to England." It was a frustrating setback for Knopf, but instead of scolding the author for thus marking time and making no progress the publisher tactfully advised Cash to forget about the English project for the time.

Although the Knopfs got no manuscript out of Cash that year, they were still not unduly concerned. Mrs. Knopf had gone to visit the author in Shelby, had spent a day with him, and had come away much impressed with his serious intent and with what she found to be his remarkably objective outlook on the Negro question. Then a Knopf editor had suggested, quite rightly, that the existing manuscript could be vastly improved by making concrete its mass of generalizations without, at the same time, turning the book into a statistical brochure. However, the revision took so long—and besides, the author had run up against a stone wall in seeking a proper concluding section—that Knopf had to waive the contractual deadline. That summer too, while turning out his weekly book-page column, Cash had discovered in a little magazine of the South the very diversion he sought from his current writing block.

Long before *Killers of the Dream* and *Strange Fruit*, Lillian Smith and her partner Paula Snelling were making their little journal a pioneer voice of Southern dissatisfaction with the status quo. Their periodical was *Pseudopodia*, published in Clayton, Georgia. (The pseudopod, as the editors explained, is a temporary and tender projection, but after getting letters addressed to "Pseudophobia" they changed the title to *North Georgia Review* and finally to *South Today*.) The editors thanked Cash for his having encouraged them via his Charlotte *News* column and asked for a literary contribution, whereupon he sent forward some self-contained excerpts from his manuscript and bade them take their pick. Only then did he think to seek permission from Mrs. Knopf, who thought it all a bad idea but decided not to object lest it take Cash's aim even further off his target.

"The Reign of the Commonplace" was the excerpt from the author's manuscript that appeared in the Fall 1936 number of *Pseudopodia*. The excerpt was almost word for word identical to the passage in the published *The Mind of the South* (pp. 137–41, Vintage edn.). In it Cash bore down on intolerance of dissent, referring to the fierce Southern insistence upon ideological conformity, by the terms of which even such mild native-son critics as Walter Hines Page and George Washington Cable found that they could not go home again. Lillian Smith's accompanying editorial voiced high praise for Cash's forthcoming book, "which, if the excellent chapters we have read in manuscript are fair samplings, should be a best seller among literate people, and following in the wake of 'Gone With the Wind' [devastatingly reviewed by Miss Smith in the same issue] may act as an astringent to our self-pity." An editor's note prefacing Cash's excerpt remarked, all too hopefully, that the book would be published by Knopf in the spring of 1937.

That spring and summer, while Cash wrote uninterruptedly for the Charlotte *News* at the expense of his own manuscript, he and his friends were further diverted by the North Carolina gubernatorial campaign. In Shelby, one did not speak out against the leading contender, because he was the anointed heir apparent of the Gardner organization (otherwise the Shelby Dynasty), which had dictated Governor Gardner's successor and had now placed the mantle of succession about the shoulders of the former governor's brother-in-law, Clyde R. Hoey. The name was correctly pronounced *Hóo-ey*, which Cash was prone to exaggerate because he remembered Hoey's star-spangled performance as prosecutor of the Gastonia strikers for "conspiracy to murder." Mr. Hoey was the epitome of all that Cash distrusted: a prohibitionist, a Bible-class teacher, a joiner of fraternal organizations, a rafter-ringing orator. His hightop shoes, striped trousers, and swallowtail coat (adorned with a flower) were surmounted by long white flowing hair that fell back to his collar. Yet this Shelby politician embodied all that Cash's own parents admired in a public man, and the author's bitterly self-imposed silence on the subject of Hoey was symptomatic of the trouble he was having writing down the necessarily "traitorous" thoughts that would have to go into the final portion of *Mind*.

That October furnished another diversion: a Guggenheim fellowship application. As Cash wrote Mrs. Knopf: "Mencken says he is willing to testify to the belief I'll make a good job of it, and I hope that you and Mr. Knopf will agree with him." With their assent, and after adding Gerald Johnson to the list, Cash wrote his proposal:

> I propose a year in Germany for work on a novel. Residence would be mainly in Berlin and Munich. I name Germany for a double reason. In the first place, I have a strong personal interest in its culture. And in the second place, I have a particular interest in the Nazi regime and movement as a historical phenomenon, and want an opportunity to observe it at close range.

As to the novel, it would be "a story of the Old South as it was, rather than as the legend-mongers have made it out to be." Then he quoted from his current manuscript the passage about his "stout young Irishman" great-great-grandfather (pp. 15–17, Vintage edn.) by way of setting the theme, which was, in effect, the influence on the land of the notion of class.

If Cash was beset with a writing block where his manuscript was concerned, he experienced nothing of that sort when writing his contributions to the Charlotte *News*. A regular Sunday column for the book page plus a scattering of editorials, they were of uniformly high quality: witty, erudite, urbane, and pointed. His editorials, all on foreign affairs, lashed out at the Axis aggressors with an expertise on international affairs that was virtually unmatched in his region. His columns were even more of a feast because they were even more original, sometimes taking a new book for a point of departure, more often reverting to Cash's own enthusiasms in reading. One time Cash would suggest: "Two essays which, if I had my way about it, would be read and expounded to American school boys and girls at least once every day are John Stuart Mill's 'On Liberty' and William Hazlitt's 'On Vulgarity and Affectation.'" Another time he offered a note on literary charm and wittily discussed the three books that had charmed him most: Pepys's *Diary*, Montaigne's *Essays*, and Chaucer's *Canterbury Tales*. He wrote perceptively of contemporary Southern authors like Cabell, Faulkner, and Wolfe (he liked them in that order) and of those contemporary Europeans whose Ku Kluckery, as Cash referred to Nazi ideas of race, was bolstered by a false appeal to Nietzsche.

By the fall of 1937 it became clear that Cash's bid for economic independence as a free-lance writer was not working out. Payment for his part-time Charlotte *News* work was minimal, his family had had to move into more modest quarters in Shelby, and something called a "recession" had afflicted the land. Now John Cash withdrew from the textile business altogether and got himself a job on the road as a shoe salesman, and his son Wilbur, now the only one of the children living at home, knew it was time for him to leave. He was getting nowhere with his manuscript, so he was content to take the job Cameron Shipp now helped to get him as full-time editorialist for the Charlotte *News*.

Cash was coming on the paper not from another job but

from the status of ailing and unemployed writer, so his salary was understandably modest. Even so, as he bedded down in Charlotte's old Selwyn Hotel, he probably was making a salutary physical break with Shelby, where, as "Sleepy" Cash, he was as much taken for granted as the very courthouse square. That October of 1937 he walked into the city room of the Charlotte *News* (which had moved into a new building after his departure nine years earlier), greeted old friends, and introduced himself to newcomers, with a certain firmness, as Jack Cash.

CHAPTER 4

To the Peak

The camaraderie of the city room again served as a tonic for Cash, and with his close friends he was an easy and sometimes even a brilliant conversationalist. He was that way with Cameron Shipp, whom he admired for having gotten his own job with the Charlotte *News* via a one-word letter to the publisher he had been interviewing, a letter that said only: "Yes?" Cam had the kind of bright spirit Cash valued for the warmth it cast, and Cash was more amused than put out when made the butt of one of Cam's practical jokes. The most elaborate prank involved Shipp's committing to memory the first page of the other's *Mind* manuscript, then proceeding to "read" a blank first page that had been substituted for the genuine one. The other newsmen crowded around and nodded assent at Shipp's "reading" the blank page, the while clucking sympathetically over Cash's fading eyesight and approaching blindness. With his economic problem "settled" (at about forty dollars a week, with thirty dollars a month going to his parents) and his acceptance by his peers, Jack's chronic lack of confidence began slowly to recede.

Many years after his friend's death, Cameron Shipp recalled of him: "Cash was an odd one, a grim one, often a silent, strange man, who took little part in the playfulness of the city room. Only a handful of us were fortunate enough to know him well and to relish his wit." Still, Shipp was writing years afterward and neglected to mention how he used to call his friend "Dr. Wilbur Joe" and how their humorously brilliant passage of words made the whole newsroom light up. They showed off in company, and never had any professional vaudeville pair a better justification for doing so. Although not self-assertive, Cash could nevertheless be activated by the right question to pour out all the arresting conclusions he had gathered in a lifetime of observing people and devouring books. Now that he had a little money to buy books and worked for a newspaper that assigned him others to review, Cash was reading more than ever.

Cash never bought a novel or anything new, concentrating instead on the basic works in inexpensive editions, but even so he bought "more than I can ever read," he mourned to Alfred Knopf. Reporter Pete McKnight, hearing of Cash's prodigious reading, tested him on a batch of old *Saturday Review* literary quizzes loaded with obscure references. Jack turned out to have almost total recall, as he gripped his bald forehead with one hand and unerringly came up with the correct answers. In the room he moved to several blocks farther uptown, in the Frederick Apartments, he assembled a then-advanced phonograph rig and a good collection of 78-r.p.m. records. To Knopf he reported: "I think Beethoven's C Minor Symphony is still the greatest music ever written, like Mozart and Sibelius about equally [a common aberrant judgment of the 1930's], find nothing startling in Strawinsky, read heavy old books almost exclusively nowadays."

Cash's phonograph was equipped with a changer that would replay the last record in the stack. When his neighbor Pete McKnight heard a finale of some symphony repeated, he would know that Cash had either fallen asleep or passed out. When the latter condition prevailed, especially on week-

PART I: *To the Peak*

ends, Pete would enter Cash's room with his own key and put him to bed. Cash was well aware of McKnight's helpfulness but never mentioned it on mornings after. Cash did not hesitate to invoke his music as a weapon against philistinism, and whenever the female secretaries across the hall offended his hearing with their hit records by radio crooners, he would respond with "The Ride of the Valkyries" at such thunderous volume as to peel the very paint from the walls. One of his friends remembered the apparition of Cash lowering in his doorway in his gray underwear, howling imprecations at his lady neighbors.

At the office Cash would typically sidle down the aisle to his desk, often late, glancing quickly over his shoulder as he went. He would seat himself at his typewriter, stare at it until he began to write, and finally turn in his copy just before deadline. His editorials, as before, were of a uniformly high order and dealt almost exclusively with the international scene, which, to the *News*'s management, was then a form of Afghanistanism that could safely be relegated to Cash. His well-known low opinion of the establishment and, generally, of the "successful" in public life made it seem advisable to give Jack the "unimportant" Franco–Mussolini–Hitler beat. An evening paper had to set great store by early-morning punctuality, and unfortunately Cash was often missing for the strategic Monday-morning stint. Editor J. E. Dowd repeatedly determined to fire him for not showing up for work, but never made good the threat. As to free rein for his anti-Fascism and tolerance for his personal shortcomings, Cash was bound to admit, as he did to Paula Snelling: "The News gives me more latitude than I ever expected to get on a Southern newspaper."

However much Jack Cash carried "the wound in the heart" that so many of his generation bore away from the Spanish Civil War, and however much that tragic conflict dominated his early editorial thinking, he continued to express himself with unexceptionable moderation, keeping his emotion under tight rein. When, in December 1937, he was assigned a by-lined article in which to answer a reader's query "about the war going on in Spain now," he wrote a thousand words of the most judicious balance. After first conceding that he knew nothing firsthand about Spain, he proceeded with a neat summation of the "hands off" attitude of the West, the bluntly aggressive intent of the Axis, and a third view that the Spanish Republic was legitimately entitled to support from the free world. Even this third view, with which he basically agreed, might not be "free of propaganda and distortion," he warned. Emotion might cause people to lose something of perspective. He added: "It is entirely possible, for instance, that they unduly minimize the alliance between the Spanish government and the Spanish Communists and Moscow." Here, surely, was anything but white-hot polemic.

Nor was Cash out of line in jeering at "The Eternal Optimists," as he editorially termed Britain and France, for taking Mussolini's word that he would not intervene in Spain. The Duce was ready to ban further "volunteer" enlistments for service in Spain in return, it was said, for recognition of his Ethiopian conquest. "Is there no such thing as the cold shoulder in the relations of states?" Cash wrote. With Francisco Franco the editorialist was more downright, because in the war effort of the Spanish *caudillo* were bound up the fortunes of all the totalitarian dictators. Even if the Spanish Loyalist side was guilty of some murders, Cash maintained that it had not, like Franco, adopted a policy of the ruthless extermination of civilian population; "it has no Guernica on its shield." But Cash never took his eye off the prime menace, the evil genius of Hitler, even when Cash the editorialist tried to shrink him down to size as "Adolf Hitler, sitting oddly upon the throne of Barbarossa."

Sometimes Cash would turn his attention to the Far East,

writing: "I am not interested in the gentle and polite world of books today, for I cannot forget the thing that the Japanese pigs did in Shanghai last Monday." Or he would seek comfort in an anti-Nazi warning by the Vatican "that if Nazi paganism were not checked, the blood of Catholic priests might be shed as it was in Spain." But in the end it all came down to the fanatical Fuehrer, who, just as Cash was demonstrating that Hitler had foretold his every aggression, was annexing Austria to the Third Reich. Why, Cash asked in March 1938, does no American publisher bring out a complete English translation of *Mein Kampf*? (Two of them did so the following year.) Jack had not read the original *Mein Kampf*, but he had seen here and there certain freelance translations of it—not the "authorized" and emasculated *My Battle* published in England—and he found these translations "almost incredibly hot stuff."

So what did the future call for, as decreed by Hitler? Cash spelled it out quite plainly:

> . . . the recovery first of the "ancient realms" of Germany and Austro-Hungary. That means Czechoslovakia, Hungary, hunks of Jugoslavia, Rumania, and Poland. After that, he proposes to grab the Ukraine and Russia. And will he let the west off scot free? Not according to his program. The Netherlands and Belgium are to be absorbed. And then it will be France's turn. One of the original objectives of the German Army in 1914 was the annexation of the northern province of France, with a view to the Channel ports. And that, says Mr. Hitler, he means to realize in his lifetime. And Alsace-Lorraine? He told France recently that she need have no fear for those provinces. But he did not say that in the book, and his word is notoriously worthless.

This wholly rational fear of Hitler's evil intentions became, whenever Cash had been drinking, a mortal fear of Hitler the man. Now that he was re-established in Charlotte, he again spent many hours with his urologist friend, Dr.

Squires. Invariably the author would question his ability ever to marry because of his supposed impotence and, as he took a few drinks, express his fear of Hitler. Cash was well aware that he was far beyond the average in intelligence, and after a few drinks he was quite likely to tell his doctor so explicitly. Again, as in 1926–8, Dr. Squires admired Cash's punctilious use of English and his carrying a thesaurus under his arm. He also chauffeured Jack both ways on the occasions of their talks, and he gave him scientific papers to edit in lieu of payment. By this time Jack knew full well that he harbored some neuroses because of his endocrine disorder; his object now was to learn to live with his affliction.

Another affliction was the *Mind* manuscript, which did not prosper because of Cash's writing block. Certainly he tried to break free, to "talk out" his problem of bringing his book to some sort of logical terminus. With a newspaper crony and fellow native of South Carolina, John A. Daly, who soon learned to avoid mention of Hitler, Cash would repair to the Little Pep Café after work each day for two glasses apiece of fifteen-cent sherry. A typical question from Cash: "Do you reckon the South did all it could have done with the Negro after he had been freed?" After a discussion of Southern industrialization, Cash would advance some such question as: "How did the ex-slave get along during this time?" He talked of myriad affairs; of the building of railroads, of Ford's revolution achieved by motorizing the buggy, of the role of the telephone in "civilizing" the South and cementing family life, of the cotton mills urbanizing the tenant farmers, of the status of mill villages and villagers. Through it all, Cash was impressed with what he would describe as the South's resentment of criticism, constructive or not, its status as a colonial economy, its fate to make only uneven and tortuous progress. And, above all, he was oppressed by the sense of "no way out." As he later confessed to Alfred Knopf: "I have never been able to approach the task of continuing it [*Mind*] without extreme depression and dislike."

Even so, Cash was now more at ease and was otherwise fitting in better than in his impossible earlier role in Shelby. He enjoyed being teased by Cameron Shipp, who prefaced an article of Cash's titled "This Is How We Talk—Babel in the South" with a spoof about Cash's own fruity Southern accent. Shipp added: "Mr. Cash himself is a linguist. He speaks French with a Wake Forest accent, German as if it were American Mercury slang, and English with the magnificent periods of a boy who was raised under the influence of Cleveland County oratory and George Jean Nathan."

On wintry December days, Jack would awake and head downtown toward a lonely breakfast, perhaps unhappy with "a commonplace job in a commonplace town," and yet perhaps find himself converted on the way. In one such *causerie* editorial, he wrote of the unsuspected beauties of the city's early morning, claiming "that all towns are white and gold and purple towns—that Charlotte also is beautiful with the beauty of the earth at eight o'clock on a fine December morning. And you go on, not minding very much even that you have to put words on paper to ends that remain obscure."

Despite his own lack of self-confidence, Cash was already something of a personage to Charlotte people. If his manuscript was incomplete it had already been recognized with a Knopf contract, and the redoubtable Mr. Cash, in addition to his editorials, wrote lucidly about every imaginable intellectual subject for Cameron Shipp's book page. Letter writers to the paper would inquire after him, like the one who asked for a complete briefing on the Spanish Civil War. In a humorous vein another reader asked the editor: "Do you suppose that distinguished savant, Mr. W. J. Cash, will develop a crop of gray hair just because he inadvertently spelled Nietzsche incorrectly?" To which the editor's note replied: "Mr. Cash complains mournfully that he'd be willing enough to develop a gray thatch if only that were possible, seeing that, alas, he is already considerably bald and steadily growing balder." And in the spring of 1938 came the Carolinas Book Fair.

The Book Fair, a one-shot cultural explosion, took place in Charlotte's huge old armory-auditorium, in which books, publishers' representatives, and authors busily rattled around. Cameron Shipp was general manager, and he managed to get the mayor of Charlotte to introduce playwright Paul Green, the opening speaker, but had no luck attracting Governor Hoey. After the fair, Cam wrote about having invited the governor, who "stalled so long that we stopped asking him. He was probably right—no votes at a book fair." Tim Pridgen and Jack Cash were introduced among local authors with books in the making, and the four-day affair wound up in good shape, as Shipp said: "All the writers got along beautifully, no fights." At one midnight talkfest at the Hotel Charlotte coffee shop with a group from the fair, Cash spoke penetratingly to Jonathan Daniels about the South. He spoke not of his own stalled project, but of Daniels's *A Southerner Discovers the South*; Cash predicted that, in the context of F.D.R.'s deeming the region Economic Problem Number One, the book was bound to earn good royalties.

Book Fair Week also brought Cash the friendship of Mary Ross Northrop, a sometime contributor to the *News's* book page whom he had been wanting to meet. She had been curious about him, too, first from having read his gorgeously colored blast against Charlotte in the *American Mercury*, more recently from seeing his picture in connection with some Book Week publicity. She had been intrigued, looking over the Book Week planners, to see this one man. She had thought him some peppery oldster from his writing, but he was only six years older than she, this grown man with the wonderfully impish grin of a boy. Cameron Shipp introduced them at an evening session of the fair marked by a party given by the Charlotte novelist Marian Sims. Mary had been taken to the fair by her uncle, Tom Ross, who was immensely pleased to meet the man whose articles he had so much enjoyed, and now Mary tried to study Cash without staring outright. She saw a rather badly dressed fellow in a shiny brown suit, developing a small pot belly, going bald, and sporting a terrible haircut for the sake of the few remaining bristles on his crown. Jack sat there most of the evening, his face cupped in his hands, talking, but mostly staring at Mary. She could remember not a word of the talk except her uncle's whisper as he excused himself: "Babby, you have a new beau." Moreover, Mary somehow knew that this new beau was going to "take," and she laughingly told her mother next morning: "Last night I met a fat country boy I'm going to marry."

He and Mary began seeing one another steadily, often meeting after work in the Little Pep, converging there from the Charlotte *News* and from Mary's editing job with the Federal Writers' Project (the one Jack had applied for). At first Jack was somewhat distrustful of her craftsmanship, for Mary had won a local short-story prize five times running. He feared she might be the type who wrote the kind of stuff that was acceptable to the rich woman who donated the prize. After Mary convinced him that she had competed for the twenty-five-dollar prizes because she needed the money, he was thoroughly disarmed. Within a month he announced, in some wonder, that they would be married.

Mary, an attractive brunette, was very much a breezy and easygoing person. In these respects, her temperament was directly opposed to Cash's, and perhaps for that reason she was all the more attractive to him. He took an interest in her writing, recommending her to the *North Georgia Review* this way:

> At my suggestion, a friend of mine here, Mrs. Mary Ross Northrop, is submitting you some sketches she has done about

people she knew in two years in a tuberculosis sanatorium in
this county. She is first family in Charlotte, but the depression
bankrupted and killed her father, and a marriage in New
York ended in divorce. So, when the rains came, she had to
go into a ward, the rest of whose inhabitants were what we
so bravely call white trash.

Mary had been somewhat panicky at the notion of letting
Cash read her sketches, collectively titled "Women's Ward,"
but on hearing him say that the two of them would be married, she knew the ordeal had to be faced. Mary and her
mother lived at the Blandwood Apartments in a once elegant
neighborhood gone to seed. The apartment units had big
kitchens, high ceilings, front porches, and back entrances;
they were so comfortable, in fact, that they were fated for
the wreckers' ball even then. Cash came in early one night
after his own odd-hours dinner—before that of the ladies—
and Mary all but forced her manuscript on him while she
and her mother ate. Table conversation was understandably
desultory, but it ceased altogether with Cash's first chuckle.
Mary and her mother finished dinner while Cash kept right
on reading and nodding approval until he had read all the
sketches. Mary had never been so relieved in her life, she
avowed. He was too, and said so, grinning at her. Their
understanding, already reached, was that they would be
married when Cash finished his book.

In a personal communication to the present writer, Mary
recalled what had drawn her to Cash:

> The first attraction was instantaneous and was nothing more
> than the old Boy Meets Girl business. As I came to know him,
> the second attraction showed up in his genius with the
> spoken words: he was a wit and a spellbinder. And that—after
> my marriage to a handsome non-reading boating enthusiast—
> was God's own special blessing. Here was the one I could
> grow old with and with whom I'd never know a bored mo-
> ment. I was enchanted.

And as I came to know him well the real clincher appeared. He *needed* me. Outside that small orbit (rut) he was in—to the Charlotte *News* office, the Little Pep, back to the Frederick Apartments—he was on a little island and it was my joy to be his bridge to the mainland. He was a shy man and, from many standpoints, far too humble. He needed me as buffer, bumper, secretary-manager, ego-booster, a familiar face in any crowd, an ever-handy liar, and a love. Because he liked my brand of nonsense and respected my opinions, I also had an audience. It all added up to one thing: we fell in love.

At first Cash would sit on the front porch at Mary's place, beaming artlessly and talking little. Then, bit by bit, a few cracks appeared in the great dam of his earlier silence, until finally the wall burst and a flood of talk came through. The topic was, invariably, W. J. Cash, his life and times; but "this to hear would gentle Desdemona seriously incline," and her admirer did his best to oblige. He laughed to tell Mary of his experience in Gaffney as a twelve-year-old beset with uncontrollable and painful giggling in church. Now he knew it as his frightened reaction to the sermon, which had seemed to single him out as the lone sinner in all that Baptist throng. Later he mocked his youthful agony during the only football game he ever played, when a few townspeople watched him gallop mindlessly all over the field regardless of team, ball, or scrimmage—and Mary joined him in helpless laughter.

Still later Cash good-humoredly dissected, for Mary's benefit, his old and hopeless romance with Peggy Ann. It was not the beauteous college freshman he scoffed at, but himself. Once, he told Mary, he had noticed a little "matter" in the corner of Peggy Ann's eye, and although he had tried to call it to her attention he found himself helpless to do so. Enshrined there on her pedestal she obviously could not be made of the same humble clay as he. Talking to Mary about it, Cash took a common-sense "who did she think she was?" backward look at his old inamorata. He had to laugh at himself, as now he could, for having so guilelessly succumbed to Cabell's Code of Domnei, or woman worship, at which his mind had scoffed but in which his emotions had become ensnared.

Cash listened to Mary with as much attention as she listened to him. To a criticism she once ventured about his old hero Mencken, Cash replied, "You say the things I've always wanted said." Again, in a more romantic mood, he responded to something she said with, "It was you I was crying for all over Europe." Of course it was the fatal beauty of Peggy Ann that had kept the Chevalier Cash in thrall during that European trip, and Mary knew it, but she wisely kept her own counsel until her admirer came to laugh at himself. Once, when Mary's Gothic table-model Philco gave forth moonily with "My Wonderful One," Cash looked up smiling and remarked that it was the song to which he used to be most vulnerable because it always reminded him of Peggy Ann. "Which one reminds you of me, you big ape?" Mary put in. She knew what he would say, because it was the same song that reminded her of him. She had recently exposed him to the Ella Fitzgerald version of "A-Tisket A-Tasket," and he had been tickled by it. Cash now cut his eye at Mary sideways and laughed with her at the predictable answer: "A-Tisket A-Tasket."

At the time, Mary set down Cash's poor physical coordination as the plain awkwardness of a man who had been brought up in countrified surroundings. The choking to which he had been subject from boyhood, the throat constrictions, were more of a nuisance than anything serious. That, at any rate, was how Cash himself explained them, and indeed they now seemed like routine manifestations of nervousness, like making an involuntary face or pulling an ear. As if to underline his ability to turn a harassment into an asset,

Cash somehow learned, through his throat constrictions, to produce a sonorous voice that would have been mesmeric in any pulpit. Once he began reading a fashion article to Mary, giving it the "treatment" full of measured cadences and organ tones, rolling on about *peau de soie,* shoulder pads, and peplums. They both laughed over his purported ability to convey a sublime conviction of some great faith, to make converts of the very headhunters.

Mary contributed to the Charlotte *News* occasional book reviews and commentaries, the latter by "Tillie Eulenspiegel." The amused Cash responded with a rare humorous effort of his own (reprinted in this volume) by "W. J. Eulenspiegel," in which he parodied the plot of an Agrarian novel, portrayed himself as "Mr. Casshe, the villain of the piece," and studded the rest with references to such folk as Sally Lou and Jim John, "the best shrimp fisher at the landing." Cameron Shipp, who was distantly related to Mary, referred obliquely to the romance in his book column: "Mary says she hears that our engagement has been announced, which is flattering, but was as much news to us as it will be to Mrs. S. Must be some other writin' man." And of course he meant Cash, who was seeing Mary regularly, going for long walks at the end of the trolley-car line, and taking her encouragement seriously enough to resume his long-stalled work on *The Mind of the South.* Editor J. E. Dowd chipped in with two weeks off in addition to Cash's regular one-week vacation that summer.

In October 1938 Cash sent forward pages 20 to 508 of new manuscript, and the Knopfs crossed their fingers before what their house reader termed this "unforgettable portrait of the Southern psychology." Retaining his original introduction, Cash had rewritten his first draft and had added to it in promising quantity—through Book Three's Chapter II, Section 8 (p. 273, Vintage edn.). He had, after all, only a chapter and a half to go to complete the entire work. He had completed his treatment of progress during the twenties in the South, and now he was about to pick up the role of the textile worker after World War I. From Chapel Hill, where Dr. Howard Odum's opinion had been sought by the publisher, came the advice that the manuscript should be published at once, "that the body of the text not only approximates a brilliant interpretation, but reads like a story." Instead of Cash's rather commonplace introduction, "To Begin With–," Odum suggested that the author "pen a very fine little preview note" and entitle it "Preview to Understanding." So it was that *The Mind of the South* came to contain exactly such a preface with exactly that title. Finally, Odum cautioned the Knopfs not to seek detailed changes in Cash's manuscript; "better take it while it is moving smoothly."

In the off hours those days Cash usually was to be found at his "club," the Little Pep, talking a blue streak to Mary and sipping the establishment's brawny sherry. That October 30, a Sunday, was the day of the famous Orson Welles "Invasion from Mars" broadcast, which Jack and Mary heard only as a murmuring background from the Little Pep's wall radio, beneath which they sat. They knew the play was science fiction because they had heard just enough of the introduction, and thus they were unprepared for the later reaction. When they learned of the widespread panic set off by the radio play, as the incredible stories came pouring in, Cash was first dumfounded and then, in turn, sympathetic, perturbed, and at last roaring with laughter. Indeed, he laughed himself into a choking fit. Characteristically, he grew thoughtful later while pondering the report about a Princeton student who, believing the Martians were swarming over New Jersey, broke into a grocery store and commenced to gorge and gorge.

Cash was now meeting, and liking, individual "country-clubbers" to whom Mary introduced him. He still felt self-conscious in such company, to be sure, but he had only to remind himself that Peggy Ann, and also Mary, for that matter, had belonged. And Cash's confidence was just beginning to show through. While having drinks with a group of Mary's acquaintances, the talk got around, as it always did in those days, to the New Deal. One man, who was allied in business with some big money and had therefore been rescued by the New Deal, snarled his opinion that Roosevelt was "insane, insane!" When Cash mildly disagreed, the other turned on him and said quite seriously: "You must be on relief." Mary held her breath, but Cash replied, with the nice courtesy and care one uses with backward children: "No, I'm the editorial writer for the *News*."

To Mrs. Knopf, who was now keeping after him about the balance of the manuscript, the author wrote that December:

> This thing, somewhat to my horror, is stringing out to greater length than I had planned—or I should have been through by now. I've turned out sixty pages since I sent you the body of the manuscript, but I see a good deal of work still in front of me yet. Nor do I know how it can be avoided; to telescope the book too abruptly at this stage will simply make it look foolish, I'm afraid. It might have been remedied at an earlier stage, but within the design as it is already drawn by the material you have, it seems impossible to do anything but go ahead and give the material such treatment as it appears inevitably to demand. Naturally I shall lop off everything that I can, for I am most impatient to get done with it and see it in print.

It was December 14, 1938; as an outside deadline for completion of his manuscript, he set the following February 1.

At the opening of 1939, Alfred Knopf got tangible evidence of the "depression and dislike" with which Cash faced his writing task. The author reported that he had slipped on some ice on his apartment-house steps and "smashed my face up pretty dreadfully. Fortunately, my head seems to be pretty thick and so there were no very serious results." This was supposed to explain the author's not having sent in any copy, and "in this instance it was of course beyond my control." On February 15, Mrs. Knopf was heartened to receive fifty-one more pages of copy, and was the manuscript now complete? Not yet, came the answer from Charlotte. Cash was getting a week's leave beginning the very next day, a leave that presumably would result in a completed manuscript. He did not explain that he had again prevailed on Editor Dowd, who this time let Cash anticipate the week's vacation he was due that coming summer.

After another exasperating delay, during which the Knopfs tried to remind Cash that other books about the South were now being published and his own would suffer, the author and his publishers met for a Sunday confrontation at the O. Henry Hotel in Greensboro, North Carolina. It was already April, and the Knopfs were understandably eager to turn over a completed manuscript to the printers in time for publication by the year's end. The Knopfs were offering an additional advance, despite the fact that they had already given Cash $250, because the author now had sixty more pages to show them and it was all obviously excellent material. They had agreed on a lesser amount in Greensboro, but Cash wrote Alfred Knopf after their meeting, on April 16, 1939, "Can you make that advance $200?"

> Since seeing you, I have cast up my debts and find that I owe about that much which I'd like to get rid of. It will, of course, be quite all right if you don't feel like increasing the figure I first named. But [and here he got to the heart of his argument] I think it will help in getting the book finished.

By return mail Knopf agreed:

> Mrs. Knopf and I both think you mean business this time and so I am enclosing a check for two hundred dollars on account

in the firm belief that we are going to get your book out this year. I hope you can send on the sixty pages already written immediately, and follow them with the balance by the middle of June, at the latest.

By late May, Knopf was still looking for the sixty pages from Cash's closing section of book manuscript, and the publisher was—as he informed the author—making plans for *Mind's* appearance on his fall list. Cash replied with a tortuous explanation that his Charlotte stenographer had a husband whose illness now demanded her entire attention, that she was a needy middle-aged woman who had trouble finding employment, that the sixty pages could wait, since the entire manuscript was not yet ready. Nevertheless, and in view of Knopf's impatience, the author would find another stenographer without further delay.

I have been working at the manuscript as much as possible [he had told Knopf that he had not been feeling well] and can report that it is well along in the last chapter. I have no thought of turning it loose again until it is completed, and two or three more weeks should see the end. Hence I hope you will go ahead with your plans for it.

Alfred Knopf was leaving for London that June, and the only cheering bon-voyage note he got from Cash was the first twenty pages of the manuscript, the "Preview to Understanding" that Dr. Howard Odum had recommended. As usual it was easier for the author to rewrite his old copy than to come to grips with the problems of the modern South now that war in Europe—which meant a second World War—was plainly inevitable. To be sure, he did send along ninety-three pages to complete his penultimate chapter, but the scope of the book kept ballooning, with the ending still as far off as before. So, when chided by Mrs. Knopf for missing still another deadline, Cash testily insisted that

what I promised was to get to work on the job and stay at it until it was completed. I have kept that promise, and am keeping it. And I shall not hold up the preparation of the book longer than is absolutely necessary. Merely, it has again turned out to be a little longer than I had hoped. And I cannot write it faster than the time at my disposal will allow. The end is in sight, and I'm giving it every minute I can. That's all I can do.

And there was nothing the Knopfs could do, for not only had they committed themselves financially but the reader's report on the author's latest installment came through as "very satisfactory indeed." Meanwhile, instead of fighting the "extreme depression and dislike" that he felt for the subject he must confront, Cash dissipated his strength in ceaseless worry about the European crisis. That June marked the wedding of his sister Bertie, who wanted nothing more than to have her big brother Wilbur take a part in the ceremonial. Cash would do no such thing, of course; he sat there, as Bertie recalled, sober as a judge, with the tears streaming down his cheeks. And that same month Jack went up to Asheville to visit Mary, who had just been transferred there in those final weeks before the death of the Federal Writers' Project. Mary's office was opposite the entrance to Riverside Cemetery, and so the two of them went in to let Jack wipe his eyes at the grave of the novelist Thomas Wolfe, whom Cash admired and whose premature death had greatly shocked him the year before. In his cups, and sometimes out, Jack would confess a brooding fear of death and of "the cold grave."

During the weeks Mary was in Asheville, Cash's weekly letters to her were scarcely more, in effect, than punching the time clock to show her he was still there. He hated the posing represented by "literary" letters, and thus kept his missives deliberately prosaic. At any event, all the old-time *Weltschmerz* he had suffered with Peggy Ann was out of his system now. Besides, at any sign of such mooning Mary would have teased him for being such an oaf, an irreverence that always tickled him. Knowing his distaste for the seemingly simple act of manipulating typewriter keys, Mary felt somewhat complimented that his letters were as frequent as they were. She was not permitted to be so casual. Cash had to hear from her at least every other day, and any lapse meant a telephone call asking her what the hell was wrong and what did she mean worrying him that way.

At the end of July Cash made a special effort and wrote a lengthy feature article (reprinted in this volume) after his interview in Charlotte with Thomas Wolfe's sister. But he was able to send forward only a token contribution of copy for the final chapter of his manuscript, and when Mrs. Knopf returned from a trip she was understandably dismayed at the status of a book already on the firm's fall list. To her anxious inquiries the author replied apologetically on August 10, 1939:

> Since July 10 I have been ailing with chronic bronchitis, about the most unpleasant Summer experience I have encountered. Most of the time I have gone on working here at the office, but I have felt too exhausted to do much with the book—else I should long ago have had all the manuscript in your hands. And this week, until yesterday, I have had to stay in bed. However, I think I am pretty clear of the thing now—and expect to get back to work on the book Sunday. Only six sections remain to be written. And I think I can manage those in about ten days.

The "chronic bronchitis" was simply another excuse, false like most of the others, for not completing the manuscript. The overriding reason for the delay was that he had lost his vital interest in the book; the earlier commitment had been superseded by his passion and horror at the approaching holocaust in Europe.

Ten days might have sufficed if he had had ten days to spare, but in those August days as the war clouds lowered over Europe he was totally involved in the international crisis. He wrote editorials busily—and brilliant ones they were—that bore ample testimony to his utter absorption and to his great store of information. If he wrote about Admiral Horthy's Hungary, as he did on August 18, he spoke of Germany's desire to occupy the Carpatho-Ukraine in case of war and of Hungary's desire for the return of her lost Transylvanian territories. If he wrote about Hitler's taking over of Slovakia, as he wrote on the 19th, he wrote knowingly about the Polish Corridor, Danzig, and Gdynia as being next in line. He continued:

> And nothing is more certain than that if this succeeds, it will be only the beginning. If this succeeds, England's alliances in Central Europe and with Turkey will crumble at once—the Eastern Front will be done with. The old German dream of an empire stretching from the Scandinavian Peninsula to the Persian Gulf will be realized. And with that achieved, the demands of Hitler will be the most extravagant ever dreamed by man. Worse, England will be so weakened that she probably can no longer hope to oppose it. And France—France will have no choice but to become a satellite of Germany on her own account.

It was a grim and terrible choice for Hitler's foes, Cash wrote: war casualties in the millions or, through Nazification, the return of Western man to barbarism.

On the first of September, Hitler launched his blitzkrieg against Poland. With the issue thus joined, Cash found it impossible to deal with *The Mind of the South*. Instead he wrote a long and skillful editorial (reprinted in this volume) entitled "A Fanatic Menaces Civilization." Just as he exposed the myths of Old South and New South, Cash now demolished the myths of the Fuehrer as supposedly nothing more than a shrewd bluffer, of the supposed power of the "realistic" German generals to curb him, of Nazism as supposedly nothing more than "a civilized philosophy made a little grotesque by a few wild aberrations." He took apart calmly and analytically every pretext that had been raised to lend color and sanction to Hitler's aggressions. And then he set forth, for other editors to copy admiringly, Hitler's unabashed aim of establishing his tyranny over all Europe and the western world, "as you can read in his 'Mein Kampf' and in Mr. [Hermann] Rauschning's 'The Revolution of Nihilism.' "

Later in September the author was avowing to Mrs. Knopf that "bronchitis" and the war had been holding up the book manuscript. "I suppose I seem both incredible and incurable," he apologized. "But I have been genuinely ill, else I should have had it in your hands long ago. Mr. Dowd, the editor here, will bear me out in that." In point of fact, Dowd was then damping down the enthusiasm of an admirer of Cash who wanted to propose the author for a Nieman fellowship at Harvard. Admitting that Cash was brilliant, had an enormous fund of knowledge, and was one editorial writer in a million, Dowd warned that it would probably be fatal to Cash's writing project to provide him now with an additional distraction. So there was no Nieman fellowship for Cash.

And while the manuscript about the South went unfinished, the author kept writing his heart out about what was happening in Europe. Of the anti-Jewish pogroms he wrote in a book-page column:

> I should not like to be a Jew just now, for to be a Jew is a hard thing in this present world. But the thing I should dislike most of all is to be a German and have been exposed to living in the fanatically distorted world Adolf Hitler has made for the moulding of German minds.

And to Mrs. Knopf, who was now at a loss for further words about the missing manuscript, he wrote on the last day of October:

That chronic bronchitis has held on all this time, with the result that most of the time I have been quite unfit for anything that called for a clear head and energy. I'm not clear of the thing yet, but I do feel a good deal better since the cool weather has at last set in down here—so much better than I think I'll be able to go ahead with it each afternoon after another day or two. It is down to the point now where about forty more manuscript pages will see the end of it. I hope I can give you the last of it in about ten days or two weeks at the most. Please believe me that I shall do it just as rapidly as I can, for I am sure that I am even sicker of the everlasting delay than you are.

Sick of delay or no, Cash was not replying to agonized tracer letters from New York that November and December, so on January 4, 1940, Alfred Knopf called on the last weapon in his arsenal. Declaring that the continued delay was making them both appear ridiculous, the publisher proposed that unless Cash met a deadline of mid-April, Knopf would feel entitled to publish the book in accordance with manuscript already in hand. This hard-nosed letter finally brought a reply from the author (two weeks late), explaining that this time he had been down with the flu and that, yes, it was all right to begin setting up the book because the balance of the copy would be in by early February anyway. He added:

> I dislike being rewritten, save in the case of obvious awkwardness or bulls. But, as I think I told you in Greensboro last Summer, I don't mind cuts which can be made without altering the sense. From looking over the manuscript, I am sure that from 15,000 to 20,000 words can be cut out with profit—perhaps more. And there are a few alterations I want to make. I had hoped to do all this myself, but it seems desirable to me to get the book out now while the Gone With the Wind picture is whipping up interest in the South. So you are at liberty to cut at discretion, with the understanding that if

there is any disagreement we'll thresh it out when the proofs are ready. The alterations I have in mind can be made in the proofs without running up composition costs to any great extent, I think.

Cash wrote that letter to Knopf on January 22, 1940; the publisher did not hear from him again until the following June 19.

First Cash took time out to oblige his friends of the *North Georgia Review* by writing a book review (reprinted in this volume) of a tolerably unimportant Southern novel, which he compared unfavorably with *Gone With the Wind* (he found the latter no prize winner either). Then the Nazis began to menace Norway, and the prescient author saw what was coming and could think of nothing else. His editorial of February 20 clearly discerned that Norway, in complaining of Britain's violation of her territorial waters in the *Altmark* case, was seeking to deprive the Nazis of an excuse to attack her. Cash would stand by the radio during the Nazi attack on Norway, as he had done in previous Hitlerian aggressions, gnawing his fists in frustrated rage, and then perhaps he would walk the streets all night. He had not listened to his radio the morning the Low Countries were invaded, and when he came to read the news on the teletype printer at the office he gave a great bellow of rage and proceeded to frighten some of his newspaper friends with his shouted abuse of the Nazis and their appeasers.

He calmed down enough to write his father the following day, May 11:

The first job is to get planes enough to the Allies to smash the German armies in the western countries, then enough to bomb every town in Germany into an ash heap. That is what will be done if he is thrown back. The next three weeks should tell the tale. If the Allies can avoid absolute disaster for that period, then they can hold him for the six months necessary to build the planes. In any case, I don't think France will ever

give up, and I'm sure England won't. Both know what it
means.

At the same time Mary and Cash sent off a telegram to
President Roosevelt urging him to provide all possible mili-
tary aid to the Allies. They composed the telegram in the
Little Pep, where they got after George, the immigrant
Greek waiter, to send a similar wire to the White House.
George looked at them wide-eyed, saying: "Can *I* wire the
President?"

The Little Pep took a proprietary interest in Cash as
resident sage, and when he acquired a white linen suit no
one was more proud of him than Mary, the Little Pep's big
comfortable waitress, to whom Cash and "Miss Mary" belonged. One night the waitress called Mary aside, apologetic
but very firm. "Miss Mary," she said, "excuse me for mentioning it, but Mr. Cash came in for breakfast this morning in
that white suit and right on the shoulder, plain as day, was
this little red mouth. You know he never notices his clothes,
so you're gonna have to be careful for him." After that, Cash
and Mary both noticed. After Cash's death and after Pearl
Harbor, both Marys went into the WAAC, as it was still
called, and set off in the same detachment for basic training.
At Fort Oglethorpe there was a touching sort of difficulty
getting the waitress to call her fellow buck private plain
Mary. Cash had been to her "the greatest man I ever knew,"
and she felt uneasy about getting familiar with his widow.

The subject of the unfinished book manuscript was obviously a long way from Cash's passionate involvement with
the European crisis. Even so, his "international" editorials,
always moderate by comparison with his superheated conversation, acted as a pressure gauge and provided a salutary
emotional outlet. Otherwise Jack would meet a friend in
the street—someone like LeGette Blythe of the *Observer*,
who later recalled it vividly—and proceed to a violent and

arm-waving oration on the menace to the United States of Hitlerism, which often resolved itself into the menace that Adolf Hitler personally posed to W. J. Cash. As the author later explained to Alfred Knopf, the international crisis made it impossible for him to think of anything else. "Worse," he wrote, "I was left hanging in the air as to how to wind up that book and increasingly convinced that some of the things I had said belonged in a different perspective." Why had he not written since January as he now wrote on June 19? "I ought to have written you long ago, I confess, and my apologies for what must have seemed a gross lack of regard [nobody mentioned the broken deadline of mid-April]. The explanation is that I was living in a fog of anger and defeatism."

After a month of blitzkrieg and the fall of France, Cash became a calmer spirit and could now quite serenely reconcile the two kinds of writing he was called upon to produce. In an editorial attacking Mussolini for the "stab in the back," he said simply that the Duce was finished whether Hitler won or lost.

> Let us not, however, assume that Hitler is going to win in the end. To say that is to say that the spirit of man has died, to grant that we have grown so soft that to keep on living we will accept the destruction of every value by which we have lived and consent to become brutalized slaves for the glorification of a gang of swine sitting in the great ugly city of Berlin.

And even if it was now too late for the United States to prevent Hitler's engulfment of Western Europe, Cash wrote, it was still possible for individual Americans to provide material help for the three million refugees in France.

By mid-July, a month after the fall of France, Cash had labored to such effect that he had gone over his manuscript four times to cut nearly 15,000 words, reducing the "over-florid effect" of his prose without rewriting, and moving toward a proper ending. "I now lack about 3,000 words of having the sort of ending I want," he wrote Knopf. "And that I know you want. I'll be able to hand it to you by next week at latest, completely ready for the printer so far as I am concerned." At the end of that week Knopf came back at him with the broken promise quoted verbatim, but on the 26th the author sent the publisher a triumphant telegram proclaiming that the completed manuscript had been sent off by express. He wrote the following day:

> At any rate, the thing is at last done and I am as relieved as I know you are. The history of that book is strange stuff. I am a lazy fellow but I think the people with whom I work down here daily will testify that I am not as astoundingly lazy as the story of the book indicates.

On August 1, Alfred Knopf thanked Cash for his telegram, his letter, "and, God be praised, the manuscript."

It was a first-rate manuscript, too. Not only did it encompass its breathtakingly ambitious subject with style and force, but Cash's painstaking corrections came almost invariably on the side of point and moderation. If he was seething within, it never showed in the beautifully controlled tone of his writing. He titled his second chapter "The Man at the Center" in place of his original "The Peasant at the Center," which would have been disastrously misleading in tone and context. He erased a "coon" that he had inadvertently let ride through, kept "nigger" only to convey the feeling of those who regularly pronounced it that way, got rid of the expression "lint-head," and cut down on his overuse of "hell of a fellow." In one instance Mary prevailed on Cash to throw out an overly sarcastic "country-clubbers" paragraph, which apparently savored too highly of sour grapes to pass muster as sober analysis. He also got rid of invidious personal references like the one to George Mc-

Duffie, South Carolina's "Orator of Nullification." In that instance Cash was trying to show the generally humble origin of Southern "aristocrats," which he did quite persuasively with the list of Virginia governors (p. 39, Vintage edn.). He now realized he did not need to invite rancor by adding the allegation, of doubtful authenticity at that, that McDuffie "arose from the estate of bound boy."

Cash's excision of certain purple patches in his extant manuscript gives evidence of consistent self-restraint in style and content. Thus, in speaking of the tribal God whom Southerners envisioned (p. 135, Vintage edn.), Cash decided against using the following extravangant figure:

> Glorious in gray and epaulettes, He had raised the rebel yell at Bull Run, swept through the Valley campaign, wrestled with the incomprehensible Grant, sadly bowed His head to the bawling of the guns at Vicksburg, stood with Jeff Davis and read the telegram which announced that the Confederate States had joined the company of the nations that were and are not, tramped the weary road homeward (splendid still in rags), trembled to hear that Lincoln was dead and Thad Stevens free to work his will, burned to see His stable boy reeling to the polls while He Himself stood by voteless, ridden with the Klan. Oh, He knew, He knew.

Again, apropos of the intellectual stagnation that once saw Southern awareness of the Darwinian doctrine restricted to a small company of medical men (p. 144, Vintage edn.), Cash excised the following:

> For, barring the schools, there were comparatively few places in the South in which to be known to have a copy of *The Origin of Species, The Descent of Man* or *Man's Place in Nature* in his library, was not warranted to bring down upon a man—even though he was known to vote the Democratic ticket and to go regularly to church—almost as horrendous social consequences as though he had been caught addressing sonnets to a wench of color.

On the other hand, he pressed home with an apt quotation his indictment of the disingenuous Southern idealization of white womanhood (p. 89, Vintage edn.), writing into the manuscript in his own hand:

> "Woman!!! The center and circumference, diameter and periphery, sine, tangent and secant of all our affections!" Such was the toast which brought twenty great cheers from the audience at the celebration of Georgia's one-hundredth anniversary in the 1830's.

The author also took care to moderate the tone of the final section of his book, the one that dealt with contemporary developments, virtually bending over backward in the direction of restraint. Thus, after saying quite plainly what he thought of the Gastonia strike (p. 362, Vintage edn.), he thought it superfluous and thus excised: "The number of men who spoke out plainly enough to make it perfectly clear that they thought the strikers had a case could be counted on the fingers of one hand." Similarly, after exposing the tacit connivance of the "best people" in Negro lynching, the author thought it better to omit his angry personal estimate (intended for p. 311, Vintage edn.):

> Given their enormous power over the minds of the common people, I do not believe there has been a single ten-year period since 1910 in which, if the master group of every local area in the South or even the master group of each state as a whole had set themselves to the purpose, lynching could not have been fully extinguished in the entire region.

What troubled Cash about the role of the Negro was now implicit in his manuscript as he had made explicit in the Charlotte *News* as early as June 13, 1937. In a review of Paul H. Buck's *The Road to Reunion* Cash had differed sharply with the Harvard professor, who implied that "Uncle Sam's other province" would readily take the reunion road. Cash wrote:

We know very well down here, we who have looked at the land in which we were born and bred, that our treatment of the negro is something more than a "discipline" [Buck had so termed it]. We have our grave doubts that this "discipline" is worth the price of the staggering burden of evils—and evils for white men—which we are beginning to realize we pay for it.

And in 1940, despite the moderation of his language, Cash's message, relevant to the Negro revolution that was still unthought-of in the South of that day, came through quite clearly when he spoke of the South's characteristic vices (after duly summarizing its virtues) on his last published page: ". . . above all, too great attachment to racial values and a tendency to justify cruelty and injustice in the name of those values."

He himself thought the manuscript "mild stuff," as he wrote Jonathan Daniels a week after its mailing, "with little relation to my old American Mercury manner and with the okay of Howard Odum on it." For Jack's first order of business now was to seek a change of scene, an editorial job that "would pay a decent salary," he wrote Daniels. Cash thought that his book, however mild, would prove too strong meat for conservative Charlotte and his own conservative publisher. As associate editor for more than two years, Cash had come on the paper "at virtually nothing a week. I think I need not tell you that I am still working for a little more than that [$50 a week], though I have been writing most of the editorials for the past three years. By now I am damned sick of it." His editor, Jack explained, was also making Willkie noises that election year of 1940, whereas Cash remained loyal to Roosevelt. Actually, Editor J. E. Dowd and his associate editor put out an "Inter-Office Memo: Willkie or Roosevelt?" on October 13, in which Dowd and Cash backed their respective candidates in parallel columns (Cash's contribution is reprinted in this volume). Jonathan

Daniels sensibly advised Jack to wait before making any job change, to wait for publication of his book to generate new opportunities.

At last freed of the yoke represented by the *Mind* manuscript, and having had his publicity portrait made with a new ten-dollar Panama hat covering his baldness, Cash was full of confidence and energy. To Alfred Knopf, who wanted to be kept informed of his writing plans, the author confided (1) that he had abandoned his earlier plan for a novel about the ante-bellum South, (2) that he had for years nursed "the idea of ultimately doing a huge novel of the Civil War," but would now undertake a novel of the cotton-mill South, and (3) for the immediate future, and so as to keep his name before the public, he would like to write a biography of Huey Long. Cash had indeed written perceptively of the Louisiana kingfish in his book (pp. 290–4, Vintage edn.) as "the first Southern demagogue largely to leave aside nigger-baiting" and someone who had also done something tangible for the common people of his state. Knopf already had an author under contract for such a book, however, and when Cash spent a week in New York in mid-September the publisher concentrated his attention on the New South novel. The author was hoping for Knopf's backing, and he got it, for a Guggenheim Foundation fellowship on the basis of the *Mind* manuscript.

As to his qualification to write a novel, Cash wrote in his fellowship application:

> I have published no fiction and have submitted none to a publisher. Nevertheless, I have always been, and remain, confident that my primary talent lies in that field. *The Mind of the South*, I am sure, is properly described as "creative writing." But I am well aware of the difference between social analysis and fiction. I believe I can do the latter better than the former. And I expect to have enough of the novel ready by

the time the fellowship selection is made to offer proof of my belief.

Of his working plans he wrote:

I propose to write a novel, which is in fact already in progress [wishful thinking]. Primarily, it will be the story of the character and development of a certain Andrew Bates, born the son of a wealthy cotton mill family in piedmont North Carolina in 1900 [Cash's own year of birth], down until the outbreak of the second world war in 1939.

Over and beyond that it will be also the story of his father and grandfather. And beyond that, again, the story of the rise of an industrial town in the South after the introduction of the idea of Progress after 1880.

While the novel is being written I should like to live in Mexico City. The place has been chosen with an eye to both my journalistic future and my hopes for a career as a writer. It seems to me that Americans who deal in the printed word are going to have to pay a great deal more attention to Latin America in the future than has been the case in the past. And Mexico City seems to me to be the best place to get acquainted with it.

The novel will run, I think, to about a hundred and fifty thousand words. I expect to complete it by January 1, 1942.

Aside from his continuing distress at the ordeal of Britain during its fateful "Year Alone," the period between the fall of France and Hitler's invasion of Russia, Cash was almost a new man. A book that compiled outstanding pro-British editorials was published at that time, *What America Thinks,* and it contained no fewer than ten from the Charlotte *News,* all written by W. J. Cash. His name went forward on a nomination for a Pulitzer Prize, adducing as evidence a group of editorials headed by his memorable "Sea Fight" (reprinted in this volume) on the sacrifice of the *Jervis Bay* to save a wartime convoy. Now Cash, and Mary, his patient Griselda, could think of marriage, but the thought of a wedding dismayed them both. Mary had been divorced, could not be married in her own church in Charlotte, and she quailed at the task of arranging a full-scale church wedding elsewhere. On the other hand, her mother's scheduled departure at the start of 1941 for a job as a fraternity housemother at the University in Chapel Hill would give the newlyweds a place to live. All things considered, the mechanics of the wedding ceremony had them both feeling gloomy.

On Christmas Eve of 1940 they were moodily trimming the tree at the home of their friends the Frank McCleneghans, when Frank was struck with the happy inspiration of attending to all the details and hurrying off Jack and Mary to get married then and there. Cash was wildly enthusiastic. In Charlotte they were close to South Carolina, where the marriage laws of the time involved waiting some ten minutes for the preceding couple in line to get themselves married. Mary agreed, provided they could avoid York, South Carolina, the local Gretna Green of teen-age elopers. So Frank McCleneghan got on the telephone while another tree-trimmer came in and went along as an additional witness. They wound up, almost inevitably, in York. Mary and Jack were sandwiched in between two incredibly young and starry-eyed couples, but to Mary's amazement, the simple service by the marrying justice of the peace was solemn and quite moving. They used Frank McCleneghan's SAE fraternity ring for the ceremony.

Although Cash gave no advance notice to his parents, he did inform his sister Bertie and brother Allan, both of whom lived nearby. And right after Christmas Jack triumphantly wired Alfred Knopf:

JACKET ON MY BOOK SAYS MR. CASH HAS NEVER MARRIED. HE HAS NOW. MRS. MARY ROSS NORTHROP OF CHARLOTTE AND I WERE MARRIED CHRISTMAS MORNING.

CHAPTER 5

Appointment in Mexico City

The new year dawned bright with promise, and it brought a letter from Paula Snelling congratulating Cash on his two good fortunes. The first was his marriage; the other was the imminent publication of *The Mind of the South*, which had been foreshadowed by the appearance in the *Saturday Review of Literature* (December 28, 1940) of a good-sized excerpt from the manuscript, called "Literature and the South." This material (pp. 145–7 and 384–94, Vintage edn.) includes the author's criticisms of the Nashville Agrarians, who were thus alerted in advance and who later became the only real nay-sayers in the almost unanimous chorus of critical acclaim for Cash's book. Miss Snelling thanked him for the reference to *North Georgia Review* in the *Saturday Review* article and invited the newlyweds, on behalf of Lillian Smith and herself, to visit them in Clayton, Georgia. "Last spring in conversations with Dr. Odum," Miss Snelling wrote Cash, "he referred to you more than once in terms of highest praise . . . which may not be news to you, but perhaps it is not disagreeable to hear it again."

By the time Paula Snelling wrote this on January 10, the

Cashes were comfortably established in Mary's apartment at the Blandwood. Before that, however, they had been denied even a two-day wedding trip because Cash had to be at his desk the day after Christmas. Their first week of married life had to be spent in his two-room no-kitchen bachelor flat at the Frederick Apartments, where the bridegroom was half-sick with the flu and generally miserable. But they moved to the Blandwood after the anticipated departure of Mary's mother, and he began taking the greatest pleasure in doing little things like going to the grocery store. After two weeks his bachelor's adjustment was complete, for he admitted to Mary that he had misunderstood his "henpecked" friends who used to drift home from the Little Pep after a single glass of sherry. Now he understood that they really wanted to get home, as he now did.

As a married man he was the happiest person Mary had ever seen and the most surprised at being happy, for he had looked gloomily at the approach of marriage and had advocated the idea, she felt sure, only because he was law-abiding. Jack found that he had a perpetually willing audience at home; he could talk all afternoon and most of the night, and frequently he did. He was tickled at calling his wife "honey," at following his new cook from room to room, at committing little extravagances at the supermarket. He was the best man in the world to give presents to, delighting in 78-r.p.m. phonograph records ($1.25 maximum), inexpensive editions of the classics, an ingenious rig for his cigarette ashes (most of which still hit the floor), and a pair of bookends that were not meant to be funny but were. He marveled to Mary that he was no longer alone, that "there's somebody always on *my* side." He was delighted to find that what he would have been the last to call romance did not wither and die five minutes after the marriage ceremony. Most of all he felt tremendous relief at finding himself just another average man and a complete man, that his intermittent fear of impotence turned out to be unfounded because his marriage was going well in every respect, including the physical.

Cash's appetite, jaded from eating at the Little Pep (it might just as well have been called the Little Dyspepsia), perked up at the way Mary dressed up his meals with the help of parsley, capers, paprika, lime juice, mint, and chives. He took great interest in a novel for which Mary began making notes, material she had collected while working on the Federal Writers' Project publication, *These Are Our Lives* (University of North Carolina Press, 1939). The idea was concerned with the kind of mesmeric evangelism to which the South's poor whites were exposed and addicted. Cash also encouraged her on still another idea they discussed for a novel, this one based on a Charlotte city block on which Mary had lived as a child and which had since turned into the hub of the city's vice and organized crime.

At the same time Mary could not help taking more notice, of Cash's poor physical coordination. She noticed that he would reach for a water glass and miss it, then continue to fumble for it while the overturned glass spilled water over the table. He would grope helplessly for the little chain that turned on their reading lamp, and the lamp would go crashing to the floor. His depth perception in particular was extremely poor. One night at a street crossing he cried "Look out!" and yanked Mary out of the path of a slow-moving car a full block away. His talk of buying a car, perhaps driving it to Mexico, gave her the horrors, because she had never learned to drive and he was perhaps the world's worst driver. However, these familiar symptoms, intensified only because she now saw them every day, did not alarm her very much. She simply made a mental note to have her husband's eyes examined one of these days, or perhaps his inner ear.

In apparent contradiction of his newly secure position, Jack began to drink more whiskey than beer and sherry. He was not an alcoholic, and in quantity he did not even remotely rank as a guzzler, but alcohol continued to have an inordinate effect on him. As for the quality of the liquor then to be had in Charlotte, it was simply the cheapest grade of raw blended whiskey smuggled across from "legal" South Carolina and sold by Tar Heel bootleggers for five dollars a pint. After downing a half pint of the strong waters Cash would lose whatever coordination he still possessed, warning: "Look out, little table." Nevertheless, his book was in the press, he had every reason to expect a Guggenheim fellowship on the strength of the book, his job was secure even if underpaid, and he had a wife, he bragged to his family, who "could do anything." By the same token his wife bragged about him to his family. When his "Sea Fight" editorial won honorable mention in the competition sponsored by the State Press Association, Mary did not fail to report to her husband's parents that "Sea Fight" really was adjudged the best editorial of them all but was finally disqualified because the judges thought the winner should be on a local subject.

Mary had retained her family's beautiful old silver and some furniture, all of which pleased her husband as a new "householder." Mary was really quite a good cook and made a great hit with her Old South oyster stew, but she wrote brightly and self-deprecatingly of her housewifely skills to her in-laws (January 21, 1941):

> Wilbur hasn't complained yet about anything I've fixed for him. He wouldn't anyway, but he seems rather to enjoy most of what has been put before him. . . . This is the first time I have ever done any housekeeping to amount to a row of pins and I find myself liking it. It would be easier if the Blandwood were a new place and clean and modern. The kitchen sink is almost down [on] the floor and I have to bend over double to wash dishes, but I have a little radio in the kitchen and so I have a lot of fun tapping my foot and wondering whether Evangelist Dobbins is right when he hollers

at me that I will go to hell if I go to the movies, which I do without a guilty conscience. . . .

The book will be released for sale on the tenth of February. A Knopf salesman was here yesterday . . . and he reports that he thinks it should have a pretty good sale, but is too literary to be a popular best seller. Curiously . . . he says there will be no trouble whatever selling it in the North. They buy $3.75 books up there.

On the afternoon of publication day, Monday, February 10, 1941, Cash took up his unaccustomed role of celebrity in Efird's bookshop, autographing copies of his new book while nervously awaiting the reviews in the metropolitan press. That night he "just glanced" at *Dracula*, which he had somehow missed reading and which was one of four books Mary presented him on publishing day, and he awoke her for reassurance at two A.M.—he was just plain scared. To be sure, his friend Cameron Shipp, now a movie publicist in far-off Hollywood, contributed an admiring review for his old paper, the Charlotte *News*, a review which ended with the words, "Mr. Cash, I thank you." And now quickly there arose a chorus of praise for this unknown writer, praise from *The New York Times*, from *Atlantic Monthly*, from the two *Suns* in Baltimore, from *Time*. The roast in the Communist *New Masses* was both predictable and helpful. Herbert Aptheker criticized the author therein for jettisoning Marx's class struggle and describing instead a massive alliance among white men to force the Negro to stay in his "place." Otherwise, Mary and Jack examined the laudatory reviews in a whirl of excitement. Cash felt himself initially reassured, especially when he read in *The New York Times* that *Mind* was on its "best seller" list in Atlanta. But how would the entire South react? He had been dreading what might come from Southern reviewers, and he nervously subscribed to a clipping service so that he would miss no significant comment.

Reviews in the North Carolina papers were uniformly flattering, but the author regarded most such praise as deriving from a species of civic pride. His relief was tremendous, therefore, at the reviews that came in from the rest of the South, reviews that recognized that *Mind* was a sharp critique written by a man who nevertheless loved the South. He was grateful as he read admiring reviews in the Southern press: John Temple Graves in the Birmingham *Age Herald*, Mark Ethridge in the Louisville *Courier-Journal*, Henry Nash Smith in the Dallas *Morning News*, Thomas Lomax Hunter in the Richmond *Times-Dispatch*, and other admiring voices in the New Orleans *Item*, the Houston *Post*, and the Jackson (Mississippi) *Clarion Ledger*. Mary wrote to Cash's parents on February 20:

> What pleases me most is that Southern reviewers are whooping it up almost to a man. I had expected a lot of opposition there. It's all very exciting and I can't tell you how relieved I am. If it had fallen flat, heaven only knows what effect it might have had on Wilbur's self-confidence.

Cash's self-confidence was, in fact, so buoyed up at this point that he even resented momentarily a review that he felt was not laudatory enough. Virginius Dabney, whom Cash admired as a commentator on the South, had volunteered to review *Mind* and did write an appreciative critique in *The New York Herald Tribune Books* of February 9. But the author was angered when he read therein: "The book's rather tedious pace is stepped up in the last couple of hundred pages." First he wrote an angry letter to Dabney, but Mary talked him out of mailing it and he destroyed it. On the following Sunday afternoon, however, he called a bootlegger and, suitably fortified, wrote Dabney another abusive letter and mailed it before Mary could stop him. Cash's letter implied, in substance, that Dabney's review damned him with faint praise and was generally motivated by jealousy. A few days later, Dabney received another letter from the author, asking him to forget the first one and to accept his apology. His critic answered the letter containing the apology, gladly accepting it, and repeated that he had liked the book in the first place.

When Alfred Knopf arrived in Charlotte on February 20, en route from Nashville, he brought word that the Agrarians at Vanderbilt—Donald Davidson, the principal spokesman, and one of his lieutenants, Richmond C. Beatty—were outspokenly hostile to *Mind*, which they considered "monstrous." This hostility was to be expected, however, for the author had repeatedly attacked the Agrarians' ideology as "neo-Confederate," and the pre-publication excerpt from *Mind* had reinforced Cash's specific rejection of that ideology. As for the "pouting" of the Agrarians, Cash grinned delightedly. Moreover, he wrote a cordial note of thanks that very day to one Vanderbilt professor, Edwin Mims, who disagreed with his colleagues and had actively praised Cash's book.

Knopf took Jack and Mary to dinner at the Hotel Charlotte (Cash brought a bottle of liquor in a brown paper bag), and a cameraman from the *News* snapped them in a photo that was published next day along with Pete McKnight's interview of the publisher. Knopf believed his author had a great literary future but would not overcommit himself on Cash's forthcoming project of writing a novel. "It's up to Cash," Knopf was quoted. "He knows himself better than anyone else. And the best way for him to find out whether he can write novels or not is to try. If he can, swell. Nothing will be better news for us."

Cash probably never saw Donald Davidson's critical review of *Mind* (in the *Southern Review* for Summer 1941) but even that critic conceded that the book was "enormously instructive even in its errors." The late Richmond Beatty's roast appeared in the Nashville *Banner* of February 26, but

Cash did not see it until Knopf sent it to him in early April. The first sentence of that review read: "Mr. Cash is a geographic Southerner, but there are all sorts of Southerners; the descriptive terms for some of them are unprintable." *Mind* was composed, Beatty surmised, "with a shrewd eye for the lucrative northeastern market." At first Cash reacted angrily only to Beatty's raised-eyebrow comment that the author had reached middle age unmarried (based on information on *Mind's* original dust jacket, quickly changed), and Jack expressed that resentment to his brother-in-law. Then Cash sent the review to Margaret Mitchell in Atlanta, whom he had met shortly before. She was amused and commented that her fellow author would learn, as she had, to put up with critics reviewing books that had never been written. At the end of April, Cash wrote Knopf that he had read Beatty's review with amusement: "Apparently his standard of gentility is ill-nature." Finally, Cash virtually blew Beatty to smithereens with a mighty blast in the May 10 Charlotte *News*, in a review (reprinted in this volume) of another Knopf book, William Alexander Percy's *Lanterns on the Levee*. Cash was unduly gentle with Percy's bland Southern paternalism, but instead turned his heavy artillery on Beatty. Cash knew that Knopf had once rejected an impossible manuscript that Beatty had submitted, and from that Cash inferred that Beatty was insinuating that one had to pander to the Yankee in order to get a Yankee publisher to accept one's book. So demolishing Beatty was all the "bitterness" Cash ever suffered over reviews of his book; he returned far more shot and shell than he ever received.

The first days of March 1941 gave the Cashes their "Georgia weekend." In Atlanta, which was the only city where *Mind* was a strong seller, they were to appear at an author's luncheon promoted by the book department of Rich's Department Store. In the meantime they accepted an invitation for the day before from Lillian Smith, who had asked them to visit her mountaintop home at Clayton, Georgia. So it was that, on a Saturday, the "best-selling" author and his wife boarded a bus and made their way southwestward to little Clayton, Georgia, where they spent an uncomfortable night in the town's only hotel. On Sunday, tired and headachy, Cash began to revive when he encountered some warm friendliness on Old Screamer Mountain, where many friends of the *North Georgia Review* were greeting the guest of honor, Dr. Karl A. Menninger, the noted psychiatrist. Mary Cash could not help but wax enthusiastic at the prospect of meeting Margaret Mitchell in Atlanta, but her husband was in no hurry because, as he had written Lillian Smith on February 26: "I remember that, when nearly everybody else was going off the deep-end for the book, you were taking what turned out to be the correct measure of *Gone With the Wind.*"

Lillian Smith always remembered that Sunday, March 2, and the picture of Cash walking with her across the top of Old Screamer's ridge. He felt a calming serenity there and, when he left, suddenly turned to Miss Smith and said quite sincerely: "This has been the happiest day of my life." Thanking both editors of the *North Georgia Review* in a letter of March 10, Cash wrote:

> Dr. Menninger I thought a capital fellow, all the rest of the company was interesting, you have obviously captured the perfect cook, and I am still muttering about that mountain and that house. . . . After reading that chapter from the novel I think Lillian Smith should finish that novel at all costs. It is moving stuff.

The novel was *Strange Fruit*, published in 1944 after rejection by seven publishers. To his fellow novelist at Clayton, Cash confessed anxiety about his own forthcoming novel and the challenge of the Guggenheim grant that he was applying for (by that time negotiations with the Foundation made it virtually certain that he would receive a grant). "You know, Lillian," he said to his hostess, "I feel so drained and emptied."

The following day, Monday, Mary and Jack were in Atlanta, where their morning session opened with the author's interview over Radio Station WSB by Helen Parker, book buyer for Rich's Department Store. Then came an interview at the hotel with Frank Daniel of the Atlanta *Journal*, during which Cash suffered a violent spasm of coughing and choking. Daniel was impressed, nevertheless, with the author's imperturbability in the face of possibly hostile criticism and with his general balance. Then came a luncheon for about twenty persons in the private dining room of Rich's, where Ralph McGill of the *Constitution* jokingly asked Cash why he had had a gangster picture made for his publicity photo. The writer smiled as if bemused but remained uncommunicative, while Mary privately expressed concern about her husband's exhaustion. In fact, Cash was naturally shy in new company, and on such occasions he usually spoke only when spoken to. Also, the author was afraid of a recurrence of his morning's spasm "before all those people" and thus was quieter than usual. Mary had to carry in her purse a bottle of her husband's favorite patent medicine for coughing spasms, Brown's Mixture.

In that day Atlanta was already a "branch-office" city containing many newcomers to the South, a city oriented to the future rather than to the past and altogether receptive to serious books of the kind Cash had written. The autographing session began in midafternoon, after some additional interviews by reporters in attendance, and after the dining room had been converted to a handsome "drawing room" by pulling back the room dividers, setting out flowers, and bringing up a complement of elegant lamps, chairs, and sofas from the furniture department. As the crowd milled about, Mary stood beside her seated husband and passed him copies of *Mind* opened to the flyleaf. It was supposed to be bad luck to blot signatures at an autographing party, so she fanned them dry as Cash signed every copy of his book in stock. It was nearly five o'clock before he could break away, and "the drinks practically saved our lives," he later wrote gratefully to Margaret Mitchell.

She and her husband, John R. Marsh, took the Cashes to their club for cocktails, and in that more relaxed atmosphere Jack blossomed out with talk both fast and funny. He and Miss Mitchell had a good laugh over the naive Yankee faith in the Old South legend, a legend that *Mind* sought to demolish as earnestly as *Gone With the Wind* to perpetuate. Miss Mitchell had searched for years through antiquarian lore, she said, and had uncovered exactly one pretentious columned mansion in ante-bellum Georgia. That was "Tara," just the thing for an Irish *nouveau's* house, which, to Miss Mitchell's glee, was fastened upon by the whole literate world as the prototype of the Old South mansion. The two authors delightedly compared notes of what life was really like in ante-bellum and Reconstruction days. The latter period Miss Mitchell had caricatured outrageously in her book, whereas Cash sought to correct that slanted picture of Reconstruction. He had not upgraded his earlier opinion of *Gone With the Wind*; it was just that, as a fellow craftsman, he enjoyed the company of that novel's author. Indeed, Cash had let fall the pejorative word "sentimental" in mentioning her book in *Mind*, and later he explained to Miss Mitchell (letter of April 23):

> About that "sentimental" crack: thinking it over, I have an idea that what inspired that carelessly thrown-off judgment was the feeling that your "good" characters were shadowy. On reflection, I think the feeling may have proceeded less from themselves than from the fact that they were set beside that flamboyant wench, Scarlett. There were good women all over the place in the South, of course. But Scarlett

is a female to go along with Becky Sharp, wholly vivid and convincing. Beside her everybody else in the book, including even [Rhett] Butler, seems almost an abstraction. I hope you don't mind my saying it; I know how stupid the judgments of others on his creations sometimes seem to a writer. Indeed, I am often madder at the critics who are trying to be kind than to those obviously out to do me dirt.

Back in Charlotte, where Cash had to return to his desk at the *News*, the mail was piling up and the pace quickening. Knopf's first sales report to the author mentioned 1,400 copies, "little likelihood of a runaway, but at least we have nothing to feel ashamed of." It was better than Cash had expected, but, as he wrote to R. P. Harriss of the Baltimore *Evening Sun* on March 20, "I'm utterly worn out. We have been going at a terrific pace for the last five weeks." Then, just as Jack's sister Bertie entered a Charlotte hospital for an operation and he was distracted, along came word from Henry Allen Moe, in a letter dated March 12, that the author had been granted a Guggenheim Fellowship at a then-princely $2,000 for one year. "I could no longer stand it," Cash wrote Harriss, "got roundly drunk, and the next day was a fit subject for the hospital myself. Everything, as it happened, turned out all right, save that, worse luck, I forgot to mail in my income tax returns and now will have to pay a penalty. And I am not yet feeling that anything is really worth a damn."

Continuing his letter of March 20 to Harriss, Cash wrote:

The Fellowship is for the writing of a novel. The Foundation explained that they had no proof I could write fiction but were so impressed with the *Mind* that I could do what I liked, changing my project when and if I wanted to. We plan to spend the year in Mexico City, though that plan may be changed. We will leave here about May 15. I plan stubbornly to do the novel. I have always wanted to do that, and still think I can do a better job of it than of anything else.

And now the news of the fellowship grant brought a greater flood of mail than before, some from old Wake Forest friends like Professor Hubert M. Poteat and President Thurman D. Kitchin, some from total strangers writing in simple admiration of the book or the fellowship or both. One piece of mail was a brochure from an innkeeper near Guadalajara, Mexico, who urged him to settle there in a "writers' paradise." The monthly rate for the cottages was too high for the Cashes to do anything but whistle unbelievingly, but they were surprised at the aptness of the advertisement. Their plan for Mexico had not been announced. They made some jokes about a Nazi spy ring preparing to exact vengeance for Cash's outspoken anti-Nazi editorials. Cash certainly took such talk as a joke, but he may have tucked it into the back of his mind, where it could have awaited its release in Mexico City.

With the publication of his book and the award of a Guggenheim fellowship, Cash acquired a new self-confidence in the face of the belated success he had flirted with all his adult life. He still had to write Alfred Knopf for an advance of $100 when *Mind* went into a second edition. And he remained uncertain about his novel, writing Margaret Mitchell on April 23: "I agree that to wish that the second book shall come easily is the best thing one author could wish another. I observe that I said 'author,' a word that always has tickled me." But the fan letters kept coming in, and important writers began to notice him. He and Mary had lunch with the novelist Carson McCullers in March, and the pioneer of the South's literary renascence, Ellen Glasgow, wrote appreciatively from Richmond about *Mind* as a book for those who like to think.

People now sought out the sapient Mr. Cash to such an extent that he took to accepting every speaking invitation and then begging off sick, with Mary's connivance, as deadlines approached. He was sought out by CBS News, through

Radio Station WBT in Charlotte, to contribute a commentary about the *chetnik* resistance to Hitler following Yugoslavia's invasion in early April. Jack got drunk, whereupon Mary composed the eulogy to Draja Mikhailovich—duly broadcast—full of allusions to David and Goliath. At the local Queen's College, where he was corralled on April 17 for an hour's visit to an English class, Cash did not look directly at the young ladies but gestured choppily with his hands and concluded, according to one of his audience: "You just have to have some ideas and *say* them!" At the Charlotte Bookshop, which conducted a book-and-author session, he was more downright. Asked whether, as *Mind* seemed to warn, Cash expected actual physical violence to erupt over the Negro issue in the South, he replied: "Certainly I do."

Meanwhile, the welter of physical violence already flooding Europe engaged most of his energies in his Charlotte *News* writing. On April 3 he contributed an enthusiastic review of R. H. Markham's *The Wave of the Past*, a booklet that he found to answer and controvert Anne Morrow Lindbergh's *The Wave of the Future*. He found Mrs. Lindbergh's a tired Spenglerian view looking to Nazism for renewed strength. He found Markham's reply showing, as Cash said, "that far from being anything new, Nazism is really 'The Wave of the Past' . . . as old as Sumer and Babylon, as old as Cro-Magnon man and his Neanderthal predecessor." He similarly gave the back of his hand to the collection of isolationist columns published by General Hugh "Ironpants" Johnson, whose book Cash called "bad, misleading, even dangerous" (review reprinted in this volume). In the midst of it all, by a letter dated April 9, came a congratulatory message from Cash's long-lost early love, Peggy Ann, now married for the second time. Jack showed the letter wryly to Mary, answered it politely enough, then got back to more pressing matters. He fired off a telegram to Senator Claude D. Pepper, the Florida Democrat, supporting that pioneer of all-out aid to

Britain in his latest proposal to prevent Britain's being starved out by submarine.

On April 28 the Charlotte *News* proudly headlined a news story "Cash Invited to Talk to Texas U. Graduates" and quoted President Homer P. Rainey's invitation to Cash. "I have been for a number of years studying and thinking about the problems of the South," Dr. Rainey wrote, "but in all of my reading I have not found any analysis that I think is so courageously penetrating and so fundamentally sound as the analysis which you have given." Accordingly, the University of Texas would be pleased to have Cash make the commencement address that June 2 and would pay a gratifying $200 and expenses. Jack was flabbergasted at the honor and delighted with the windfall, and he gratefully accepted. The only alteration in plans would involve going to Mexico City by rail instead of taking a ship at New Orleans for Vera Cruz. Cash had long since decided that, since Europe was at war, he would spend the following year south of the border in Mexico, where the peso would buy a dollar's worth of goods and services and where one dollar would buy five pesos.

The month of May was spent in a whirl, what with leave-takings, packing, and Cash's full-time duties at the *News* (he could not afford to quit) until the very day of departure. He began the month with a serious, almost somber letter to his father (published in this volume) in which he acknowledged his father's fears for him but explained how much the sojourn in Mexico and the award of the fellowship promised for his writing future. In the event of war or other emergency, the son assured the father, he and Mary would be protected with round-trip tickets home.

On the first weekend in May, Mary and Jack were in Chapel Hill. There they made their farewells to her mother while Jack spoke informally to the collegians in Phillips Russell's creative writing class and somewhat more solemnly to the high-schoolers attending the Scholastic Press Institute organized by Walter Spearman. As he confessed to Mary's mother, Jack was momentarily tempted to chuck the whole Mexican expedition and spend his fellowship year in Chapel Hill, but somehow that impulse passed. The leavetaking in Shelby, the following weekend, was an emotional one; both Cash's parents were fearful at his leaving them, and he was embarrassed and impatient with his mother's tears. On the 20th he wrote Alfred Knopf of his now-concrete plans:

> My plans at present are to use the first four months in Mexico in working on that novel I have in mind. The material is already pretty well in hand, and in that period I think I can settle the question of my ability to do that kind of thing. If I find the answer is that I can't, I'll switch over to a nonfiction project, and probably come back to the United States to work on it. I already have the permission of the Guggenheim Fellowship to make the change when and if I desire to do so. I have a number of things in mind tentatively, but the time to discuss them will of course be when and if I find the switch desirable.
>
> Will it inconvenience you to let me have now what may be due me in royalties on the Mind up to the present? I dislike to ask it, but I am going to need it pretty desperately in getting out of here for Mexico. [Cash got $100 by return mail.]

On May 30 the Charlotte *News* published a photo of the Cashes doing their last-minute packing and captioned it: "Off to Mexico City on a year's Guggenheim Fellowship, Mr. and Mrs. W. J. Cash plan to come back with a novel about a family of Southern textile workers." The associate editor of the Charlotte *News* had resigned from the paper, sold his phonograph records to the obliging McCleneghans, packed their few clothes and some books in Mary's old school trunk and some handbags, and then left on that morning's 4:27 a.m. streamliner. Dismounting from their daycoach at New Orleans, the Cashes stayed, predictably, at the St.

Charles and took luncheon at Antoine's. The food was simple enough but Jack could not keep it down, for he was really ill in that damp heat where the ceiling fans failed to help. The sidewalk radios were blaring the current nonsense hit, *The Hut Sut Song*, and Cash told Mary: "The words in that song are exactly what I feel like—a brawla brawla soo-it." On the train bound for Texas he had a curious and violent fit of anger, stamping a newspaper on the floor and biting his fists. What made it so curious was that he could not remember the cause of it; it was quickly over, but Mary was puzzled.

She was nervous, too, about the commencement address, because she feared that her husband might suffer one of his constrictions of the throat right there on the rostrum. At first Cash was tired and worn out—not nervous, like Mary—but he became positively buoyant upon again being surrounded by faculty people. Then, too, the Driskill Hotel—destined to become an important news center in the Johnson administration—was a Texas pioneer in air conditioning, and the coolness there made Jack feel somewhat better. On the outdoor platform before some thirteen hundred graduates that evening of June 2, 1941, Cash spoke on "The South in a Changing World" (published in this volume). Obviously quoting from the speaker's prepared text, the Dallas *Morning News* and the Austin *Statesman* quoted him as saying that the South's "wall of idealism, romanticism, and of refusal to face the unpleasant" had resulted in a quarantine of new ideas "at the Potomac and Ohio." But he actually said nothing so provocative and inflammatory; he put aside his prepared script (which has not survived) and spoke ad lib with less than impressive results. The University authorities made a recording of that address, as delivered, and so it is that Cash's voice has been preserved. The old set of 78-r.p.m. records has been tape-recorded, and both recordings are now in the Southern Historical Collection at Chapel Hill.

The train trip along the spine of Mexico was long and exhausting for the Cashes—two days and nights, a full forty-five hours. The U. S. Consulate referred them to a popular refuge of *norteamericanos* in Mexico City, the *pensión* of a handsome old widow who dosed Mary and Jack, sent them to bed, and gave them the classic advice for newcomers (nothing to drink; cook it before you eat it). After a few days she found them a small apartment off the Paseo de la Reforma, close to the hill topped by Chapultepec Palace. It was then a newish neighborhood built on the edge of the advancing city, the area of streets named for rivers (theirs was the Calle Río de la Plata). Their little place was furnished in an impersonal denationalized sort of way, and they thought the furniture and the house, which was built flush with the street around a flowered court, had been designed for midgets. The manager was an eighteen-year-old Indian girl with enough English to direct the Cashes to the market and to a maid, tiny Sacramento, who lived with her tinier baby and small husband in a lean-to depending on the back wall of the house.

Right away Mary and Jack made their way to the vegetable counters and the meat markets (a chicken-wing store next to a chicken-breast store facing the filet-mignon store across the alley) and bought a market basket. Cash minded not at all that he was openly derided for his lack of *machismo*—male pride— in deigning to carry his wife's purchases. They filled the basket with pottery dishes, unknown vegetables, and, for about fifteen cents, filet mignon from Argentine beef. The vegetables Mary threw into a pot with a few bones, and the combination turned into a delicious everlasting soup (one adds to such a soup and it never grows less). Sacramento, whom Cash called the Holy Spirit, taught Mary to use garlic and oil in cooking frijoles, which the Cashes liked so well that they had them even for breakfast.

The soup was a boon to Mary because, in a state of

chronic internal upset and dizziness from the altitude, she had little energy to play the busy housewife. Cash was in even worse shape than she with diarrhea and dizziness. Sleep came easily enough but was light and unrefreshing. Their neighborhood was deserted at night and was patrolled by policemen who signaled and reassured one another by whistling in a minor key eerie little scalp-tingling tunes on what sounded to Mary like reed pipes. The Cashes did climb pantingly up to the palace under trees that awed them, past stone idols being eyed by small quiet people whose lids never blinked, up to the formal and unlovely seat of Maximilian and Carlotta. Their saving sense of the ridiculous did not fail the Cashes thus far from home. On one of their infrequent tourist forays they ventured into the National Museum, where, on turning on a light switch in one chamber, they found themselves in a gallery filled with pre-Columbian phallic idols and deities. The Cashes were still gaping when they realized, first with consternation and then with rising amusement, that they had been followed into the gallery by a party of lady tourists (navy blue georgette and rimless glasses). Mary and Jack began to laugh, so hard and so painfully at last that they had to leave. But on the whole they did relatively little sight-seeing for lack of energy. Even the beer, the excellent *cerveza*, did not taste right to Cash.

Nor did his work prosper. He could not accommodate his hands to the small keyboard of the new portable typewriter he had bought in San Antonio. While Mary was brushing up on her Spanish she would hear a peck, another peck, then a jangled chord of pecks as the keys jammed when he speeded up, and then the howl of his "goddam"—and she knew he was biting his fists. Cash also was frustrated by his inability to wrap his Anglo-Saxon tongue around even one word of Spanish. In Europe in 1927 he had been able to get along passably in French and German, but in that Mexican summer of 1941 nothing seemed to go right. He could not concentrate on his work because of his trouble in adjusting to alien speech, food, customs, water, air, and currency, and because of the unshakable diarrhea that sapped his strength.

His morale was given a boost, nevertheless, when a barber at the Hotel Reforma transformed him into something resembling a man of distinction. Cash had self-consciously preserved, over the bald front of his head, the forlorn and untidy wisps and bristles of hair that were the ruins of his collegiate pompadour. With no Spanish to direct otherwise, he watched anxiously as the barber, who, happily, knew his business, briskly shaved the bald area and shaped a kind of widow's peak on the top of Cash's head. Mary was delighted on seeing her husband thus given a fascinating Mephistophelean cast, and said, while Cash grinned happily, "Whee, *el diablo!*"

On June 10 he managed to dictate a "Wilbur and Mary" letter to his parents by way of reassuring them. "We have seen so much," he reported, "that I shan't even try to describe it now. But we want you to know that we are all right and comfortable. And don't worry. Mexico is a civilized if a somewhat backward country, and we have encountered nothing but the kindest treatment." By way of describing the physical environment, he added:

> The first day I spent in bed because of the dizziness caused by the altitude. Up here at first all you want to do is to sleep. It is brilliantly sunny in the morning, but about three o'clock it begins to rain, not hard but steadily. Everybody knocks off about three and sleeps until five or six, then everything opens up again until nine or ten. In the mornings it is almost hot, the nights are cool and sometimes even cold. We sleep under at least one blanket all the time.
>
> The climate still bothers us somewhat, makes us awfully tired by midday, but we are beginning to adjust to it now. And both of us like Mexico (they never call it anything but that

here) a great deal. The city is immensely beautiful and colorful. And the Indians in particular are interesting. We have a little servant in the apartment house (not our private servant but that of the whole house), who works for nearly nothing and who is charming in her eagerness to please. The Indians are the Negroes of Mexico, but they have it even harder than our Negroes, and they are more prepossessing.

The only writing Cash composed in Mexico City, apart from that letter, appears to have been an undated article that survives among his personal papers, "Report From Mexico" (published in this volume). Obviously intended as a free-lance contribution to U.S. newspapers, the article discusses the Mexican capital in a soberly informative way, then touches upon the political situation. Cash made specific reference to swarms of Nazi and Communist agents in the cities of Mexico, but attributed the information to a U.S. government employee whom he apparently had met during his temporary stay at the *pensión*. Furthermore, Cash used the same source as authority for saying that the Fifth Columnists had been "decisively defeated and reduced to gnawing their nails in rage," while Mexico gave its active support to United States foreign policy. Far from being unnerved by the Nazi attack on Russia on June 22, Cash waxed jubilant as Mary translated the news story in a Mexican newspaper. He had warned against the future Russian power from the moment of the Hitler-Stalin pact, and was in no way sorry to see Hitler diverted from further expansion to the west.

Then came the night of Monday, June 30. Cash suddenly asked Mary if she could hear those people talking outside. The Cashes sat in their small foyer–dining room, which gave onto the street entrance to their apartment house. They had often heard people talking in the hallway outside, and Mary assumed that he heard some now. He did not then show any fear but only acted as if he were eavesdropping. Then he started to whisper the substance of their talk: They were

Nazis who were planning to kill one or both of the Cashes. Mary stood as still as stone, straining to hear, and still heard nothing at all. It was a nightmarish moment in which she thought the trouble was with her, not Cash, and not until her husband began pushing furniture against the locked door did she realize that the "voices" were all in his mind.

She reasoned with him. She didn't hear any voices and, if he would take thought for a moment, Cash would realize that he didn't either. He was tired when he got to Mexico, she reminded him, and now he was sick and overwrought. And why would anybody in the world want to kill them? Then Cash would subside for a few minutes, thinking about it, but the "voices" would resume. The Cash apartment was on the ground-floor front, but its small windows were high off the street. An intruder would have to climb a ladder to break in. But by this time Cash could hear Mary only intermittently, for the "voices" dominated his consciousness. He furtively locked the windows from inside, she recalled, maneuvering so that his arm would be visible only momentarily to an assassin on the street.

Alarmed as Mary was, she really got terrified when her husband snatched up the only weapon in the apartment, a sharp carving knife. Her own thinking now became chaotic, because he had become quite irrational and there was no apparent way out of the nightmarish episode. They had no telephone, and Mary dared not cry out lest Cash turn the carving knife on the first person who entered their door. So she tried to laugh him out of countenance. She laughed at him for playing the Terrible Turk, Wild Bill Hickok, Attila the Hun. She reminded him that they were now in an impregnable fortress, and that now he could put down that carving knife and go to bed. She would read to him; what would he like? So at last they wearily got ready for bed and Cash picked up his Bible and said: "Read Ecclesiastes, baby." And so Mary read to him from the worldly-wise preacher, of there being a time to every purpose under heaven: a time to be born, and a time to die; a time to kill and a time to heal. Cash fell asleep while listening to the mighty and comforting words.

Next morning, the fateful July 1, he was himself again. He remembered the whole appalling episode, and he apologized to Mary and explained that he had been "sick" the night before. He had had too prolonged a bout with tourist sickness, he added, and had been inordinately upset because he hadn't been able to get a grip on himself. He readily agreed that he must see a doctor, and Mary left him picking at a late breakfast while she went upstairs to ask some San Antonio people who had befriended them to recommend a physician. Mary told the whole terrible story so they would know the kind of doctor needed, a psychiatrist or the closest thing to one. On their telephone Mary then called the doctor they recommended, reported the facts about Cash's irrationality the night before, and made an appointment for two that afternoon. When she returned to their apartment Cash was not there, and when he returned a while later Mary was horrified to see that he was pale and shaking, that his delusions had returned. He had placed their papers—tourist cards, fellowship credentials, almost all their money—in a safe-deposit box in a downtown bank secure from the "Nazis" who were trying to "kill" them. Mary reminded her husband that he had already realized that he had been "sick" the night before, but he would not listen. She told him they had an appointment with an American doctor at two o'clock, and at length Cash reluctantly and fearfully consented to go.

At the physician's office Cash vehemently refused treatment of any kind and jerked his arm away from the hypodermic needle like a child. Mary had to talk him into submitting to the injection, which he did unwillingly and suspiciously. On top of everything else, Cash confided to Mary as they left the physician's office that the injection had been poison. The doctor later identified the injection—and he seemed embarrassed doing so—as nothing more than vitamin B₁.

The Cashes returned home but did not stay there, because now the "killers" were beginning to close in. They would have to go to a hotel for greater safety. After Mary reconnoitered and reported that no one was lurking outside, Cash came out and they hurried down the block to the Paseo and caught a taxi heading downtown. Because Mary was wearing a red hat she had to crouch on the floor of the cab; according to Cash, the hat was too conspicuous a target for assassins. During that frantic afternoon they went to four different hotels, only the last of which Mary could later remember—the Geneve. In their room there, Cash no longer thought of arming himself, as with the carving knife of the day before, but, uncharacteristically, he cowered terrified in a corner. Their situation was plainly impossible: Mary had to seek help.

Mary did not want to call on the U. S. Consulate or Embassy, because she felt that her husband, once again recovered, would never have forgiven her for so humiliating him. Mary remembered the chief of the Associated Press bureau, where they had called a few days before, and she asked Cash to let her telephone the bureau chief. No, she must not telephone because the "Nazis" would intercept the call, so Mary had to go after the AP man personally while Cash locked himself in their room. When she returned with bureau chief Ben F. Meyer and one of his men they found that Cash had fled the hotel. By now Mary had almost lost her own control, and it was with immeasurable relief that she watched Ben Meyer unhesitatingly call the police. Since Cash was under the delusion that he was being hunted by "Nazi killers," he could be dangerous to anyone he encountered.

The room at the Geneve began to fill up. While a police

alarm went out about four o'clock, Ben Meyer was calling a list of hotels that might now be harboring W. J. Cash. Meyer first called the Hotel Reforma, where Cash had approved the barbershop, but neither the Reforma nor any of the others could confirm his presence there. It was nearly ten o'clock that night when Ben again called the Reforma and this time was told that Cash was now registered there. So detectives, uniformed police, some unexplained people, and Ben Meyer and Mary set out from the Geneve bound for the Reforma. Mary's knock on Cash's door got no answer. The hotel manager, standing in the van of what she recalled as a horde of silent people, refused to open the door but handed Mary the key. She entered the room and saw Cash hanging by his necktie from the bathroom door. He had been dead, it was later established, for several hours. Mary's scream brought them all inside, and then official routine took over.

Within five minutes Mary was telephoning reporter Pete McKnight at the Charlotte *News*, asking him to break the news as gently as he could to Cash's parents, whom he knew, and to Mary's mother through a friend. Ben Meyer's wife stayed with Mary at the police station during the unreal night with the police and Mexican Intelligence, while she tried to answer their questions as courteously as they asked them. At that time, Mexico City, like every important capital in the world, harbored some real Nazi agents, and it was some time before the authorities were convinced that Cash's "Nazis" were hallucinatory. At the conclusion of the all-night questioning at the police station, Mary was more than ready to accept an invitation to stay at the U.S. Embassy. The invitation came from an embassy staff member, who materialized as a personal escort like some welcome genie.

Ambassador Josephus Daniels of North Carolina, then in his eightieth year and dean of the diplomatic corps in Mexico, had been a lifelong friend of Mary's grand-uncle,

Benehan Cameron. The handsome Mrs. Daniels was by birth a Bagley, and so she and Mary were distantly related. The Danielses' son Jonathan was an acquaintance of Cash's and had sponsored his Guggenheim application. So although Mary had never met either of those wonderfully decorative old people, they greeted her as one of their own, and she gratefully threw herself into their arms.

Mary always felt that those two saintly representatives of the United States of America who took her into their Embassy residence probably saved her own reason. She tried to write them later but went to pieces each time. She finally explained her long silence to the wise Mrs. Daniels the following December, on the Friday before Pearl Harbor Sunday. Mary was in Raleigh to accept the Mayflower Cup for literary excellence, which was being awarded posthumously to Cash. At Mrs. Daniels's home Mary confided to her that she was afraid of breaking down during the presentation and would prefer to let Cash's father, who was there, accept the award. Mrs. Daniels, saying what Mary found to be the beautiful things that needed saying, gave the younger woman the courage to go through with the task that only she could fittingly perform.

At first meeting the Danielses in Mexico City, Mary was in emotional shock, and the concerned Mrs. Daniels fretted, referring to the given name that made them kin: "You should have the relief of tears, Mary Bagley." Understanding her situation, the Danielses diverted her by sending her to a Villa-Lobos concert at the Bellas Artes, where she sat in the ambassador's box. They had their chauffeur drive her around on her last sight-seeing tour of Mexico City, and cannily let Mary use their official limousine, splendidly emblazoned with the Great Seal of the United States, when she went down for additional questioning at police headquarters. She thought their wisest and most charming act was to seat her among the orchestra musicians, in plain view and therefore invisible, at the Embassy reception for the global diplomatic corps and Mexican officialdom on the Fourth of July.

The ambassador had to telephone Washington to extricate Mary from her "stateless" predicament: She could not leave Mexico without her tourist card, and she could not get it from the safe-deposit box without having been declared Cash's executrix by a court in the United States. Through Mr. Daniels's intervention she was presented with a beribboned document that they all had to laugh at because of its gaudy pretentiousness.

Mr. Daniels also helped arrange for Mary to accompany the remains of her husband back to North Carolina. The ambassador suggested cremation, with the return home to be made by air. For the first time Mary remembered that Cash had once remarked sourly that he would prefer cremation to embalming as the lesser of two evils. So she agreed, then flew out of Mexico City on her lone homeward journey on Saturday, July 5.

It may be well to record here the only known on-the-spot account, other than newspaper obituaries, of Cash's death. This account, in the Library of Congress, is that of Ambassador Daniels, dated July 7, 1941, and is part of a weekly diary-letter he was accustomed to send to members of his large family:

> Early in the week we came in close contact with one of the most baffling tragedies. Mr. and Mrs. Wilbur Cash, of Charlotte, had come here two [three] weeks before. He received a Guggenheim award for his book "The Mind of the South" which appeared early in the year, and he and his wife had come here, first as tourists, for he needed a rest, then he expected to gather material for another book. En route here they stopped at Austin, Texas, where he delivered the commencement address at the University. We did not know they were here until a short time before he hung himself with his

cravat in a room in the Reforma. It seems he had been extremely nervous and could not sleep and then was weakened by an attack of dysentery or diarrhea. His wife told me that in the CHARLOTTE NEWS he had written very critically of the Nazis and had the delusion they were after him. She said that after the beginning of Germany's invasion of Russia he walked the floor and talked of nothing else and bemoaned the fact that he had no paper in which to express himself. [That Cash "had no paper" referred to his loss of an editorial outlet via the Charlotte *News*. Cash's widow, who was Mr. Daniels's authority, has told the present writer that the ambassador misunderstood the impact of the Nazi-Soviet conflict on Cash, and that the onset of Cash's "voices" did not occur until June 30; i.e., the entire period of Cash's delirious state was twenty-four hours.] His delusion that Nazi agents were after him grew as he became more and more frenzied.

While his wife was at the Geneve, with Mr. and Mrs. Meyer (he is the Associated Press correspondent here), he went to the Reforma, engaged a room, where his wife found he was registered. Knocking at the door brought no response. When the door was broken open, they found he had hanged himself in the bathroom. It was, as you may imagine, a terrible blow, increased by the fact that she was in a foreign country and, I think, without money. Mr. and Mrs. Meyer took her home with them that night [a mistake: Mrs. Meyer stayed at the police station with Mary all night] and the next morning we invited her to come and stay at the Embassy. Your mother [Mrs. Daniels] gave her affectionate sympathy. She [Mary Cash] is a cousin of Belle and Sallie Cameron and her maiden name was Mary Bagley Ross and is a cousin of your mother on her father's side. Consul Wilson looked after everything for her. The Guggenheim Foundation sent her some money. His body was cremated and she left here with the ashes by aeroplane on Saturday [July 5].

Because of the uncertain hour of Mary's return, the funeral arrangements in Shelby had not been definite, but on Monday, July 7, 1941, Cash's funeral was held at the First Baptist

Church. His ashes were later interred in a vault in Sunset Cemetery. Jack's newspaper mates acted as honorary pallbearers, and one of them, LeGette Blythe, said he would never forget how queer he felt walking down the church aisle behind the funeral director who bore that little mahogany box. Assisting the regular pastor was one of Cash's Hamrick cousins from Charleston, South Carolina, who proceeded to apologize both to God and the congregation for Cousin Wilbur's ideas.

That preacher cousin must have read some of the author's sharp pieces in *The American Mercury*, because he first apologized for Cash's having maligned so many of the powers that be before assuring all present that Wilbur really had been a very good boy. Mary half-rose in her pew, but her mother physically restrained her as if fearing she might make a scandal. Mary was able to smile in later years, knowing how her husband would have whooped at it all, but at the time, as she later recalled, "I was outdoors mentally burning down that church."

Having looked at herself with a cold eye over the intervening years, Mary's conclusion was that if she had had any inkling that Cash was headed for suicide, she might have done something differently. But she was never able to give that something a name.

CHAPTER 6

Why?

E *ven for* the most tentative exploration of the tortuous "why's" that becloud Cash's fate, one must first demolish the manifold myths that have grown and flourished around his name. For this writer such demolition comes hard, because it necessarily involves the impossibly frustrating chore of trying to prove a negative. Even as the Warren Commission's report on the Kennedy assassination had no answer for those who still prefer to believe that the late President was the victim of a minutely organized plot, so this volume has none for the reader who has somehow convinced himself that Cash died at the hands of Nazi assassins.

In justice to the truth, however, the task must be attempted, and consequently I list here the three false myths about Cash that have come to my attention: (1) that Cash's death was murder at the hands of Nazi agents; (2) that his death was truly suicide but that he was suffering from an incurable brain tumor; and (3) that there must have been foul play of some sort because, when he was found hanging by his necktie, his feet were touching the floor.

The third myth can be dismissed at once. Mary was the first to see Cash's shadow on the bedroom wall; she examined his face in a flash that convinced her instantly that it was too late to do anything. She turned away and never looked back again. Authorities explain that a suicide's feet can, and indeed in the majority of instances do, touch the floor, because the suicide has only to double up and then relax in death. In fact, unless the suicide stands on a chair (and Cash used none), it is almost impossible for his attempt to succeed *without* his feet touching the floor. The police who questioned Mary for several days after her husband's death never once brought up the subject. And if she could not remember in later years whether or not the suicide's feet were touching the floor, how could such a "fact" present itself to the student author who "reported" it in the *Wake Forest Student* (the student magazine at Cash's alma mater) in the issue of November 1959? In sum, the allegedly sinister "fact" of Cash's feet touching the floor (and this "fact" is not recorded in the death certificate or any of the other pertinent documents) is irrelevant.

The second false myth, about the "incurable brain tumor," is so much alive that Ralph McGill, the publisher of the Atlanta *Constitution*, who picked up the story quite innocently, repeated it in a recent letter to me. The story is utterly false. An autopsy was performed upon Cash in accordance with Mexican law, as explained by U. S. Ambassador Josephus Daniels to Cash's father in a letter of July 3, 1941. That autopsy revealed no brain tumor of any kind. However, Mary Cash wired her father-in-law from Mexico on July 3, thinking to spare him and his wife additional pain: "Doctor thinks brain tumor may have been responsible." This possibility had been seriously discussed before the autopsy report was received. A similar story was invented independently by someone else at the funeral, Cash's old friend Everett Houser, who gave it out that an incipient brain tumor had been detected years before when Cash had been examined at the Johns Hopkins Hospital. It was all pure fiction, but it seemed to comfort many of the mourners, who proceeded to retail the fiction by word of mouth.

Nothing, however, served to comfort the suicide's devout and heartbroken parents. Nothing could make them believe that a complex of physical illness and psychological pressures could have induced in their brilliant son the dreadful "suicidal fit" that did in fact occur. Their inability to face up to the facts undoubtedly contributed to the final myth, that Cash's death was engineered by Nazi agents instructed to exact vengeance for those consistently anti-Axis editorials in the Charlotte *News*.

The author's parents, devout orthodox Baptists that they were, never could or would bring themselves to believe that their son did in fact take his life. His mother, a saintly woman whose grief brought on a series of heart attacks that finally ended her life in 1959, told Mary quietly that suicide is *the* unpardonable sin, so therefore her boy Wilbur could not have committed it. If he had committed suicide, there would be no chance for them to meet in the Better Land, and her faith was unshakable that she would one day meet her Wilbur in heaven. Mary tried to tell her that Wilbur had not "been himself," that under the circumstances God surely would not fail to forgive him. But she got nowhere with her reasoning; Nannie Hamrick Cash would not be moved.

The same was true of Cash's father, John William Cash, who lived almost a quarter century longer than his son (he died on November 16, 1964, only a few days short of his ninety-second birthday). Mary Cash reported later that she had never been directly confronted by the myth that her husband had been murdered by Nazi agents, but she came to believe that the tale got started among those who could not accept the fact of her husband's suicide. The nagging conclusion of foul play harbored by Father Cash (no one suggests that he deliberately set out to circulate it) finally took published form on August 14, 1964, in the *Cleveland* (County) *Times* of Shelby, North Carolina. The interviewer quoted John Cash: "'It was publicized that he committed suicide, but he didn't,' says the father firmly. He has always believed that his son's death was caused by foul play, thinking it connected with his strong editorial and newspaper stand against Hitler and Mussolini."

That the Nazis were hunting him down personally was precisely the tragic delusion under the influence of which W. J. Cash took his life. And it was a delusion bred of a disordered mind, as Ambassador Josephus Daniels personally wrote on July 10, 1941, to his son Jonathan, one of Cash's friends:

> It was a real tragedy. She [Mary Cash] must have known his mind was unhinged when he was obsessed by the thought that the Nazis wished to get him. *It was purely imaginary for nothing of the sort occurred.* [my italics.] I know nothing sadder than for a bright mind to become so unhinged that death seems the only course open.

Moreover, the official documents, the reports of death issued by Mexico and by the United States (and Cash's widow procured certified true copies of both), were conclusive as to the absence of foul play. That of Mexico registers the death routinely as No. 2337, Page 108 in Book No. 10 in Office No. 2 of the Civil Register, Mexico, D.F. It is dated July 3, 1941. Even the immediate news story coming out of Mexico, as filed by the Associated Press and dated July 2, 1941, reads: "Commander Alvaro Basail, of the Capital's radio police patrol, asserted Cash committed suicide." The U. S. State Department document, the "Consular Report of Death of Wilbur J. Cash," is based upon the Mexican one, being dated August 19, 1941. Completed after the thorough police investigation, it contains the notation: "Remarks— Applicant's mind became impaired and he hanged himself."

Because these myths have almost always been circulated by word of mouth, they have been infinitely harder to cancel through a process of elimination than, say, a clearly wrongheaded observation by a published author. An instance of the latter was furnished by a noted political scientist, the late V. O. Key, Jr., who in *Southern Politics in State and Nation* (New York: Knopf; 1947; p. 664) sought to generalize about suicides in the South: "A depressingly high rate of self-destruction prevails among those who ponder about the South and put down their reflections in books. A fatal frustration seems to come from the struggle to find a way through the unfathomable maze formed by tradition, caste, race, poverty." But how many suicides, exactly, did Professor Key tabulate and thus consider "a depressingly high rate of self-destruction"? His principal assistant in composing *Southern Politics*, Alexander Heard, put this question to his senior and has since informed me that Key had named exactly three: one whose name Heard could not recall, then Clarence Cason, and finally W. J. Cash. Since the incidence of three suicides cannot rightly be construed as "a depressingly high rate of self-destruction," Key's engagingly written generalization must be set down as artistic license, no more.

It has been generally accepted that Clarence Cason's suicide in 1935 was occasioned not by depression born of "no way out for the South" but by mounting fear of what he thought would be his colleagues' and neighbors' censure in Tuscaloosa, Alabama. About the unnamed third man we cannot speak, but if citing him bears out Key's observation no better than does the Cason suicide, then the inability of Dr. Heard to remember that third man's name is quite understandable.

What, then, about W. J. Cash himself? Is it not conceivable that his suicide is traceable to depression over the South's future, and that he could no longer live with the contradictions he had uncovered? The answer, almost certainly, is no. In point of fact, Cash's obsessive concern for the South became measurably less once he had gotten the monumental manuscript off his chest and into the mail in the summer of 1940. By that time, as we have seen, his angry frustration at the fall of France merely pointed up what had been true in him for the past several years: his obsession with the totalitarian evil in Europe had taken the place of his older concern for the South and its problems. It is probably true, of course, that a certain uneasiness over playing "traitor" to his native region served to inhibit Cash and to delay completion of his manuscript in the years from 1937 to 1940. But complete it he did, and the supposedly fearsome vengeance of a hypersensitive South was not exacted.

If it were not that we had already documented the almost unanimous chorus of critical acclaim with which *The Mind of the South* was greeted everywhere, it might seem plausible that Cash was upset about public reaction to his book. One such notion was, in fact, published in an otherwise perceptive article by Dewey W. Grantham, Jr., entitled "Mr. Cash Writes a Book" (*Progressive*, December 1961). Professor Grantham took occasion to write: "Indeed, the violent criticism and the personal abuse Cash encountered almost certainly contributed to his tragic suicide." What "violent criticism"? Only two hostile reviews were published, one by Donald Davidson, which Cash probably never saw, and another by Richmond Beatty, to which he replied with an attack infinitely more scathing than the one he had sustained. And what "personal abuse"? Professor Grantham has since conceded to me that the Carolinians he interviewed probably exaggerated, and one can, indeed, find some evidence of occasional and anonymous hard words being spoken about Cash. For example, one such reaction that was brought to my attention complained of writers who allegedly fouled their own nests. Another, made by an unnamed history professor after Cash's death (when the remark surely cannot have hurt him), was to the effect that he should have killed himself not after but before he wrote the book. But of personal abuse of the face-to-face variety there is not a jot of evidence; not from Cash's widow, not from his family, not from his newspaper mates.

In exploring the reasons for Cash's suicide it is perhaps most important of all to understand that, as he prepared for his fateful trip to Mexico, Cash was not a man suffering from depression—far from it. He had never shown a more positive outlook on things, never been more optimistic, never had more to live for. If his personal physician often had found Cash depressed, that was now in the past, and Dr. Claude B. Squires informed me that he could testify only to the period before Cash's marriage. Even if Cash occasionally alarmed friends like LeGette Blythe with his violent tirades against the Nazis, that was no manifestation of depression. The evidence is all on the side of Cash's looking constructively and hopefully to the future and involving himself with it and with society.

For example, in the letter written to his father (*c*. May 1, 1941) published in this volume, Cash avowed that this time his bid for economic independence would be far different from his earlier failure. "To ask for a job," he wrote, "as one who is unknown, broke and down and out, who hasn't had a job for several years, and to ask for one as a Guggenheim Fellow with a solid record as an editorial writer and as the author of a book which has made a great reputation—these are very different things." To be sure, he had shown a flagging of spirit that March 2 when he confessed to Lillian Smith that he felt "drained and emptied." But that was before the Guggenheim had come through, and before the thrilling realization that he was now important enough to be invited to speak at the University of Texas commencement. That extemporaneous speech of June 2 ends on a decided upbeat, firm with hope for the future, as Cash's voice rumbles in the old 78-r.p.m. records (emphasis added):

Yet *we* [in the South] face now a need for renewed sacrifices. As the country moves into the national defense program and *we* prepare to resist totalitarianism, *we* are going to have to make up *our* minds there are hardships: but I see no reason at all why *we* should make up *our* minds to more hardships, more sacrifices than are necessary under the circumstances. . . . As far as individualism goes, why it can be a great virtue . . . but it can also be very dangerous if it isn't kept in check by the realization that man after all is a social creature and that none of *us* has the right to stand outside the social organism.

By italicizing the pronouns in the first-person plural, and by appreciating the thrust of that final sentence of his speech, we can readily see to what extent the speaker identified himself with his fellow Southerners and Americans. Nothing could be clearer than the evidence from Cash's own lips that he was not withdrawn, not depressed. As late as June 10, the approximate date on which Cash composed his unpublished "Report From Mexico," we see a perceptive and evenhanded reporter who interviews people giving evidence on both sides of the question of a totalitarian menace to Mexico. Cash wrote quite clear-headedly: "I offer these opinions entirely without prejudice, having, as I say, formed none of my own." There is not a trace of withdrawal or depression in the paper written in Mexico, any more than there had been in the speech delivered in Austin, Texas.

Let us change direction in this ongoing process of elimination and ask this question: Is it possible to shed light on Cash's end by comparing it, as Ralph McGill did, with a well-known "success" suicide like that of the novelist Ross F. Lockridge, Jr. (1914–48)? Like Cash, after all, Lockridge did not long enjoy the fame which his book, *Raintree County*, brought him; like Cash, Lockridge committed suicide shortly after publication of his famous book. But Lockridge's novel was a best seller and brought the Indiana author considerable wealth, so there the "success" comparison ends. In addition, the mode of suicide was different (Lockridge's was by asphyxiation in a closed car with the motor left running), and the two men were worlds apart temperamentally. Or perhaps the poet Hart Crane (1899–1932)? Like Cash, Crane had won a Guggenheim fellowship, and he had also spent it in Mexico. But not only was the Ohio native's personality very different from that of Cash, but Crane jumped to his death from shipboard on returning from a lost year during which he had failed to write his great dreamed-of poem, whereas Cash had not yet set out on his projected novel. Neither in the suicide of Frances Newman of Georgia (1928), nor in that of Ernest Hemingway of Illinois (1961), nor in those of other sensitive and neurotic literary people are we likely to find details suggestive enough to make the search truly productive. Our process of elimination has left us—and it is better so—with the unique suicide of a unique human being.

What else needs to be eliminated? Obviously, Cash presents a tantalizing case history for the psychiatrist inclined to speculation. Lacking authenticating data, to be sure, a psychiatrist might nevertheless be tempted beyond his depth with the figure of the shy, sympathetic, sentimental, nonconformist, self-doubting, perfectionist Cash, and his book that "psychoanalyzes" the South. What is one to read into his "clash" with his dogmatic and orthodox Baptist father, his somewhat greater rapport with his mother? Surely we cannot make John William Cash the villain of the piece just because he happens to fit some preconceived *dramatis personae* in his son's "identity crisis." The data at hand are too slight to support too-pat conclusions, and virtually all the principal characters have left the stage and are no longer responsive to questioning. We have, too, a hint of independence and rebelliousness that begins when young Cash changed Joseph Wilbur to Wilbur Joseph.

That impression is heightened in the light of his youthful iconoclasm at Wake Forest and the avidity with which he seized, for his hero, upon that inspired troublemaker H. L. Mencken. But the same was true with hundreds of thousands of contemporary collegians, and Cash was moved to admit later that his misogynist idol "grew up" when he took a wife. The same lack of data warns the researcher against drawing unwarranted conclusions from, perhaps, the adolescent Wilbur's pursuing books rather than girls (despite his disclaimer to his publisher years later), or the young man's initial amatory failure with Peggy Ann. The same applies to his sometime experience with sexual impotence on the one hand, and his longtime friendship for the young woman whom he later married and with whom he enjoyed a satisfactory physical relationship. His hyperthyroidism and other endocrine disorders were accompanied, as is almost invariably the case, by psychological symptoms, but Cash had learned to live, or at least to co-exist in peace, with them. Indeed, on the one occasion that Dr. Squires referred him to a Charlotte colleague who was then the city's sole practitioner of psychiatry, and that on a part-time and "learner" basis, that physician found himself unable to improve on Cash's self-help. What with his own extensive reading in psychiatry and psychology, Cash probably was as well able to help himself as his would-be psychiatrist.

Eliminating still further, we must deal with the question of alcoholism. To some extent Cash's end was consistent with that of one who is intoxicated by drugs or alcohol. He was a drinker, we know, and the long succession of missed Monday mornings at the Charlotte *News* suggests a man who will retire for a "lost weekend" of solitary drinking. Alcoholism and suicide do go hand in hand, to be sure, but Cash, on the testimony of his personal physician, was no alcoholic. Even if the influence of alcohol is taken into account in Cash's suicide, one can say without much fear of contradiction that alcoholism was not *the* cause. The withdrawal symptoms in true alcoholism occur typically within seventy-two hours and not, as in Cash, after a three-week period during which he could not even bring himself to swallow the Mexican beer. Similarly, it seems safe in this elimination process to rule out any of the primary psychoses. None, certainly, was suggested by the psychiatrist-in-training who examined Cash in Charlotte. Because Cash made no other attempt at suicide, and certainly never went around threatening it, it is safe, for example, to rule out the manic-depressive psychosis. If he had shown a withdrawal from life and public affairs, Cash might be suspected of schizophrenia, and indeed at the end Cash turned to behavior consistent with this psychosis, but he was far from withdrawn from the arena of common humanity. He was not withdrawn in Austin, Texas, when he identified himself with Southerners and Americans preparing to defend themselves against the threat of totalitarian aggression, and he was not withdrawn when he coolly assessed the Nazi threat in Mexico and wrote about it dispassionately for an American audience. He was not withdrawn as late as June 22 when he reacted excitedly to Hitler's invasion of Russia and complained, as if in frustration, that he could no longer editorialize about it in the Charlotte *News*.

But suppose some aggravation of his thyroid condition had set in, and Cash was suffering from thyrotoxicosis, an acute hyperthyroid attack? Insomnia and even paranoid delusions and hallucinations are consistent with such an attack. Of course, if Cash suffered a greatly increased metabolic rate, this might very well have been a contributory factor in almost any toxic state. But detailed medical records of Cash's hyperthyroidism and its diagnosis have not been found, as of this writing, and so a diagnosis of thyrotoxicosis would be highly speculative. In such a state Cash's pulse would have been racing at a pace sufficient to alarm the blandest examining physician in Mexico, and he would have shown the intense sweating and tremulousness that accompany a severe attack. Moreover, the majority of physicians consulted, including Dr. Squires, who was aware of Cash's difficulties with depth perception and physical coordination, consider the possibility of thyrotoxicosis as highly unlikely.

At length, then, perhaps the only satisfactory hypothesis can be derived by working backward; that is, from the suicidal state itself. That state was characterized by (1) disorientation, (2) difficulties that were worse at night, (3) paranoid delusions, (4) auditory hallucinations, and (5) a great state of fear. Going back a bit earlier, we find an apparent decline in Cash's mental capacity, marked by his inability to master so much as a word of Spanish although he had actually served as a teacher of a related Romance language, French. He could not even remember the tourist tips on Mexico volunteered by his helpful upstairs neighbors from San Antonio. At the very end, of course, the picture is marked by a state of delirium.

The symptoms enumerated above are classically descriptive of a condition that, in modern psychiatry, is termed "acute brain syndrome." Such a syndrome can develop gradually, over the space of an entire year, but typically becomes critical in a relatively short period, as in Cash's case. As happened to Cash, the higher centers of the brain are the first to be metabolically attacked, leaving the primitive ones (e.g., the sexual) unaffected, as Mary Cash testified to her husband's examining physician in Mexico. Cash's final delirium was, of course, a state of cerebral incompetence, but it was almost certainly toxic in origin. The man had suffered brain damage, true, and his brain was operating marginally, but he was not insane.

The toxins operating on Cash derived, in all likelihood, from an infection, the nature of which is, of course, unknown to this day. Such toxins have been known to originate outside the system from drugs, medicinal or narcotic, although there is no evidence of such drugs in Cash's case. Again, outside the system, such toxins might have originated from the explosive mixture of alcohol and altitude, although alcohol is partly discounted. The altitude factor, contributing added difficulties for a man with chronic respiratory troubles, may well have represented the "last straw" in a worsening of Cash's overall physical condition. Obviously, the toxic agents also could have been produced by a whole series of endogenous factors, including central-nervous-system disease. In any case his difficulties were toxic rather than psychic: Cash's old neurotic problems, with which he had learned to cope over the years, seem to have played no more than a secondary role in his acute final illness, which was based primarily on cerebral incompetence.

In Cash's tragic last twenty-four hours we see a man who is plainly in a deteriorating mental condition but whose brain still is operating enough for him to be dimly and frantically aware of his plight. Predisposed to hypochondria by his past sufferings, he must have felt especially threatened by the mental incapacity that had been afflicting him of late. His fine mind, which was the personal quality he prized most of all, was not only incapable of retaining a word of Spanish or tourist information but could not or would not begin focusing upon the new writing task at hand. Physically sick as he was, Cash may very well have believed, in some dim and marginal way, that he was falling apart inside.

On his last Monday night he was still "rational" enough to seize a carving knife in order to defend himself and his wife against the "Nazis," but the following day saw a further deterioration in his terrified cowering at the Hotel Geneve. In all this there is no evidence of a protracted depression or of premeditated suicide on his part—no stealthy procuring of a suicide weapon. The two distinct phases of his suicidal act are wholly consistent, mechanically, with what some psychiatrists have come to describe as "suicidal fit"; in the first phase the patient impulsively flees the scene of stress, and in the second (sometimes after a brief pause in seclusion) seizes and wields against himself the first weapon or poisonous substance that comes to hand. With Cash the first lethal agent that came to hand, "caught" as he was in an unfurnished hotel bathroom, was his own necktie. And such was the "suicidal fit" that was triggered, as we are led to conclude in this hypothesis, by an acute brain syndrome, toxic in origin, that attacked the weakened and vulnerable Cash.

If, in conclusion, unconscious drives in Cash produced a certain pattern of behavior, it is all the more crucial to understand that an important part of that behavior was the writing of *The Mind of the South*. If Cash was neurotic in the years of his literary productivity, so were scores and hundreds of literary craftsmen before and since. However obscure his clinical history, Cash was demonstrably able to transcend his sufferings and to produce a work that, by simple inspection and by common consent, stands alone in its time as a feat of historical synthesis and creative imagination. It is enough to say that it was not a "diseased" mind but one of truly sunburst clarity that brought forth this published claim on the regard of men.

CHAPTER 7

Perspectives

THOMAS WOLFE

*W*hen *Thomas Wolfe* died a world-celebrated novelist in 1938, W. J. Cash was still an obscure editorialist. They never met, and Cash overcame his diffidence in the face of the other's fame only to the extent of shedding a tear on Wolfe's grave. Wolfe was one of three contemporary Southern novelists whom Cash, himself a would-be novelist, avidly read, criticized, and sought to emulate (the others, each set upon a successively higher plateau, were William Faulkner and James Branch Cabell). But only in Wolfe, that one of the three who predeceased him, did Cash find the dark intimation of mortality, because only in Wolfe, the fellow Carolinian, was there a close parallel in family background, in education, even in almost-exact contemporaneity (both were born in 1900, Wolfe on October 3, Cash on May 2). The death of the months-younger Thomas Wolfe made a deep impression on Cash; his already vivid fear of death was further accelerated to shudders at the prospect of what he called "the cold grave." Although Cash did not know it, Wolfe had had an intimation of tuberculosis, a species of which later killed him, as early as 1920, thus somewhat paralleling the hyperthyroidism of Cash in 1923.

The two Carolinians came of the same ethnic stock, German on one side of the family and Ulster Scotch ("Scotch-Irish") on the other. They were born within one hundred miles of each other, Cash in the Appalachian foothills and Wolfe in the true mountain country. Both encountered the orthodox religion of their parents, both found it unacceptable intellectually, yet both found a need for religion in a personal sense, and both came independently to favor Ecclesiastes above all else in the Bible. Both changed from children into adolescents of comparable sensitivity, and both suffered through a miserable first year at college, Cash at Wofford and Wolfe at Chapel Hill. Though Cash never quite became the Big Man on Campus that Wolfe did, he matched the other in his love for bull sessions, in his service as campus journalist, and in a gamy indifference at times to soap and water.

As of 1938, the year of Wolfe's death, both men were bachelors. In falling honestly and desperately in love, both had suffered the pangs of an early and unhappy romantic attachment. As they emerged into the post–World War I era, both were pretty well characterized by the "romantic aestheticism" of Eugene Gant that Wolfe outlined in his speech at Purdue University in 1938, "the wounded, sensitive, the extraordinary creature in conflict with his environment, with the Babbitt, the Philistine, the small town, the family."

Of course, where Cash and Wolfe diverged was in their responses to the world crisis of the 1930's. In analyzing Marxism and its premises, Cash found himself in thorough disagreement, and he looked to Roosevelt's New Deal—recognizing its limitations, to be sure—as the way out of the Depression. His anti-Nazism began with a horrified but reasoned repudiation, lock, stock, and barrel, of the totalitarian method and its view of man. The more emotional Wolfe had to be shocked into anti-Nazism by what he experienced personally in Germany, just as he was shocked into his New Dealism. Therein lay the basic divergence in the "style" of each man: the rhapsodic novel *Look Homeward, Angel* (1929) looked for inspiration to James Joyce; the astringent article "The Mind of the South" (1929) was influenced by H. L. Mencken's grand sense of the ridiculous.

The would-be novelist Cash looked on hungrily in 1929 as Wolfe's *Look Homeward, Angel* was published to such critical acclaim that Sinclair Lewis dubbed the Tar Heel giant as "possibly the next great novelist." That impressive first novel, published in the same month as Cash's "Mind" article in *The American Mercury*, evoked in Cash an attitude described by his fellow reporter Katherine Grantham as "three parts envy and six parts sneer." The envy is easier to understand than the sneer, for Wolfe was not to be classed with the *poseurs* of Cash's world, the group of Nashville poets who had founded *The Fugitive* (1922–5) and who went on, some of them, to publish the symposium *I'll Take My Stand* (1930). Nevertheless, after his own ill health and poverty, after his own immersion in the dread loneliness of fighting a book onto paper, Jack read with new tolerance Wolfe's second novel. In 1935 he read *Of Time and the River* and Wolfe's book of short stories, *From Death to Morning*, and he was ready to dispense a more even-handed literary judgment than many of Wolfe's critics.

Thomas Wolfe was a frequent subject of Cash's book-page columns for the Charlotte *News* (all the Cash articles mentioned in this chapter, unless otherwise identified, were published in that newspaper). One of the earliest columns, that of December 15, 1935, addressed itself to the question: "Wolfe: Genius or Not?" The columnist observed that the pro-Wolfe and anti-Wolfe critics allowed themselves extreme judgments in either case, the former being ready to rank Wolfe with the immortals and the latter damning him for a literary output characterized by great sprawling ineptitude. Cash defended Wolfe vigorously against any imputation of mediocrity, against the stock charges that his books were too long, that he was too free in his resort to rhetoric, or that his material was not worth all the effort expended. To Cash, Thomas Wolfe was, to answer the columnist's own question, indeed a genius.

There was a saving qualification. Cash would define the Tar Heel giant as a genius of high order "in the sense that all men who are truly artists are geniuses—which is to say, creators." Furthermore, Cash was distinctly cool to the judgment that confidently ranked Wolfe with the company of immortals. One had only to read any comparable portion of Wolfe's work and compare it with the story of Hutwood in Dreiser's *Sister Carrie*, "and it is immediately plain that he [Wolfe] somehow fails to measure fully up—that there is some secret of massivity, or rendering life fully in the round, and some penetration of essential beauty here to which he has not quite reached, and which is the guerdon of immortality." Having said all that, however, Cash found Wolfe towering above the other novelists his age (he mentioned Faulkner specifically), who were not "remotely his equal in force, in color, in accurate observation, in beauty."

The following spring, in Volume 1, Number 1 of *Pseudopodia* (later the *North Georgia Review*), Paula Snelling published a critical analysis of Thomas Wolfe that Cash specifically endorsed in a letter of October 15, 1936. After having read the first two novels plus Wolfe's *The Story of a Novel* (1936), Miss Snelling found that his vivid two-dimensional impressions and powerful young manhood, however attractive, were not producing a more mature individual either as novelist or as man. Shortly after applauding Miss Snelling's judgment, W. J. Cash followed it with a book-page criticism of his own (October 25, 1936):

The inordinately publicized Tom Wolfe has, for all his Gargantuan production, almost no sense of the novel; and what is worse, he has in him a certain soulful moonshine which, while it makes grand reading in small doses, is apt to grow somewhat appalling in the doses Mr. Wolfe himself prescribes. Worst of all the enormous Thomas has, so far as can be judged on the evidence available at present, only one story. At least, whenever he has occasionally attempted to tell some other story than this one of the lonely soul chasing its tale around this cuckoo globe, the result has been pretty dismal.

"The late great Thomas Wolfe," Cash wrote (October 16, 1938) after the other's death, "has been promised immortality by most of the people who have written about him since his death." And while avowing that that was a large order indeed, the columnist added that he put small stock in the extravagant use of any such expression as "immortality." In death, Wolfe exercised a fascination for Cash, who readily saw in him

> perhaps the greatest master of rhetoric the United States has produced, and the rhetoric he used was the rhetoric of his native land, round and huge and soaring. And immeasurably better than anybody has ever done, he got down the story of the bewildered adolescence of the generation of men to which he belonged.

For it was, in large measure, Cash's adolescence too that Wolfe had described.

"Wolfe had told the truth about Asheville—and Asheville was shocked and outraged at the spectacle." Here Cash touched upon (October 30, 1938) the impulse for criticism of his native land that he shared in common with his fellow Carolinian. The revulsion—the guilty revulsion—against his birthplace was full upon the author of *Mind* when he rebelled unconsciously against completing his overdue book manuscript. Nevertheless, Cash discerned in Wolfe's outspoken rebellion the selfsame attitude he would have to adopt with the publication of *Mind*. And, in words prophetic for the appearance of *Mind*, he wrote:

> For, certainly, Wolfe had violated every convention of friendship and acquaintance—the everyday code of reticences and pretenses by which men everywhere live. . . . If the artist is going to be a gentleman, he had better take good care to pick himself out a very small field. Else sooner or later, he is going to run smack up against the problem of having to suppress and slur over the truth or having to violate the conventions as to what he can say and tell. And when he decides to suppress the truth, he immediately ceases to be an artist and becomes merely a manufacturer of spiritual cosmetics.

Indeed, the author made the point in *Mind* that the first-rate Southern novelists of the twentieth century were able to contribute the region's first literature of any weight and substance precisely because they maligned, in one way or another, their native land. Certainly they all abdicated any role in glorifying and defending Dixie. It was an extremely personal matter to Cash that the fictional Eugene Gant actively hated the South, for in *Mind* the author discerned that such angry distaste was a function of Thomas Wolfe's inner conflict: the reverence for the Southern legend, as given to childhood by parental authority, assailed by every new idea and perception gained since childhood. If William Faulkner was not the explicit critic of the South, he did exemplify the "fury of portraiture, a concentration on decadence and social horrors," that Cash found apt to his thesis. And what about the timeless shadows, the universal tales of James Branch Cabell? Why, the Cabell rhetoric was pure Dixie, and his tender mocking irony made all the Cabell women a product of the legend of Southern Womanhood, "just as Horvendile is unmistakably related to the most celebrated character in the repertoire of the Southern pulpit [Satan]."

WILLIAM FAULKNER

Not until the appearance in 1946 of Malcolm Cowley's splendid *The Portable Faulkner* did William Faulkner emerge into widespread popularity in his own land. During the 1930's the Mississippian represented for W. J. Cash merely another gifted Southern novelist who went largely unread by his own people because, the Babbitts of Dixie complained, "He gives only one side of the picture and doesn't give us credit for anything nice." Jack valued Faulkner first for providing exactly the darker picture of the South that was a healthy antidote for the old ego-boosting literature that sought to identify Dixie with Cloud-Cuckoo land. The South had special need for Faulkner's somber tones, Cash avowed, as long as its tradition forbade it to face facts and as long as the South, collectively, played the ostrich. Faulkner was only three years older than Cash, and in Cash's view both had emerged into postadolescence thinking that they hated the South. It was their first adult reaction against the sentimentality and South-worship to which they had been exposed as boys. "Faulkner," Cash wrote (October 9, 1938), "has never confessed to any such thing. But he doesn't need to; it is written on every page of his earlier books." To be sure, the columnist added, the impatient scorn of many young Southerners for their native land was softening and becoming more compassionate now, for it was to be discerned plainly enough in Faulkner. Moreover, Cash wrote, "I can see it in myself."

In his very first column for Cameron Shipp's book page (November 17, 1935), Cash used Faulkner to support his thesis that a Southern rearing had conditioned a set of novelists whose emotions were ranged all on one side, intellects all on the other. There was not the slightest doubt, the columnist added, that Faulkner's conscious purpose was to write as realistically as Dreiser himself. Indeed, the Mississippian's descriptions were realistic with a vengeance; his pictures of the sort of houses inhabited by poor whites, even the character of the poor white himself, was realism done to a turn. Yet, Jack pursued his argument, the primary and fundamental Faulkner would always come roaring through, in every case "extravagant and melodramatic—which is to say romantic." Faulkner went beyond, that is to say, what was strictly necessary to picture truly an already extravagant and melodramatic region, and he employed so violent a palette because it was his true and characteristic medium. Cash went on:

> And if that is not enough—well, has nobody ever observed that the motive which most obsesses Faulkner is, of all the fish that fly, precisely that preeminently southern and romantic one: honor? To be sure, our Mr. Faulkner will point out all his hero's warts; to be sure, he is very likely to make him drunken and futile and most absent-minded about the seventh commandment. Nevertheless, the obsession may be traced in virtually everything he has done—including exactly that terrific book, "Sanctuary."

So Cash valued Faulkner highly—above Thomas Wolfe, at the last—and certainly would have sympathized with the Mississippian's reference in his Nobel Prize speech in 1950 to "problems of the human heart in conflict with itself." The Carolinian would also have applauded Faulkner's expanded list of universal truths enunciated at Stockholm: "love and honor and pity and pride and compassion and sacrifice." Indeed, the Nobel laureate's newfound clarity of expression would have startled Cash, who had long resigned himself to struggling through the syntactical mazes devised by the Faulkner he knew. And Cash discovered a greater flaw in Faulkner, which he did not hesitate to expose: The Mississippian avoided like the plague any consideration of social forces. It was as if Faulkner had immured himself in the Delta country, blissfully unmindful of the new urban and industrial South, treating Memphis, which was the metropolis of his little world, like a plain cotton town writ large.

What triggered Cash's criticism was "the jitney-sociologists," an epithet struck off by Laurence Stallings in praise of Faulkner, precisely because the Mississippian could not be so described. Cash conceded freely in his column of April 5, 1936, that social forces had no business in a novel purely as social forces. Furthermore he added, "I could dispose with the much touted performance of T. S. Stribling [a writer of novels concerned with the South] without too great a pang, on the plain and obvious ground that Stribling is more interested in his background than in his figures." Yet if the proper concern of the novelist is with the human protagonist in his battle with God (and Cash held that it was, even if one were to speak more circumspectly) and if the novelist must picture God's creature in the trap of his special passions and hopes (and Cash agreed he must), then the novelist must also show his protagonist held fast, above everything, by the social fabric and the social inheritance.

Precisely because Faulkner omitted this part of his proper work, Cash held, his reader was plumped down, as it were, in the midst of a weird group of psychopaths. Did Faulkner exaggerate? Didn't his poor whites perform their roles truly, and didn't his decadent aristocrats behave exactly as portrayed? Yes, of course, Cash replied, but "The whole fault here is just that he shows us what without in the least telling us how and why." The flaw that Cash detected bore upon Faulkner's allowing himself to be trapped by the hoariest of white-invented myths about the Negro: that the submerged Negro is happy with his lot. To be sure, Faulkner endowed his Negroes with a vivid individualism, he destroyed the stereotype, he portrayed the Negro as one who persevered and endured. But in *Reivers* (1962), published in the last year of William Faulkner's life, the author put into the mouth of his sympathetic Negro, Ned William McCaslin:

"If you could just be a nigger one Saturday night, you wouldn't never want to be white again." Cash would have scorned such a portrayal as cheap and unworthy.

JAMES BRANCH CABELL

During the late 1930's, when Cash was writing his literary criticism, James Branch Cabell's position, with the popular reader as well as with the critical fraternity, was in almost total eclipse. Only in the late 1940's, in the wake of Edmund Wilson's perceptive reassessment, did there begin a revival of interest in Cabell, who was Cash's personal favorite. Such a choice in favorites is instructive, because the complexity, the many-sidedness, the humanistic philosophy with which Cabell challenges his readers can be inviting only to a sophisticated and catholic taste.

Like his enthusiasm for Joseph Conrad, Cash derived his enthusiasm for Cabell from Mencken, who proved so influential to those of Jack's college generation. Nevertheless, when Mencken shared Cabell's eclipse in the late 1930's, Cash chose to abide with Cabell rather than with the Baltimore Sage, whose understanding of the Depression era was limited to mocking at the New Deal as a huge swindle. Cash delighted in Cabell as a literary craftsman, to be sure, but for two thematic reasons besides. First, Cabell's *The Rivet in Grandfather's Neck* (1915) and *The Cream of the Jest* (1917), which Cash particularly relished, made an ironic hash of the various romantic ideals in the American South. Second, Cabell enunciated in *Beyond Life* (1919) the essentially humanistic aesthetic and credo that were closest to Cash.

All this is not to say that Cash neglected Cabell's mythical kingdom of Poictesme in the south of France, for he figuratively sought it out when he visited that region in 1927. Moreover, he read the notorious *Jurgen* and many of the

other romantic chronicles of the time of Dom Manuel with
the keenest enjoyment. "The peculiar object which obsesses
the peculiar Mr. Cabell," our columnist delightedly wrote
on July 11, 1937, "is, of course, the spectacle of humanity in
the hours after the throes of the odd combination of passion
and sentiment which we call love—the spectacle of man and
woman, remembering themselves in the transports of desire
and what men name romance."

The degree to which Cash relished, and reveled in,
Cabell's mythical world can be gauged by these words from
the same article:

> And the world which he [Cabell] inhabits is a world of
> half-lights and strange melancholy repose. Its sunlight falls in
> soft chiaroscuro through clouds and over mountains which
> never existed for other men in this world save in the paintings
> of forgotten medieval painters—into forests which are secret
> with a secret that now and then another man may have once
> glimpsed for a passing illuminated second of his childhood,
> and upon castles that shine with a deeper inward translucence
> never boasted by any other castle save, perhaps, only Joyous
> Garde. . . . The streams of this world flow in silver and not in
> gold; they tinkle merrily and yet a little sadly. Always some-
> where in the distance there sounds the sudden breathless
> mirth of women, falling and falling through the bottomless
> abyss of memory. Always there sounds too the echo of some-
> thing that is most marvelously like a sort of muted belly-
> laugh—such a short, sardonic laugh as old Silenus might give
> did he suddenly find himself entirely sober and in love. And
> always death peeps through the cadences of slow and more
> than earthly music, dying through the shadows and the long
> blue reaches.

Cash wryly acknowledged that Poictesme was not for
the pious, that limitation being the root cause of Cabell's
almost total neglect by his fellow Southerners. Analyzing
why this most eminent of Southern writers should be unread

in the South (in "Jurgen in the South," June 20, 1937), Cash found, first, that Cabell offended "our sentimental and over-nice Southern Puritanism." He added that Southerners were all too prone to confound the Medicean Venus with French postcards and were decidedly more shocked by *Jurgen* than by *Fanny Hill*. In the second place, Cabell was not only a bawdy fellow but a subversive one, forever indulging in such troublemaking as wondering, questioning, and rehears-ing odd paradoxes. Thirdly, the author slipped in some unwelcome melancholy, and he let people hear "behind the sighs of his lovers the coming of stealthy-footed death." Finally, Cabell committed the sin of irony, Cash wrote, and "not only suspected of laughing at the human race, he is suspected of laughing at the South itself. It is a treason we have never tolerated and probably never will."

CLARENCE CASON, *90° in the Shade*

In all probability *The Mind of the South* could not have been written in an earlier generation, for it depended on the social scientists of the 1920's and 1930's to supply the underpinning of fact and theory upon which Cash could build his penetrat-ingly personal inquiry. Indeed, the author could have writ-ten such a book in an earlier generation only if he had been prepared to leave town. The very fact of *Mind's* cordial reception by Southern critics indicates a stirring of change, a certain relaxation of the old iron conformity that Cash would have been glad to acknowledge had he lived. As we have indicated, the writing contemporary of Cash who most dramatically acted out his fear of the earlier conformity was Clarence Cason of Alabama, who in 1935 put a bullet through his brain three days before publication of his *90° in the Shade*.

Cason's intelligent and unpretentious book is pretty well forgotten today, but it deserves attention if only to serve as an intellectual yardstick for *Mind*. It is proper to speak of *Mind* as an achievement unprecedented in Southern studies. No professional historian with daring enough to attempt so audacious an intellectual feat had ever come forward with an analysis of the Southern mind in its totality. Neither had Clarence Cason, really, but he was the contemporary whose book most closely approached Cash's, at least in intention, and with which *Mind* may usefully be compared. Both authors were journalists, but their "journalistic" methods varied widely. Cason was journalistic in the sense that he seized upon news events, alive in everyone's mind at the time of writing, to the detriment of a longer view. Cash was journalistic only in the best sense, that he couched his sophisticated thought in simple and clear language, free from jargon.

Even though he was bold enough to label deep-South politics "Fascism: Southern Style," Cason devoted less space to fundamental patterns of thought and action in the South than to the detailed rascalities of such as Heflin, Vardaman, and Bilbo. As in discussing the Bryan–Darrow confrontation, or the New Deal's TVA, or the Gastonia textile strike, Cason often managed to be persuasive without being conclusive. He lacked organization, and therefore he lacked coherent argument. This is not necessarily to denigrate Cason's achievement, for the man who taught journalism at the University of Alabama had set out to provide no more than a casual and only incidentally penetrating reportorial account of how it was with the South during the early New Deal. Within the limits he apparently set for himself, he managed quite well.

Yet it is instructive to note how many of Cash's great themes Cason touched upon tentatively, unobtrusively, without achieving anything like the same impact. Born and bred in the South, Cason touched, like Cash, upon the survival of plantation patterns, the role of the cotton mill as civic enterprise, the South's hypersensitivity to criticism, the "white-supremacy" gambit, the sham of the Old South myth. It was merely that in Cason these elements were only mentioned in passing. He pilloried many evils that needed exposure—the brutality of Southern loan sharks, the exploitation of "cheap Anglo-Saxon labor," the toleration of lynching by the "best people"—yet, he blunted the force of his analysis with a humorous or otherwise pleasant turn of phrase. At the end of his book Cason even called for a "nice, quiet revolution." But then he changed his tune, disclaiming, as if he had to, either a Communist or Populist revolt, and went on to a series of "revisions," "clarifications," "recognitions," and "redirections."

Cash's intellect was too ruthless for that sort of thing. Instead of wasting his strength on the minutiae of current affairs, he wrestled skillfully with the great imponderables, the universal values. If the South of 1940 was trapped in a maze of its own devising and he could see no way out, he was not going to prescribe anything so reassuring and concrete as a "nice, quiet revolution." Cash's ominous silence, in the context of his implicitly pessimistic "no way out," made readers lay down his book in thoughtful disquiet.

THE NASHVILLE AGRARIANS

When in the late 1920's Cash began scoffing at the poets and litterateurs who made up the Fugitive Group of Nashville, a core of Fugitives, notably John Crowe Ransom, Donald Davidson, and Allen Tate, were already pushing on toward Agrarianism. The Fugitives originally had been praised by none other than Cash's idolized Mencken, who saw in them evidence of a long-overdue Southern literary renascence. Their paths diverged from Mencken's, of course, starting in 1925 with the Scopes anti-evolution trial in Tennessee. As Menckenians and "outsiders" poured boiling oil of pitiless ridicule on the heads of fundamentalists, the Southern intellectuals who were the Fugitives slowly swung around to a stubborn defense of the anti-intellectuals because these were "their" people. This type of rationalization led gradually to an idealized and romanticized picture of an Old South that never was, a newer version of the Old South legend that had been created earlier by writers like Thomas Nelson Page.

As the Southern agricultural depression fell to a new low in late 1930, "Twelve Southerners" (including the Fugitive core) published their symposium, *I'll Take My Stand*. The argument, distilled from the separate statements, was for a reconstruction of American society on the basis of an agrarian policy suggested by the family farm of the Old Middle South. Almost entirely innocent of any of the social sciences, particularly economics, the Agrarians made a sentimental rather than a logical appeal and were, on the whole, pretty well cut up by the critics. It was open to simple inspection that they were brimming over with nostalgic yearning for ancestral ways, that they ludicrously overvalued the supposedly ennobling satisfaction of farm work, that they saw the hated "foreign" industrialization only in its worst aspects, and that they wanted, with King Canute, to arm themselves with imperiousness and sternly order the sea to sweep back upon itself.

In *The Mind of the South* the Nashville Agrarians fared much better than they had at the hands of the reviewers in 1930. The Agrarians had worked away at their social studies and made some knowledgeable converts, like Herbert Agar, and had published a better reasoned symposium, *Who Owns America?*, in 1936. By that time, however, they had exhausted most of their capital of goodwill, and the better book did not stir up anything like the ferment created by the weaker one. To attack the Agrarians on the basis of their assumed role of practical economists and political theorists would be too easy, too much like shooting fish in a barrel. Cash scorned that approach, just as he scorned the cheap guilt-by-association attack against the Agrarians that pictured them as Fascist sympathizers. Cash knew that their appearance in *The American Review*, bankrolled by the wealthy and eccentric Seward Collins, subjected them to their being published, quite innocently, cheek by jowl with pronouncements extolling Mussolini and Hitler. Cash expicitly disavowed such an attack in *Mind*.

What he did expose was their "neo-medievalism," which he systematically traced, and he further exposed the projection of that "neo-medievalism" upon the Old South in furtherance of an untenable legend. He showed the relation of the Nashville Agrarians to the yearning for the past that had animated certain European and American thinkers uninterruptedly since the revolt against Rousseau in the early nineteenth century. He found them influenced, in varying degree, by such conservative ideologues as De Maistre and Brunetière, such "neo-medievalists" as Belloc, Chesterton, and Eliot. And that neat dissection, published first in the *Saturday Review of Literature* (December 28, 1940) and repeated in *Mind*, helps account for the waspish reviews of Cash's book by the Agrarians Donald Davidson and Richmond C. Beatty.

Allen Tate's *Reactionary Essays on Poetry and Ideas* (1936) called up Cash's original anti-Agrarian formulation in a book-page column of March 29, 1936, in which he lauded Tate as a good poet gone wrong. In identifying Tate with "neo-medievalism," Cash was, as always, precise in defining ideas for his newspaper readers:

> And precisely what does a Neo-Medievalist argue? Well, that there is a "form" normal to human society when it is "completely human," that this form is the feudal form in use in Europe during the Middle Ages, that men can only be true men when they are arranged in castes, planted on the land instead of cities, and given great lords to be their masters. That authority is necessary to men not only in the political

realm but in the spiritual as well, that what we currently call "myths" are in reality profound emanations from the soul of humanity, which embody profound truths of subjective experience—that religion, properly speaking, is only the whole corpus of these "myths," and that without them it is impossible—and therefore the position of the Catholic Church in the Middle Ages is the only one which can be normal to the human spirit when it is "really human," and "sees life whole" and not in terms of intellectual abstraction.

Cash then showed that Tate made a special adaptation of this "neo-medievalism" in several essays, a position that Tate called Agrarianism but that Cash thought more truly a neo-Confederate position. The columnist then moved in for the kill:

> Mr. Tate did not invent this notion. In its main outlines it was invented by his former professor at Vanderbilt, John Crowe Ransom—another poet. And Professor Ransom's notion is itself, of course, only the result of the meeting and marriage of Neo-Medievalism with the ancient Southern sentimentality. At bottom, it is only a somewhat sophisticated version of the late lamented Thomas Nelson Page's dream of the old plantation—his confusion of the Old South with Cloud-Cuckoo-Town.

Southern Agrarianism did not long outlive Cash, and in 1945, John Crowe Ransom himself officially abjured in the *Kenyon Review* (Autumn issue). He remarked that the agrarian economy then threateningly prescribed for defeated Germany, an agrarianism that he once would have regarded as a blessing, was now rightly seen for what was intended: a heavy punishment. In point of fact, the economic and political myopia of the Agrarians has mattered little in the face of their significant contributions to literature and letters. Cash was fully aware of that contribution when he wrote on March 20, 1941, to R. P. Harriss of the Baltimore *Evening Sun*:

I'd forgive the Agrarians all their crimes if they could persuade [Carl] Van Doren to bring out that edition of [Harriss's] "The Foxes." And I think I understand why they like it. It has in it something that both Caroline Gordon and Robert Penn Warren, especially, have tried to do—to catch the flavor of country life as lived in the South.

THE CHAPEL HILL REGIONALISTS

By contrast with the Nashville Agrarians, the Regionalists of Chapel Hill commanded the author's admiration, an admiration he expressed in his newspaper pieces as well as in *The Mind of the South*. It was not that Cash believed that the Regionalists had "the answer" where the Agrarians did not. It was, rather, that he eschewed answers, even Clarence Cason's "nice, quiet revolution," and preferred to hammer away at the South's proclivity for wishful thinking and self-deception. Whereas he rejected the Agrarian answer of reposing all reform hopes in the bankrupted Southern agriculture of the 1930's, he never accepted wholeheartedly the Regionalist answer, the direction of which was regional in scope and rational in approach (always skirting the dangerous word "planning"). He liked the way the Chapel Hill Regionalists attacked the old and narrow sectionalism, but most of all he valued their prodigious research in, and description of, Southern society.

Cash's brightest light in the Chapel Hill constellation was Howard W. Odum (others were E. C. Branson and Rupert B. Vance), who had personally played his aforementioned key role in the development of *Mind*. Indeed, the year after the publication of the article "The Mind of the South" in *The American Mercury*, Odum came out with his book *An American Epoch* and adopted therein an impressionistic approach to Southern life, concentrating on the realities of folk life in the New South. The vividness that

Odum achieved through the use of his semifictional characters "Uncle John" and "the old Major" was a device that commended itself to Cash, who appears to have derived from Odum the hypothetical "man at the center" appearing in *Mind*. As a skilled literary craftsman, Cash could not, of course, admire the older man's special language ("Odumese," the sweating sociology students called it). Cash felt impelled to write (December 22, 1935) of "Howard Odum, whose sociological treatises, I must admit, and despite an interest in the subject, leave me cold, but who fully establishes his claim as a writer in the saga of Black Ulysses." Odum's three small books about Black Ulysses, *Rainbow Round My Shoulder* (1928), *Wings on My Feet* (1929), and *Cold Blue Moon* (1931), were delightful compendiums of Negro folklore and first attracted Cash.

With the appearance of Odum's monumental *Southern Regions of the United States* (1936), Cash had to overcome his distaste for the "Odumese" in which it was couched in deference to its value as an unparalleled source book. Like other admirers of *Southern Regions*, Cash strove with the statistical and other data with which Odum magisterially measured the South against the five principal bases of a great civilization (natural wealth, human wealth, technological skill, capital, and institutional services) and found his native region deficient in the last three. As to "human wealth," Odum showed not only that hate and fear had resulted in appalling waste of the energies of whites and Negroes, but he prefigured the theoretical basis of a Southern society into which the Negro could be integrated. He wrote, and Cash noted it carefully, that instead of speaking of the "Negro problem," which connoted abnormality, one should regard the Negro's role in the South as "normal" and go on from there.

On this particular point Cash went Odum one better in plain talk. He spoke of the South, which had just been labeled the nation's number-one economic problem, and of the complex of historical forces whose outcome had bred the problem (July 17, 1938):

> One of those [historical forces] is slavery and what has come down to us from slavery—a social system in which economic ends are continually obscured by considerations of racial feeling—a surplus of labor cheaper than that to be had anywhere else in America—the competition of the Negro with the white man, and the consequent beating down of the living standard of the latter—the army of cheap Negro labor living in slums, dealt out a most inadequate justice in our courts, and left to wallow in poverty, crime, and disease, with inevitable results on the social status, the crime-rate and health of the white race.

Cash most certainly did not share in the cry of rage that went up in the Southern press at the region's designation by President Roosevelt as "Economic Problem Number One." "And down in the tall grass a lordly statesman raised his noble head," Cash jibed at Senator John E. Miller of Arkansas, who "brought out that ancient chestnut which has it that all the South needs is to be let strictly alone." Here again was evidence to Cash of a hotly patriotic and hotly sensitive South that was almost morbidly suspicious of all change. Yet the President did not have to invent any part of his description, because, Cash pointed out: "Most of it came straight out of a book called 'Southern Regions,' written by a native Georgian Howard Odum, now on the faculty at the University of North Carolina."

GUNNAR MYRDAL, *An American Dilemma*

Myrdal's classic study—"The Negro Problem and Modern Democracy" is its subtitle—makes for provocative contrast with *The Mind of the South* if only because both books were published on the eve of decisive change in the subjects they had described. The dramatic change in the Southern "mind" since 1941, brought about both by rapid industrial-technological change and by federal support for civil rights, has been matched by the radical improvement in the status of the American Negro since publication of *Dilemma* in 1944. Cash's book never enjoyed the distinction, as did Myrdal's, of being cited in a decision of the United States Supreme Court, but *Mind* is cited and quoted again and again in *An American Dilemma*. Indeed, the Court's particular citation of Myrdal in the public-school-desegregation decision of May 17, 1954, had to do with a theme that Cash had written about repeatedly in the Charlotte *News*: the harmful effect of prejudice and discrimination on personality development.

As professional sociologists, the authors of *An American Dilemma* counted themselves fortunate in being able to examine that dilemma as, in effect, objective anthropologists. Gunnar Myrdal was a Swede, and of his two assistants, Richard Sterner was also a Swede and Arnold Rose was a native of Chicago. Certainly, their writing about the American South would not be inhibited by the reticence of a native son. Yet Professor Rose has confessed to me his admiration for Cash's most unusual gift of being able to examine his native region with no hint of defensive rationalizing, just as if he had never set foot in the South. On the other hand, of course, Cash's obvious affection for the South drew the fangs of critics in the ranks of militant white supremacists. His cool detachment played a role, as Professor Rose has assured the writer, both in confirming the basic approach adopted by the authors of *An American Dilemma* and in clarifying for them a number of Southern obscurities.

Thus it was that Myrdal went out of his way, in footnotes, to credit Cash for important insights. For example, in *An American Dilemma* (New York: Harper & Row; 1962; p. 1355) Myrdal attributed to Cash his understanding of the cult of white womanhood, and how this inflated status resulted from sex relations in the Old South of white men with Negro women. Or again, deferring to Cash's observations as a veteran newspaper reporter, Myrdal cited him (p. 1361) in reporting that "when the red light districts of Southern cities were suppressed, prostitution took to hotels." Further, when he wanted to get at the commonsense of the element of cruelty in slavery, Myrdal (p. 1338) quoted two long paragraphs from Cash's book (pp. 85–6, Vintage edn.). And finally, when Myrdal set out to define his regional terms and encountered trouble in fastening upon a precise-enough definition for the South, he quoted (p. 1071) from Cash's introduction, "Preview to Understanding." Although it might be maintained that there are many Souths, as Cash conceded, the Swede used the Carolinian to bolster his position that in considering the Negro problem one could justly speak of the South as a reasonably homogenous unit.

Even though Myrdal began his epochal study as early as 1938 there is no evidence that there was any direct contact between him or his many research assistants and the obscure Mr. Cash. Myrdal approached his subject from the viewpoint of a European, and, as was true also of that greatest of European interpreters of America, Alexis de Tocqueville, he quite obviously harbored a few preconceived notions about what America was and is. Despite the stature of his work, Myrdal could make some unaccountable errors of judgment. Speaking of the Southern Negro, for example, despite his enormous compendium of factual material he nowhere found room for a single mention of Howard Odum's *Southern Regions*. Nevertheless, the Swedish visitor wrought a great triumph in identifying, from out of the great welter of sociological and psychological data, the true nature of America's racial dilemma. He isolated the heart of the matter as a great and fundamental moral question. On top of everything else, he declared himself optimistic about the future of America's race relations to a degree that no American of that day, certainly not W. J. Cash, would dare. Moreover, Myrdal lived to see his opinion sustained. Strangely enough, the optimism of Myrdal and the pessimism of Cash seem less contradictory than complementary, Myrdal finding vindication in the fact that the South has come a long way and Cash somberly echoing that it has a long way to go.

William Faulkner, who modestly rated Thomas Wolfe above himself as a writer, once said of Wolfe what applies equally to W. J. Cash: "He had much courage and wrote as if he didn't have long to live." Unlike some contemporary books written by self-styled Southern liberals of the 1930's, in which logic-tight compartments and remarkable inconsistencies flourished, Cash's work went ruthlessly to the core of the South's self-deception. His Southerners (and he loved them) valued justice, but they valued equally a way of life built upon injustice. He concluded on a note of pessimism, as well he might, because there existed a wide gulf between intellectuals like himself and the South's political leaders of 1940, who exerted little leadership and less statesmanship.

A few critics have observed loftily that Cash did not accomplish a comprehensive intellectual history of the South—something he himself never intended—as if to say that Cash's "man at the center" should have been John C. Calhoun. Other critics, more justly, have suggested that Cash may have ridden his thesis too hard, that the author's personal antennae seemed especially attuned to the continuity and the essential unity of the Southern mind. At all events, Cash began absorbing impressions through his pores on the day he was born, never letting up until he discerned the pattern that for him distinguished the Southern mind, his own mind, from those of all other men. The result was precisely his brilliant book, which, whether one praises it or condemns it, continues to be quoted on all sides. Because

Mind is personal and impressionistic, teachers have wished at times that their students would not continue to choose it as their first book about the South. In this case the students may well be wiser than they realize, for what they value as an interesting and readable book happens to be original historical writing of the highest order.

In the context of the Negro Revolution and with the advantage of hindsight, it has been suggested that Cash somehow slighted the Negro problem by not having made it the very base and center of his argument. Even that criticism, weak as it is because alien to the author's intent, fails to appreciate how well *Mind* has stood up over the years and how a rereading will reveal that Cash accorded the Negro problem considerably more centrality than had been thought. To be sure, despite the author's voluminous consideration of Negro themes, his concern for understanding the Southern mind in its total capacity for self-deception ranged over the entire landscape of Dixie. He exposed the historical falsity of the Southern myths, Old South and New; the emotional crises that led to the origin of those myths and their survival; the nonpeaceful coexistence of individualism and intolerance; the factors bearing upon class consciousness; the relation one with the other of religion, race, rhetoric, romanticism, leisure, and the cult of Southern Womanhood; and the patterns formed by demagoguery, violence, paternalism, and evangelism. Nevertheless, bearing upon the centrality of the Negro problem, Cash listed the vices of his native region upon the last page of his book and noted: ". . . above all too great attachment to racial values and a tendency to justify cruelty and injustice in the name of those values." However guarded that language of 1940, Cash highlighted in his general indictment a pitilessly searching critique of the South's treatment of the Negro.

He was a truth-seeker, this W. J. Cash, whose too-short

life yielded one fine book as its only monument. Thoughtful men will continue to honor him in the realization that, like most truth-seekers, W. J. Cash gathered his crumbs and grains of truth at the cost of his bitter toil and agony.

A READER

A READER

CONTENTS

Contents

1

POSSIBILITIES

(Editorial, *Old Gold and Black*,
Wake Forest College, May 5, 1922)

The prime target of the North Carolina fundamentalists was
Wake Forest's president, Dr. William Louis Poteat, who as a
biologist did not ignore Darwin's teachings and yet remained the
popular and devout head of a Baptist college. Editor Cash was
ever vigorous in his defense of Poteat, and in this editorial he
brought heavy irony to bear against two fundamentalist "succes-
sors" to his beloved "Dr. Billy."

Since some of the brethren seem so determined to
transfer Dr. William Louis Poteat to the "higher field
of activity and larger salary" which Editor Coffin [1] of
the Raleigh Times quite sensibly suggests will be his if he
is hounded away from Wake Forest because of his views on
evolution, we have decided to get on the band-wagon along
with the crowd, and in order to prove to the Old Guard that
we have repented of the wickedness of our ways and have
abandoned our heresy, we have been industriously searching

---

[1] Oscar J. Coffin left the Raleigh *Times* in 1926 and served for the
next three decades in Chapel Hill as head of the department of journalism at the University of North Carolina.

the field of possibilities for a "safe and sound" successor to Dr. Poteat.

First and foremost, we wish to recommend Willie J. Bryan. Few men are so well qualified for the position. Willie belongs to the old reading and 'ritin and 'rithmetic school, and his mind is a wonderful example of what the good old days and the good old ways could produce. His brain is untainted by any of the newfangled kinds of education. He has steadfastly refused to find out anything about the theory of evolution lest he place his immortal soul in jeopardy, and as late as 1896 he had never read a book on that dreadful subject, economics, which everybody knows was invented to keep the "dere peepul" from getting Free Silver and securing all the money they wanted by the very simple device of printing it on nice white paper. Undoubtedly, he would be a great success as president of this institution. Unfortunately, however, there are about three things which make him unavailable. In the first place, Willie is reported to have designs on a seat in the world's greatest assemblage of bigots, which is sometimes called the United States Senate. Then, if he were brought here as president, the student body would undoubtedly become afflicted with the wanderlust and migrate elsewhere. Lastly, Willie hasn't yet convinced himself that the earth is flat and that the sun "do move," hence, he would not be acceptable to a number of the most pious brethren.

Wilbur Glenn Voliva [2] seems to be the next most likely prospect. Without a doubt, his views would meet with widespread approval. The delightful regulations which he imposes on the celestial-minded citizens of Zion City would exactly suit the temperaments of the Baptist young men at Wake Forest. In particular would they joy in the jailing of

---

[2] Unlike Bryan, Voliva was unyielding in his insistence that the earth was flat. Voliva presided over his little puritanical theocracy in Zion City, Illinois.

all culprits found smoking or loitering at soda fountains. We trust that we will not be accused of trying to amalgamate the two schools into a co-ed institution if we suggest that Comrade Voliva also be granted the presidency of Meredith.[3] Surely the styles which he prescribes in Zion City would afford the modest maidens grateful relief from the shameless dress of modern society. And both youth and the maiden would rise up and call him blessed when he released their minds from the bonds of the heathenish doctrine of evolution with his wonderful theory that the earth is flat and that the sun—which is only thirty-five miles in diameter and placed at a distance of only three thousand miles—spins around the earth. But, sad to relate, Voliva probably wouldn't accept the job because he is very well satisfied with running Zion City.

And now, to save our lives, we can't think of another possibility. What a pity that good old Cotton Mather is dead! And, come to think of it, we guess that most of the eligible brethren died off about five centuries ago, unless perchance some member of the Old Guard aspires to the position.

---

[3] Meredith College, a Baptist college for women, in Raleigh, North Carolina.

2

THE MIND
OF THE SOUTH

(*The American Mercury*, October 1929)

*In this Mencken-published article, bearing the same title as the
book that was more than a decade away, Cash struck some of the
major chords sounded in the later work. His thesis was to remain
essentially the same: the continuity of the Old South mind with
the New. One notices at once that Mencken's smiling condescen-
sion is mirrored in Cash's use in 1929 of such expressions as "the
bogey of the Ethiop" and the "perpetual sweat about the nigger."
There is not even a hint of such language in the later book.*

O*ne hears much* in these days of the New South. The
land of the storied rebel becomes industrialized; it
casts up a new aristocracy of money-bags which in
turn spawns a new *noblesse;* scoriac ferments spout and
thunder toward an upheaval and overturn of all the old
social, political, and intellectual values and an outgushing of
divine fire in the arts—these are the things one hears about.
There *is* a new South, to be sure. It is a chicken-pox of
factories on the Watch-Us-Grow maps; it is a kaleidoscopic
chromo of stacks and chimneys on the club-car window as
the train rolls southward from Washington to New Orleans.

But I question that it is much more. For the mind of that heroic region, I opine, is still basically and essentially the mind of the Old South. It is a mind, that is to say, of the soil rather than of the mills—a mind, indeed, which, as yet, is almost wholly unadjusted to the new industry.

Its salient characteristic is a magnificent incapacity for the real, a Brobdingnagian talent for the fantastic. The very legend of the Old South, for example, is warp and woof of the Southern mind. The "plantation" which prevailed outside the tidewater and delta regions was actually no more than a farm; its owner was, properly, neither a planter nor an aristocrat, but a backwoods farmer; yet the pretension to aristocracy was universal. Every farmhouse became a Big House, every farm a baronial estate, every master of scant red acres and a few mangy blacks a feudal lord. The haughty pride of these one-gallus squires of the uplands was scarcely matched by that of the F. F. V's of the estuary of the James. Their pride and their legend, handed down to their descendants, are today the basis of all social life in the South.

Such romancing was a natural outgrowth of the old Southern life. Harsh contact with toil was almost wholly lacking, as well for the poor whites as for the grand dukes. The growing of cotton involves only two or three months of labor a year, so even the slaves spent most of their lives on their backsides, as their progeny do to this day. The paternal care accorded the blacks and the white trash insured them against want. Leisure conspired with the languorous climate to the spinning of dreams. Unpleasant realities were singularly rare, and those which existed, as, for example, slavery, lent themselves to pleasant glorification. Thus fact gave way to amiable fiction.

It is not without a certain aptness, then, that the Southerner's chosen drink is called moonshine. Everywhere he turns away from reality to a gaudy world of his own making. He declines to conceive of himself as the mad king's "poor, bare, forked animal"; in his own eyes, he is eternally a noble and heroic fellow. He has always displayed a passion for going to war. He pants after Causes and ravening monsters—witness his perpetual sweat about the nigger. (No matter whether the black boy is or is not a menace, he serves admirably as a dragon for the Southerner to belabor with all the showiness of a paladin out of a novel by Dr. Thomas Dixon.[1] The lyncher, in his own sight, is a Roland or an Oliver, magnificently hurling down the glove in behalf of embattled Chastity.)

Even Rotary flourishes primarily as a Cause, as another opportunity for the Southerner to puff and prance and be a noble hotspur. His political heroes are, typically, florid magnificoes, with great manes and clownish ways—the Bleases and the Heflins. (It is said sometimes, I know, that they are exalted only by the rascals and the dolts, but, on a basis of observation, I make bold to believe that, while all decent Southerners vote against them, most do so with secret regret and only for the same reason that they condemn lynching, to wit: that they are self-conscious before the frown of the world, that they are patriots to the South.)

When the Southerner has read at all, he has read only Scott or Dumas or Dickens. His own books have been completely divorced from the real. He bawls loudly for Law Enforcement in the teeth of his own ingenious flouting of the Fourteenth and Fifteenth Amendments. He boasts of the purity of his Anglo-Saxon blood—and, *sub rosa*, winks at miscegenation. Yet, he is never—consciously, at least—a hypocrite. He is a Tartarin, not a Tartuffe. Whatever pleases

---

[1] Thomas Dixon, a native of Shelby, N.C., was a fiery orator committed to the cause of White Supremacy. His first novel, the racist *The Leopard's Spots* (1902), was a financial success, so he retired from the Baptist ministry. Drawing on material from his first three novels, Dixon then wrote the photoplay which became, under the direction of David Wark Griffith, the famous motion picture *The Birth of a Nation* (1915).

him he counts as real. Whatever does not please him he holds
as non-existent.

II

How this characteristic reacts with industrialism is strikingly
shown by the case of the cotton-mill strikes in the Carolinas.
Of the dozen-odd strikes which flared up a few months ago,
not one now remains. All failed. New ones, to be sure, are
springing up as a result of the unionization campaign which
Thomas F. McMahon, president of the United Textile Workers of America, is waging in the region. But the U. T. W. A.
failed in similar campaigns in 1920 and in 1923 and, in the
light of recent history, I see no reason to believe that the
present drive is likely to be any more successful.

Yet the peons of the mills unquestionably have genuine
grievances, *in the absolute*. Wages rarely top $20. The
average is from $11 to $14, with the minimum as low as $6.
The ten-hour or eleven-hour day reigns. It is true that, as
most of the mills own their own villages, houses are furnished
the workers at nominal rentals. But, save in the cases of
Cramerton, N. C., the Cone villages at Greensboro, and a
few other such model communities, the houses afforded are
hardly more than pig-sties. The squalid, the ugly, and the
drab are the hallmarks of the Southern mill town. Emaciated
men and women and stunted children are everywhere in
evidence.

But the Southerner sees and understands nothing of this.
Force his attention to the facts and he will, to be sure,
appear for the nonce to take cognizance of them, will even
be troubled, for he is not inhumane. But seek to remind him
tomorrow of the things you have shown him today and you
will discover no evidence that he recalls them at all; his
talk will be entirely of the Cone villages and Cramerton and
he will assume in all discussions of the merits of the case
that these model kraals are typical of the estate of the mill-

billy. The whole cast of his mind inhibits retention and contemplation of the hard facts, and he honestly believes that Cramerton is typical, that the top wage is the average wage. That is to say, he can honestly see only the pleasant thing. That is why, quite apart from antinomian considerations, the Southern newspapers almost unanimously denounced the accurate stories of the strikes printed by the New York *World* and the Baltimore *Sun* as baseless fabrications, inspired purely by sectional malice.

North Carolina furnished an interesting case study in this phase of the Southern mind when, at Gastonia, thugs, combed from the ruffians of two States and made sheriff's deputies, were loosed on a parade of inoffensive strikers, and dotards and women were mercilessly clubbed. A rumbling of protest shook the State. The Greensboro *Daily News* and the Raleigh *News and Observer* went so far as to denounce the business editorially. Whereupon—but that was all. Confronted by the damned facts, North Carolina gaped for a moment, then hastily brushed the offensive object into the ashcan, poured itself an extra-long drink, and went back to the pleasant business of golf-gab or mule-swapping.

If I have made incidental mention of violence, let it not be inferred that, in general, the strikes have been crushed by the blackjack. It is a significant fact that only at mills owned and operated by Yankees, or, in the case of Elizabethton, Tenn., by Germans, has violence been in evidence. The native baron simply closes his mill and sits back to wait for nature to take its course. He understands, that is, that the strikes may be trusted to go to pieces in the mind of the striker himself.

That mind is, in every essential respect, merely the ancient mind of the South. It is distinctly of the soil. For the peon, in origin, is usually a mountain-peasant, a hill-billy of the valleys and coves of the Appalachian ridge. He is leisured, lazy, shiftless. He is moony, sharing the common

Southern passion for the lush and the baroque. He yammers his head off for Heflin and Blease, not because they promise him better working and living conditions—they don't—but because Heflin is his captain in the War Against the Pope, because Blease led him in that grand gesture for Human Freedom, that Storming of the Bastille—the flinging open of the gates of the South Carolina penitentiary. He crowds such swashbuckling and witless brotherhoods as the Klan, the Junior Order, the Patriotic Order Sons of America, and the American Legion. He is passionately interested in the shouting of souls "coming through" at a tent-revival, in the thrilling of his spine to "Washed in the Blood" at the Baptist synagogue, in a passing medicine show, and in the next installment of "Tiger Love" at the Little Gem. But in such hypothetical propositions as his need of a bathtub, in such prosaic problems as his economic status, he is interested but vaguely if at all.

In brief, he is totally blind to the realities of his condition. Though for a quarter of a century he has been in contact with industry, and has daily rubbed elbows with a standard of living higher than his own, his standards remain precisely those of a hill-billy. He holds it to be against God to take a bath at any other time than Saturday night. Often enough, indeed, he sews himself into his underwear at Hallowe'en, not to emerge again until the robin wings the northern way. Scorning the efforts of Y. M. C. A. secretaries to lure him into shower-baths, he continues, with a fine loyalty to tradition, to perform his ablutions in the tin tub which does duty on Monday as the family laundry.

So with everything. He is not displeased with his mill-shanty—for the reason that it is, at its worst, a far better house than the cabins of his original mountain home. And he has little real understanding that his wages are meagre. In his native hill society, money was an almost unknown commodity and the possession of ten dollars stamped a man as hog-rich; hence, privately and in the sub-conscious depths of him, he is inclined to regard a wage of that much a week as affluence. He is still at heart a mountain lout, lolling among his hounds or puttering about a moonshine-still while his women hoe the corn. He has no genuine conviction of wrong. His grievances exist only in the absolute. There is not one among them for which he is really willing to fight. And that is the prime reason why all Southern strikes fail.

III

Moreover, the mind of the Southerner is an intensely individualistic mind. There again, it strikes back to the Old South, to the soil. The South is the historic champion of States' Rights. It holds Locke's "indefeasibility of private rights" as axiomatic. Its economic philosophy is that of Adam Smith, recognizing no limitations on the pursuit of self-interest by the individual, and counting unbridled private enterprise as not only the natural order but also the source of all public good. *Laissez-faire* is its watchword.

The Southerner is without inkling of the fact that, admirably adapted as such a philosophy was to the simple, agricultural society of the Jeffersonian era, it is inadequate for dealing with the industrial problems of today. He has never heard of the doctrine of the social function of industry and would not understand it if he had. He cannot see that industrialism inevitably consolidates power into the hands of a steadily decreasing few, and enables them, if unchecked, to grab the lion's share of the product of other men's labor; he cannot see that the worker in a machine age is not an individual at all but an atom among atoms—that he is no longer, and cannot possibly be, a free agent. Under the Southern view, even a cotton-mill is an individual. If a peon cares to work for the wage it chooses to pay, very well; if he doesn't, let him exercise a freeman's privilege and quit. But for him to combine with his fellows and seek to tie up the operation of the mill until his wages are raised—that, as the South sees it, is exactly as if a lone farm-hand, displeased with his pay, took post with a shotgun to bar his employer from tilling his fields.

The lint-head of the mills, indeed, is the best individualist of them all, and for this there is excellent reason. Often enough he owns a farm, his ancestral portion in the hills—rocks, pinebrush, and abrupt slopes, but still a farm, well adapted to moonshining. If he is landless, there are hundreds of proprietors eager to secure him as a tenant, an estate in which he will not have to work more than three months out of twelve. As a result, there is a constant flow back and forth between the soil and the mills. Thus the Southern peon is not, in fact, and *as an individual,* as irrevocably bound to the wheel of industry as his Northern brother, since he may always escape to churldom. The equally valid fact that, because only a handful can escape at any given time, the mass of his fellows are held irretrievably in bondage is lost upon him. He is always, in his own eyes, a man apart. He exhibits the grasping jealousy for petty personal advantage, the refusal to yield one jot or tittle for the common good, characteristic of the peasant. If, by a miracle, he is ambitious, his aspirations run, not to improving his own status by improving that of the class to which, in reality, he is bound, but to gaudy visions of himself as a member of the master class, as superintendent or even president of the mills. His fellows may be damned.

Another excellent reason, then, for the failure of Southern strikes is the impossibility of holding in organization the individualized yokel mind. The peon, to be sure, will join the union, but that is only because he is a romantic loon. He will join anything, be it a passing circus, a lynching-bee, or the Church of Latter Day Saints. He will even join the Bolsheviks (as at Gastonia, where the strikers were organized by the National Textile Workers' Union), though he is congenitally incapable of comprehending the basic notion of communism. The labor-organizers, with their sniffling pictures of his dismal estate, furnish him with a Cause for which he can strut and pose and, generally, be a magnificent galoot. And the prospect of striking invokes visions of Hell popping, the militia, parades, fist-fights and boozy harangues—just such a Roman holiday as he dotes on. By all means, he'll join the union!

But when flour runs low in the barrel, when monotonous waiting succeeds the opening Ku Klux festivities, when fresh clodhoppers, lured by the delights of moviehouses and ice-cream joints, begin to pour in and seize the vacant jobs in the mills, and when a strike-breaker drops around to the back door to say that, while the boss is goddam sore, he is willing to give everybody just one more chance, well, the lint-head, who has no deep-seated sense of wrong, who all along has rather suspected that the business he is embarked on is indistinguishable from road-agentry, and who decidedly likes the ego-warming backslap of the boss, does the natural thing for a romantic and sidesteps reality—does the natural thing for an individualist and goes back to work.

IV

Finally, the mind of the South begins and ends with God, John Calvin's God—the anthropomorphic Jehovah of the Old Testament. It is the *a priori* mind which reigned everywhere before the advent of Darwin and Wallace. The earth is God's stage. Life is God's drama, with every man cast for his rôle by the Omnipotent Hand. All exists for a Purpose—that set forth in the Shorter Catechism. The Southerner, without, of course, having looked within the damned pages of Voltaire, is an ardent disciple of the Preceptor Pangloss: "It is demonstrable . . . that things cannot be otherwise than they are;

for all being created for an end, all is necessary for the best
end. Observe that the nose has been formed to bear spectacles—thus we have spectacles." Whatever exists is ordered.
Even Satan, who is forever thrusting a spoke into the rhythm
of things, is, in reality, ordained for the Purpose. But that in
nowise relieves those who accept his counsels or serve his
ends; their damnation is also necessary to the greater glory
of God.

Under this view of things, it plainly becomes blasphemy
for the mill-billy to complain. Did God desire him to live in
a house with plumbing, did He wish him to have better
wages, it is quite clear that He would have arranged it. With
that doctrine, the peon is in thorough accord. He literally
holds it to be a violation of God's Plan for him to have a
bath save on Saturday night. Could he have a clear-seeing
conviction of his wrongs, could he strip himself of his petty
individualism, he would, nevertheless, I believe, hesitate
under the sorrowing eyes of his pastor, wilt, and, borne up
by the promised joys of the poor and torments of the rich
in the Life to Come, go humbly back to his post in the mills.
If you doubt it, consider the authentic case of the mill-billy
parents who refused to let a North Carolina surgeon remove
cataracts from the eyes of their blind daughter on the ground
that if God had wanted her to see He would have given her
good eyes at birth. The peon is always a Christian.

The South does not maintain, of course, that, even in a
closed, ordered world, change is impossible, but such change
must always proceed from God. In the case of the lint-head,
for example, it could come about in two ways. God could
directly instruct the barons, who are such consecrated men
that they pay the salaries not only of their uptown pastors
but of the peon's shepherds as well, to give the peon better
wages and a bathtub, in which case He, of course, would be
promptly obeyed. It is clear that He has not yet resorted to
this method, which, indeed, must be described as somewhat

extraordinary. The more usual way would be for Him to communicate His wishes to His immediate servants, the holy men. These holy men hold audience with Him several times daily, so that the South is in constant touch with His plans. At this writing, the uptown pastors seem agreed that God is insistent that there must be less raging after vain things like porcelain baths and more concern with the Higher Life. With this report that of the peon's shepherds coincides perfectly.

The liaison thus maintained between God and the South through His intelligence men is the explanation of many things—for instance, the paradox that our States' Rights, individualistic, *laissez-faire* hero is the chief champion of Prohibition. Many explanations for that have been offered, but it seems to me to be pretty evident that the Noble Experiment arose in the South primarily from the fact that the college of canons went into a huddle with God and emerged with the news that He wanted a Law. The gallant Confederate, of course, was and is not, in fact, dry. But if God wanted a Law—well, He got it. That is why the South will tolerate no monkey-business with the Volstead Act. It is God's Law. And therein, indeed, is stated the South's whole attitude toward morals. Adultery, thievery, horse-racing, cock-fighting, whatnot, are wrong not because they react unfavorably on human society but because they are forbidden by God, either in the Bible or in the dictums of the chosen vessels of His Will. Individual transgressions of most of these laws may, to be sure, be glossed over by an extra dollar on the collection plate on Sunday, but to oppose the laws themselves is to oppose God. Blasphemy is the first crime in the Southern calendar.

It follows, from both his romanticism and his theology, that the Southerner is ungiven to reflection. Thinking involves unpleasant realities, unsavory conclusions; and, happily, there is no need for it, since, as everything is arranged by God, there is nothing to think about. The South, with more leisure than New England, has yet produced no Emerson nor even a Thoreau. Though the British friars shrieked and tore their garments as lustily when Darwin advanced the doctrine of evolution in 1859 as did their Southern brethren when such Catalines as Dr. W. L. Poteat, of North Carolina, bore it below the Potomac forty years afterward, yet all England accepted it within two decades, while the South, in significant contrast, is no more reconciled to it today than in 1900. All that matter of the origin of man was settled very long ago—set down in Genesis by God Himself. To question it is to blaspheme. All ideas not approved by the Bible and the *shamans* are both despised and ignored. And, indeed, a thinker in the South is regarded quite logically as an enemy of the people, who, for the common weal, ought to be put down summarily—for, to think at all, it is necessary to repudiate the whole Southern scheme of things, to go outside God's ordered drama and contrive with Satan for the overthrow of Heaven.

All problems are settled categorically. Maxim and rule are enough. Precedent is inviolable. And nice distinctions are, of course, impossible. A nigger, for example, is either a vile clown or an amiable Uncle Tom. If he insists on upsetting things by being something else, he passes, like Elijah, in a chariot of fire, and is wafted to his reward on wings of kerosene. (The Southerner, faced with any reality which refuses to fit into his rose-colored, pigeonholed world, quietly abolishes it. Lynching is not only a romantic gesture but a protective one as well.) The more serious and intelligent of the cotton-mill operatives, unlike their peers in most industrial hives, are never found pondering Prince Kropotkin, Karl Marx, or even Upton Sinclair. Their minds run rather to the problem of convincing sinful souls of the merits of total immersion. Their own case is disposed of by maxims: "The poor we have with us always," "Servants, obey your masters" and "God's in His Heaven; all's right with the world."

It is this lack of thoughtfulness which accounts for the fact that the mind of the South is almost impervious to change, that, for a quarter of a century, it has successfully resisted the steadily increasing pressure of industrialism, blithely adopting the Kiwanis moonshine—all those frothy things it found compatible—but continuing, in the main, to move through the old rhythms. I have paid much attention herein to the cotton-mill peon because it seems obvious to me that if change is to come about in the Southern mind, it must arise from him, for he is in most direct contact with industry and it is in his status that the inadequacy of the old formulæ is most clearly evident. Everywhere revision of values and adjustment of the agricultural mind to industrialism have been brought about by the revolts of the laboring classes, since it is the natural tendency of the upper classes to assume that *quand le Roi avait bu, la Pologne était ivre,* and to ask: "When all goes so well, why trouble to change?"

But the Southern peon is scarcely touched by industrialism. He accepts; he does not question and challenge. His desultory revolts have not arisen from his own convictions but from the urging of professional agitators. Even the recent spontaneous walkouts in South Carolina were inspired, not by protest against wages and living conditions, but by collision between the peon's native shiftlessness and so-called efficiency system introduced in Yankee-owned mills; they prove nothing save that he declines to become industrialized.

V

But if the much-proclaimed industrialization of the South is merely a matter of externals, the remaining ingredients of the New South formula are scarcely more than wind. The money-bags do exist, certainly—a handful of parvenus. But they have begotten no new cultural *noblesse,* nor are they likely to. Sworn enemies of the arts, of all ideas dating after 1400, and of common decency, they have imported the senseless Yankee dogma of work for work's sake, and seek rather to destroy than to increase that leisure which must be the basis of any culture. All their contributions to educational institutions, of which the Duke gift [2] is the outstanding example, have been motivated by a desire to perpetuate the old order, not to create an enlightened new one. As for the prognostications of social, political, and intellectual revolution, the prophecies of the outpouring of heavenly fire—they, like the great Woof-Woof in Kansas,[3] arise from nowhere; like the earth, they are hung upon nothing—unless, indeed, it be the cabalistic imaginations of those occult professors who write books called "The New South" or "The Rising South" or "The Advancing South."

There, to be sure, is the breaking of the Solid South, the swinging of traditionally Democratic States into the Republican column last Fall. But that was proof, not that the mind of the South had changed, but that it was unchanged. Satan had seized the Democratic party, and the oriflamme of God, as was witnessed by all the holy men, had passed to the keeping of the Republicans. The Southerner merely chose to remain loyal to the All Highest. The sadly moth-eaten Cause of White Supremacy was laid aside for two shiny and extraor-

---

[2] The Duke gift was that of James Buchanan Duke, the tobacco and utilities magnate who, in 1924, handsomely endowed Trinity College (Methodist) on condition that the institution change its name to Duke University. Mr. Duke shrewdly saw to it that the Duke Endowment was bankrolled by stock in the Duke Power Company so that the prosperity of the one was tied to the other. Thus, "adverse" state taxation upon the Duke Power Company could be, and in fact was, avoided by appealing to legislative sentiment against "harming" the beneficent Duke Endowment.

[3] This reference probably is to William Allen White, the Sage of Emporia, and to his attempts to discredit Al Smith, whom Cash had championed, during the presidential campaign of 1928.

dinarily juicy new ones—the plot of the Pope (Satan's cousin) and the scarcely less electric plot of the Rum Ring. Save among cotton-mill barons and a few Babbitts, the Hoover *élan* and Republican principles—whatever, and if, they may be—had nothing to do with the matter. As I write, the De Priest incident seems to have miraculously refurbished and revivified the bogey of the Ethiop—and the Southern Democratic bosses are engaged in identifying themselves with the War on the Pope by bellowing for Raskob's scalp and openly threatening to repudiate the national party if Great Moral Ideas are again defied. Whichever party best combines causes and monsters and clinches its claim to the banner of God will win. Party labels may or may not be changed. In any case, I believe, the mind of the South will remain the same.

There are, too, of course, Mr. James Branch Cabell, Mr. DuBose Heyward, Mrs. Julia Peterkin—a little group of capable craftsmen who have abandoned the pistols and coffee-lilacs and roses-sweetness and light formulæ of Southern littérateurs to cope with reality. It is true also that the South swells with pride in them. But—I have myself watched a lone copy of "The Cream of the Jest" gather flyspecks for two years in a bookshop not two hundred miles south of Monument Avenue. For, gloss it over as one will, it is undeniably true that Mr. Cabell's persons do things forbidden by the Bible, that Poictesme, as compared with the satrapies of Bishops Cannon, Mouzon,[4] *et al.*, is in sin, and that (O base infidelity!) he fails to view these matters with becoming indignation. Of late days, I have heard often the

---

[4] James Cannon Jr. and Edwin D. Mouzon were Southern Methodist bishops who were prominent, as was William Allen White, in the fight to retain national prohibition, Cannon attaining unprecedented influence through his political infighting against Al Smith in 1928. Later, when Cannon was shown to have been gambling in the stock market, Mouzon became perhaps his chief adversary within the church.

plaint that "Mamba's Daughters" is both pointless and untrue to the Southern Negro, which last is to say that Mr. Heyward's portrayals fit neither the Uncle Tom formula nor that of the vaudeville buffoon. And Mrs. Peterkin's "Scarlet Sister Mary" is barred from the library at Gaffney, in her native State of South Carolina, as an immoral book. The gloomy fact is that, however much patriotic pride the Southerner may take in the fame of these people, he is bewildered and infuriated by their works.

Lastly, there are such diverse factors—to mention a few out of many—as Odum's *Social Forces* and Koch's Playmakers at the University of North Carolina, Poteat's teaching of evolution in face of the stake to young Baptists at Wake Forest College for the past thirty years, and the Commission for Inter-racial Coöperation, which aims to foster a more reasonable attitude toward the Negro. It would be foolish to say that they have had no civilizing influence. But it is insanity to claim that they have had any definite effect on the mass of Southerners, to assert that there is any prospect of their engendering, at an early date, a revolution of thought in the South. The men who are responsible for these things, like the artists I have discussed, are not, in any true sense, of the Southern mind. All of them are of that level of intelligence which is above and outside any group mind. They are isolated phenomena, thrown up, not because of conditions in the South, but in spite of them.

Eventually, of course, must come change. Perhaps, indeed, the beginning of it is already at hand. For, undeniably, there is a stir, a rustling upon the land, a vague, formless, intangible thing which may or may not be the adumbration of coming upheaval. Tomorrow—the day after—eventually— the cotton-mill peon will acquire the labor outlook and explosion will follow. In the long run the mind of the South will be remade. Will that bring on the millennium which the prophets profess to see as already in the offing? Will Atlanta become another Periclean Athens, Richmond a new Augustan Rome? I don't know, certainly, but I glance at the cotton-mill barons, the only product of readjustment yet in evidence, and take the liberty of doubting it. I suspect that the South will merely repeat the dismal history of Yankeedom, that we shall have the hog apotheosized—and nothing else. I suspect that we shall merely exchange the Confederate for that dreadful fellow, the go-getter, Colonel Carter for Mr. Lowell Schmaltz, the Hon. John LaFarge Beauregard for George F. Babbitt. I suspect, in other words, that the last case will be infinitely worse than the first.

3

THE WAR
IN THE SOUTH

(*The American Mercury*, February 1930)

The timeliness of this article lay in its being published on the heels of a wave of anti-union violence in the North Carolina of 1929. Seen in retrospect, this episode marks an important milestone in the history of the American labor movement.

First and foremost among the battles in that war came the world-famed strike at Gastonia, marked by the formation of a vigilante "Committee of One Hundred" against the strikers and the arrival of a Communist leadership headed by the late Fred Erwin Beal. He was later to turn anti-Communist when doing so was unfashionable, before the Hitler–Stalin Pact killed the Popular Front, and he frankly admitted that the Communist mission in 1929 was to exploit the very real misery of the textile workers in the interest of Marxist class struggle.

On June 7, 1929, the Gastonia police chief was shot to death, and a warrant went out for the arrest of Fred Beal as the strike leader. He was not charged with committing or even plotting the murder, the state contending only that he had uttered words that had stirred other unnamed men to violence. Vigilantes of the Committee of One Hundred nearly snatched him from the arresting officers for what would have been a certain lynching. Mindful of the lynch spirit that animated the Gastonia area, the presiding judge granted a motion for a change of venue so that the trial was held in Charlotte.

After one mistrial and a protracted legal battle, Beal and six others were found guilty of second-degree murder, and Beal drew a long prison term. He jumped bail and made his way to the Soviet Union, where he remained three years (1930–3) before returning to the United States disillusioned with Communism. His later autobiography, Proletarian Journey *(1937), which pilloried Stalin's Russia and made Beal a despised renegade in the eyes of American Communists, nevertheless pictured faithfully the hate-filled atmosphere of Gastonia and the one-sided trial. Beal was extradited to North Carolina, where he was jailed in 1938. His plea for a pardon was not granted by Governor Clyde R. Hoey, who had been the private prosecutor at Beal's trial, but the pardon plea was granted by Hoey's successor in 1942.*

In the midst of the Gastonia strikers' trial, on October 2, 1929, the McDowell County sheriff and all his deputies fired tear gas into the picket lines of strikers at Marion, North Carolina. As soon as the pickets turned their backs to flee, the sheriff and his men opened fire and shot five men to death and wounded twice as many more. Each dead or wounded man was shot in the back. The sheriff was not only freed of a charge of murder but given a state job as a prison guard.

The active anti-union vigilantism in North Carolina began to subside into a more passive disapproval only with the murder of Ella May Wiggins. On September 14, 1929, with Beal's trial still in progress, a group of union members from Bessemer City, North Carolina, set out in a truck bound for a mass meeting in South Gastonia. The truck turned back on being chased by an automobile procession of vigilantes, who forced the truck into a ditch and began shooting. A bullet killed Mrs. Ella May Wiggins, one of the local strike leaders and mother of five small children. After a Gastonia grand jury refused to indict anyone, Governor O. Max Gardner insisted on a prosecution. Later the defense attorney for the accused argued that his clients ought not to be found guilty because the dead woman believed in Communism. The jury agreed; it stayed out thirty minutes and returned with a verdict of not guilty.

While "The War in the South" bears ample witness to Cash's thorough familiarity with the Southern textile industry, it marks him as unduly optimistic as to chances of unionizing Southern mills. A decade later, after an obdurate union-busting campaign that proceeded in spite of the Wagner Act, Cash recorded himself as a pessimist. In his book of 1941 he did not subscribe to the facile optimism expressed in this article of 1930: "The labor union will conquer."

*W*hen *Comrades* Fred Beal and George Pershing, of the National Textile Workers' Union and the Communist Party in America, sat down in Gastonia, N. C., last Spring to the business of organizing a strike in that lovely town, it may be imagined that, between puffs at his two-bit cigar, Brother Thomas F. McMahon, of the United Textile Workers of America, permitted himself the luxury of a horse-laugh. For Brother McMahon had himself, in his time, tried the introduction of the Brotherhood of Man into that amazing and sulphurous land below the Potomac, and, accordingly, cherished no longer even the puniest of illusions. But to great faith it is given to move mountains. And to the comrades it grandly fell to set off the war in the South.

If I say war, I do not at all mean that the situation down there at the moment, viewed in isolation, justifies the term. As I write this, there are no strikes, save for a feeble ghost at Marion, and Beal and the Gastonia strikers have been crushed with long prison terms. Indeed, it would be easy to believe that the cotton-mill barons, the police, the jackal newspapers, and all the forces of Law and Order have succeeded in putting down the rebellion of a people who, for the great part, were not even sure that they wanted to rebel. Nevertheless, Gastonia, if I mistake not, is the Lexington from which historians of the future will reckon the industrial struggle, the war of a thousand battles, which, so I believe, will convulse the South during the next decade. That war itself was inevitable. The stage was set. The entry of the Reds simply put it in motion. And, being in motion, it will now go forward inexorably. There will be lulls—long ones, perhaps—but there will be hereafter no genuine cessation of hostilities until the war is fought and done.

To understand it one must know something of its central figure, the cotton-mill baron—of his character and history. For years, he has been represented in the South as a double for the Little Brother to the Birds, and in the North as an unmitigated villain—one part Simon Legree and three parts Satan. He is neither. He is, in fact, just what he was to begin with: a horse-trader, by which I mean to include all that race of factors, cross-road merchants, and money-grubbers in general, which, in the Old South, succeeded in raising itself above the poor whites economically, without, by any means, creating a distinct middle class. Hard-fisted, pious, and full of a puerile cunning, he is a realist, but it is such a realist as the old-time Negro-drover or backwoods usurer was—a realist who had thrown away the rose-colored glasses of the South, only to fix his gaze exactly at the end of his nose. At bottom, he is naïve, even stupid. Pig-headed, colossally greedy, vain and ignorant, he is totally incapable of the notion of *noblesse oblige*. There are honorable exceptions to all this, of course, but here manifestly, I am concerned only with the average.

The cotton-mill baron's medieval character, taken with the circumstances, explains his rise to power, his displacement of the gentleman planter as head of the Southern social order. And, ironically enough, just because he cared nothing for the good of society, he has rendered the South an incalculable service.

II

Dr. Broadus Mitchell of the Johns Hopkins has pretty well established it as a fact that the gentry of the South founded the cotton-mill industry below the Potomac, not in the hope of profit but to save the poor white, unable to compete with the freed Negro on the farm, from falling to the economic level of that freed Negro.[1] But the early stages of industrialization—everywhere difficult since the level of production in an agricultural region hardly ever so far passes that of subsistence as to provide capital for factories—were fraught, in the poverty-and-debt-ridden South, with almost insurmountable perils. Mortgages and credits, extended by machinery agents from the North, accounted for most of the mills south of the Mason-Dixon line in 1880. Industry down there literally faced the task of lifting itself by its own bootstraps. And, if it is clear that the survivors of the old gentry, being the only socially conscious group in the South, could alone open the way for industrialization, it is clear, too, that they were unfitted to carry out what they had begun. At business they were babes. Their very indifference to profits inevitably would have defeated their aim. For, if the poor white was to be saved, not ten mills but hundreds of mills were needed. And, in a land bled white of capital, the only way to pay for them was out of profits.

What was obviously needed was a leadership dedicated with unswerving singleness of purpose to the till, or, if you like, the trough. That leadership the old horse-trader, alone among Southerners, was fitted to supply. He stepped upon the stage to displace the gentry, to wrest profits from the mills over every obstacle, to devote—prior to 1910, at any rate—every cent of those profits to creating more mills and still more mills, to save the poor white. For the South, it is

---

[1] Broadus Mitchell, *The Rise of the Cotton Mills in the South* (Baltimore: Johns Hopkins; 1921).

nothing that he was actuated only by the lust for greater and yet greater profits. It is everything that he created the bridge over which the white man passed to sanctuary.

Moreover, in saving the poor white, he inevitably saved something else—the ancient social-economic pattern of the South, the plantation system. That is the meaning of the long hours, the wage which requires the labor of an entire family to maintain a standard of living, the mill-village, a sort of medieval fief, where every house, every school, every church, every teacher and preacher, nay, every word and thought, is owned by, or subject to, my lord, the baron—in brief, of all those things in which the Yankee critic sees the hand of the black-birder and the galley-master, the proof of the baron's villainy. They simply represent plantation standards and practices carried over into industry. The poor white had been bred in dependence. Of his old masters he had expected and demanded all things—work, tools, houses, paternal care, freedom from responsibility. He possessed neither the means nor the inclination to get these things for himself. Between the standard of the Negro and responsibility for himself, he would have chosen the first. Necessity, then—and the naïve acceptance of the only system he himself had ever known as the only possible one—caused the cotton-mill baron to carry the system on, and even to function within it—until after 1910, at least—in very much the same way as the planter before him.

The South was immensely grateful. Ungiven to analysis, it had no true conception of the real character of the baron; it has, indeed, none today. What it saw (and, in the main, still sees) was thousands saved from the squalid standard of the Moor, and given more or less decent employment; free houses, schools, churches, salaries of teachers and preachers paid, every variety of welfare work supported; the rising prosperity which touched everybody. To its eyes these things could proceed only from a noble soul, so the cult of the baron was born. The Charlotte *Observer* and other such dreadful sheets began their daily *Te Deum* in his honor. Legislatures poured out laws to aid and please him. All power became his.

Most grateful of all were the poor whites. They looked back to what they had escaped and congratulated themselves. Their natural envy of the baron was throttled by a vast thankfulness. A hedonistic, shiftless race, ambition bothered them but little. If it did, well, there was Blankville, the heart and center of the cotton-mill South—popular account designates its founders and lordlings as having been a tinker, a peddler, and a brace of bastards! Anyone with the will might come up. Until after 1910, the baron himself lived very simply. He maintained the old easy relations of the plantation, called his workmen by their first names, feasted them at barbecues, occasionally had one in to dinner. His wife and daughters knew them familiarly and without snobbishness. Everything contributed to amazingly good feeling, and the baron moved among his subjects as hero and friend.

The inevitable result was that he came to accept these tributes, this gratefulness, as his due. Inevitably, he came to think of himself, not in the manner of the true aristocrat as under the debt of *noblesse oblige,* but as a gaudy Lord Bountiful, a sort of sun-king shedding light and leading, whose every deed was good just because it was his.

III

No Knight of the Holy Ghost ever battled for the Grail with a more profound conviction of the rightness of his cause than that with which the beleaguered baron wars in the South today. His dominant emotion is outraged indignation. It is an emotion which the South in general and even the great body of mill-workers, as at present constituted, measurably share. The labor leaders are "alien" invaders, racketeers, stick-up men, mad Yankee guerrillas waging war on the South seventy years after; the mill-workers who strike or join unions are "traitors," outlaws; both alike are enemies not only of the baron but of all Southern society. A passion of patriotism sweeps the land. Add something of bewilderment, something more of fear, count in the Southern capacity for florid fancy, and you have the complex which conjures up a Red Peril, which beholds a foe, not to be tolerated, not to be treated with, but to be stamped out, extirpated, without quarter and without squeamishness.

The renegade to this view must be torn on the economic rack, starved into submission. To that end the reserve of labor which exists in the tenant-farmer class must be preserved. The baron serves notice on the Yankee manufacturer that further removal of factories to the South will not be welcomed. (A proposal for a new $5,000,000 art cloth mill in Gaston county met with such hostility last Summer that it was abandoned.) Black-lists of all men who have taken part in strikes or joined unions are made up and circulated. Any traffic with union agents means dismissal. Spies swarm.

The police, the newspapers, officialdom—do they not exist to protect society? Well, right gladly they see their duty and do it. The killing of the police-chief at Gastonia was unquestionably precipitated by the badgering activities of his own officers. And before the shedding of blood at Marion, the zeal of the sheriff in hounding the strikers had been such as to arouse the protest of even the attorney for the mills. The newspapers bawl for syndicalism laws; and it is almost a foregone conclusion that the Legislatures of the Carolinas, at least, will enact such laws, designed to cripple all union activities, at their next sessions. Municipal corporations, as at Marion and Gastonia, may be counted on to suspend all those American rights which in these grand days have become so un-American.

The courts deal telling blows. Fair trials? For "traitors" and "aliens"? Technically, yes. In fact, no. The quizzing of the talesmen in the trial of the Gastonia strikers established the mathematical impossibility of finding an unprejudiced jury. Grant that, legally, at least, the judge was fair, grant that most of the witnesses for the defense were as obviously lying as were most of those for the State, grant even the probability that one of the prisoners killed the Gastonia police-chief, the fact remains that Beal and his men were convicted before the hearing began.

The same thing precisely holds true in the case of Alfred Hoffman, U.T.W.A. organizer, convicted, with a group of strikers, at Marion on a highly dubious charge of "rioting." The simple truth is that, whatever the attitude of the judges, so long as witnesses share the dominant prejudices, so long as juries, composed of farmers, can be swayed by the magniloquent declaration of mill-paid attorneys that "the mills are the millowners' to do with as they please, just as your farms are yours to do with as *you* please"—the Beals and the Hoffmans must always be convicted, Gaston county grand juries must always, unless under great pressure, decline to proceed against the killers of an Ella May Wiggins, and a Marion sheriff must always go free.

But the single best weapon for putting down the "invader" and the "renegade" is Ku Kluxery—the repressed sadism, the native blood-lust, the horrible mob-instinct, which smoulders among the brutal and the ignorant everywhere in the South, and, above all, and ironically, among the mill-workers themselves. It is in bringing it into play that the police, the newspapers, and officialdom render their best service. It is as though they said: "Here they are, boys—the alien and the traitor! Help yourselves!"

Of course, nothing so crude is actually said. It may even be true, as a general proposition, that these inciting agencies do not understand their own motives or clearly perceive their own objectives. But, out of a welter of passion, out of hidden depths of desire, there emerge editorials which play violently upon all this sectional hate and racial bigotry, which touch the springs which release all the classical Klan emotions. A powerful sheet advances the doctrine that since the Communists oppose the institutions of the land, they are not entitled to the protection of its laws. At Gastonia, the police stand idle while masked hoodlums destroy the strikers' headquarters. When a mob roars through the streets of Gastonia and Charlotte, the gendarmes of those towns know nothing of it—they are blind and deaf.

Meanwhile, the local newspapers excuse the mob's outrages. On the eve of a Red pogrom in which a woman is run to earth and slain, the Gastonia *Gazette* warns the Communists that if they attempt to hold a meeting on their own leased property, "the good people of the town" will meet them with violence, and, in effect, justifies that violence beforehand. Officialdom investigates and learns nothing. Collusion? Probably not. Its whole outlook makes it inevitable that it should learn nothing. And so the Kluckers are not slow to see that here is their opportunity to sport and cavort, to drain the reservoir of their simian ferocity to the last thin drop.

Nor can it be said that Kluxery is roused and loosed only against the Reds. Every labor agitator, every striker, is a Bolshevik in the South. Neither the Kluckers nor their masters draw distinctions. True, the newspapers professed a vast love for the U.T.W.A. when the Gastonia battle was at its height, but when it organized the strike at Marion they turned on it, hoof and horn, branding its organizer, Hoffman, as an "alien" and bellowing idiotically about the gold of Moscow. This same Hoffman was kidnapped by Kluckers at Elizabethton and ridden out of Tennessee. And the U.T.W.A. organizer was hustled out of Ware Shoals, S.C., while the police looked complacently on. Significant, too, is the fact

that the victims of the Gastonia whipping-mob were required to pledge, not that they would have nothing more
to do with the Communists but that they would never again
join a labor union. The Red Peril is simply the labor union
peril.

But the baron and the South—that reactionary South
which supports him—are sadly mistaken, I suspect, when
they assume that they will succeed in repelling "invasion,"
in stamping out "treason." They are mistaken when they assume that the *status quo* can be successfully maintained.
They reckon without, are almost blind to, the changes that
have been taking place down there for the past twenty years,
and are still in progress. It is those changes upon which I
predicate my assertion that the present war was inevitable.

In the first place, the conditions which they defend no
longer have any justification in circumstances. After 1910 the
Negro ceased to be an economic menace. Mills had so
multiplied as to make the position of the poor white secure.
Merely to give a man a job at a living wage was no longer
to be entitled to his undying gratitude. Moreover, the industry was now producing a surplus which was not any more
required for the building of new mills. That surplus the baron
diverted to his private use, building ghastly burlesques of the
Georgian mansions of the old South, acquiring fleets of
automobiles. His daughter came home from the correct
schools in Virginia with a gelid stare, mouthing of class. His
wife acquired a lorgnette, joined the Colonial Dames, went
abroad. The old easy relations between man and master
went aglimmering. At the same time, all the fat posts in the
mills began to be filled by the baron's sons or the graduates
of technical schools. The door was closed on the lint-head. A
vast social and economic chasm opened.

Coincidentally, there arose in the South a group of people
who began to see the baron realistically and to exhibit impatience with his outworn system and standards. They find

voice today in such excellent newspapers as the Greensboro *Daily News* and the Raleigh *News and Observer,* flourish in such institutions as the University of North Carolina, despite the yelping of such paladins of the *status quo* as Dr. David Clark,[2] editor of the *Southern Textile Bulletin.* They constitute a formidable foe to the baron and his reactionary viewpoint.

But a change even more significant than these is in process. The first truly industrial generation among Southern mill-workers has been born and comes to growth. As yet it is still, for the major part, in its teens, though the vanguard has moved into the twenties. This generation has never known competition with the Negro. It cares nothing for tradition. It can read. And in it is the restlessness, the questioning, of a restless and questioning age. About it, it hears a thousand smug professions which do not agree with the facts it sees; it becomes a little cynical, even begins to doubt the Plan of Salvation.

Bound to the bare necessities, it moodily observes the other classes about it swathed in luxuries, satiate with "flowers and furs and cheeks." It wants those things, means to have them, Heaven willing or no. It is starkly aware that the old easy rise of the doffer-boy to the presidency of the mills is a tale that is told. And, springing from the mills, it instinctively seeks its ends through group action. It is the raw material of a vast revolt.

---

[2] Cash was needling David Clark in that Menckenian style that rang with such faint praise as "Dr. Harding" and "Dr. Coolidge." The late David Clark, roundly reactionary, owned no honorary degree in 1930, but Cash was as prescient as ever, because an appreciative alma mater, North Carolina State College, was to dub Clark "Doctor of Textile Science" in 1944.

IV

Untouched by the conservatism of the American Federation of Labor, plastic, basically unsophisticated, eager, this new generation offers fertile soil for whatever promises, however vaguely or absurdly, an outlet for its aspirations and improvement in its status. That is why the Reds were not wholly mad when they fell upon the notion that the South was a promising field for their activities. And that is why, too, the war must go on, why McMahon, having taken the field, cannot withdraw; he simply dare not, for that would be to leave it to the comrades, who, while they can never hope to sell their nostrum to the Confederacy, might very conceivably, given a free hand, establish their union down there.

At the moment, the advantage in the struggle is obviously with the baron and his allied reactionaries, and it will remain there, I suspect, for some while to come. Though the youngsters begin to breathe heavily, few Southern mill-workers above thirty are material for successful unionization. They may be disgruntled, but they are not rebellious—the old tradition is too strong upon them. A Klucker frolic now and then—and they will not ask for more. But, as time goes on, the support of the South will more and more fall away from the baron; his foes at home will become more and more formidable. Indeed, the reactionary South is even now, plainly enough, making its last great stand. The old social-economic system is breaking up. As the rising generation comes to ascendancy among the mill-workers, Southern strikes will begin to be won. And the ultimate outcome is as inevitable as the cycle of the sun: *the labor union will conquer.*

That is written plain for the baron to read in the history of every similar struggle in every older industrial region in the world. But there we come back to it: he is ignorant, he knows no history. Nor would it make any difference if he did.

He would still insist, in his pig-headed way, that, in his case, at least, the demands of labor are impossible, that unionization means ruin, and that higher wages and shorter hours spell bankruptcy for the industry. On the face of it, he has an excellent case. It certainly is true that, for the past seven or eight years, the great part of the mills have continually vociferated that they were not making money, and that their balance sheets have pretty well borne out the claim. But let us see.

The post-war years—1918–20—saw the greatest boom in the history of the industry. The heavens opened: money rained. The baron was ecstatic, transported. Then that fellow accursed of all times, the tax-collector, yanked him flaming from Paradise to despair. Under the then existing laws, what amounted to a double tax was assessed against corporate earnings. As such, they were subject to the excess profits toll; as declared dividends paid to the stockholder, they were again levied on as private income. From the first there could be no escape; but the baron speedily devised a device by which to evade the second—the stock dividend. It magically converted income into capital, and had the additional merit of cutting down future excess profit levies, since these were reckoned on a basis of capitalization. Everywhere the mills resorted to it. Stock dividends of 50% and 100% were common. A mill at Greenville, S. C., declared one of 300%.

But there was no corresponding increase in productive equipment. To escape taxation the industry had simply fallen into the embrace of that Old Man of the Sea—overcapitalization. Consider the case of a typical mill. It is capitalized at $1,500,000. In the first six months of 1929, it showed a profit of $51,000 or 3%. Yet the value of the plant is (on a replacement basis) only about $500,000, and it originally cost only a half or two-thirds that much. It should properly carry a capitalization of, say, no more than $750,000, certainly not more than $1,000,000. Thus, $750,000 or, at the minimum, $500,000 of the present capitalization is not capital at all, in the sense of productive equipment or the funds necessary to the operation of such equipment, but merely, in relation to the mill, at least, idle money. And the dividend actually earned on the true capital is not 6% annually but something more than 10% or 12%.

This over-capitalization makes it possible for a host of lesser incubi to bedevil the industry. There is, for example, the so-called marginal mill, that is, one bought or built on a shoestring; one accounted for by mortgages and mortgage bonds; one which the baron expects to pay for itself, meet high interest rates, pay him a juicy salary, and still show handsome profits. There is, too, the mill which, without being marginal, swings to the opposite extreme from the general and is under-capitalized, so that it must limp along on antiquated or worn-out machinery.

Plainly enough, neither of these mills has any business existing. They largely explain the over-production which dogs the industry. Nor could they exist if the industry in general were efficient. Their own higher basic production costs would quickly eliminate them if it were not for the fact that the majority of the mills are staggering along under a top-heavy load of money bags, and so must drive up the price of their goods beyond its natural level.

Much of the over-production, to which the baron charges all his woes, has, however, no existence in fact. It is simply a psychopathic obsession, artfully played upon—perhaps created—by the baron's selling agents in the East. It is not necessary to go into a detailed analysis of their methods here. It is enough that these gentry compete among themselves by under-bidding and cutthroat methods, and, accordingly, find it to their advantage to lead the baron to pile up a large volume of goods by glowing reports of market conditions—of which the baron is profoundly ignorant as a rule—and then play on his over-production complex, his fear of a dead market and a possible receivership, until, in panic, he is ready to accept any price at all. Obviously, it is an idiotic system.

V

The simple truth is that if the cotton-mill industry in the South is not making and showing healthy profits, it is because it is the most inefficiently organized in the country. The cure for its woes is apparent: it is the New Industrialism. By that I mean the theory which not only accepts high wages and short hours as inevitable, but professes to see them as creating a vast new market and, hence, wholly desirable; which eliminates the waste caused by too many small units and casts out the unfit by means of the merger; which attacks the problem of profit from the angle of mass production and cost per unit; which adjusts its capital to its needs; and which controls its own marketing system. The doctrine has obvious limitations, but, within them, its claims cannot be doubted; consider, for example, the possible effect on the over-production of cotton goods if the wages of the lint-head were so raised that he might change his underwear twice a week rather than once, as now the custom is!

Indeed, the war in the South is, in its final aspect, a struggle between the old and worn-out Southern social-economic system and this New Industrialism, with the thrust of the latter converging relentlessly on the baron as protagonist of the former. What he needs to do is not to fight, but to set his house in order for the coming of the inevitable. But that is exactly what he won't do—what, in fact, he is probably quite incapable of doing. His talents are fitted to primitive industrialism, to the small unit, to higgling and barter, not to organization in the grand manner. For years the experts he has called into consultation have been telling him that his only salvation lies in the merger and the selling combine. But he is incapable of tearing away from the trough immediately before him long enough to see the vaster and more promising troughs ahead. Doggedly, he holds his gaze to the end of his nose. The giant merger which was proposed over a year ago failed, I am told, because most of the mills involved were over-capitalized, and because the owning companies refused to take steps to reduce capitalization to a reasonable figure. Selling combines cannot be formed because the baron is an incurable individualist, suspicious of his fellows and incapable of working in organization.

Because all these things are true, I guess that the end of the war will see, not only the victory of the labor union and the beginning of striking changes in the South generally, but also the passing of the cotton-mill baron as a type. Become an anachronism and having already served his purpose, he will vanish from the stage as inexorably as did the gentleman of the agricultural era before him. The New Industrialism will come, and with it a new race of industrial grand dukes, to be recruited, I suppose, from the commercial Babbitts of North and South alike. Now and then, of course, a baron will pass over into the ranks of the new peerage, but, on the whole, he seems to be destined to fade out. The character which made him becomes his doom.

4

NORTH CAROLINA
FACES THE FACTS

(Article, Baltimore *Evening Sun,*
August 29, 1935)

*In this article on Negro lynching, Cash unswervingly went to the
heart of the matter: that lynching had the covert approval of the
majority of Southern whites, including the "best people." Although he did not support the federal anti-lynching laws proposed during the 1930's, arguing that in the charged emotional
atmosphere of the South they would do more harm than good,
Cash later drove home his indictment of the South's "best people"
in* The Mind of the South *manuscript.*

*A*s a Southerner and a North Carolinian, I think I am
able to discover one very hopeful circumstance in
the case of the lynching of a raving-mad black man
at Louisburg, in Franklin county, North Carolina, which
took place recently. It is this: that there is beginning to appear in the South—in North Carolina, anyhow—some willing-
ness to approach the problem of lynching in a realistic spirit.

It has long been the custom, of course, for the chief newspapers in the Southern country to decry lynching as an
inexcusable barbarity. But it has also been the custom to say

that, after all, the South as such was not to be held responsible, that the people who actually lynched were only a handful of degraded poor-whites, that public opinion in general was not in favor of it, and that the "best people" in particular were dead set against it.

The claim was never true, obviously. Take this case at Louisburg for instance. A mob of twenty-five men without masks or disguises took the victim from the Sheriff of Franklin county and five of his deputies in broad day.

Not a blow was struck, not a gun was drawn. The killers simply said they wanted the man, and the Sheriff accommodatingly handed him over. Afterward, in the court of inquiry convoked by Governor Ehringhaus, the Sheriff and his deputies were seized with complete amnesia. They could not recall the makes of the automobiles used by the killers, they could not recall whether or not these automobiles had license plates, and they could not remember that there was a single face in all the twenty-five that they had ever seen before. How absurd that is will be manifest to anybody who knows the rural South, and knows that, in such a county as Franklin, it is always impossible to get together so many as twelve men without the Sheriff and his deputies being able to name at least eleven of them.

The fact is overwhelmingly plain. The hands which actually manipulated rope and trigger at Louisburg may very well have been those of degraded poor-whites. The hands which actually manipulate rope and trigger—or kerosene can and brand—in Southern lynchings generally are very often those of degraded poor-whites, though not always. But the force which really lynched at Louisburg—the force which really lynches everywhere in the South—was and is the force of public opinion.

And when one says public opinion, one shifts the ultimate responsibility straight back upon the "best people"— the ruling class. For these people everywhere very largely determine public opinion, of course. And they do so with particular effectiveness in the South—for two reasons. One of these is that, under the Southern political and economic system, social control is remarkably concentrated in the hands of a relatively small group of landowners, time-merchants, bankers, and the chief lawyers of the county seat. The other reason is historical—that, for seventy-five years, the South, high and low, rich and poor, has been absorbed with almost unparalleled completeness in a single issue; that, as a result of that long obsession, the masses stand to the master class very much as, say, the veterans of Austerlitz and Marengo stood to Bonaparte and his marshals: that they trust them with a marvelous trust, are greatly dependent on their favor for a good opinion of themselves, and look to them always for instruction as to what to think and believe and do.

I suggest nothing so nonsensical as that all Southerners favor lynching, surely. Hundreds of men in North Carolina, thousands in the South, hate it passionately. None the less, the great body of the master class does favor it. On no other hypothesis can we explain the fact that the police officers—hardboiled, small-time politicians, with a very accurate sense of the realities of their world—almost invariably behave as the Franklin county officers behaved.

But the encouraging thing about this case is that this time there were no excuses. This time not a single newspaper in North Carolina, so far as I know—certainly, none of any importance—laid the blame at the door of the poor-whites, not one said that we must be careful not to charge the crime to "the good people of the State."

On the contrary, virtually all of them spoke out with more vigor and more anger than they have ever shown before. And though many of them contented themselves with a pointless lambasting of the Franklin officers, some of them went further and more or less explicitly laid the blame in the quarter where it belongs. It was so with the three chief papers of more or less Liberal leanings—with the Greensboro *Daily News,* the *News and Observer* of Raleigh, and the Charlotte *News.* And, what is much more significant, it was true with the Charlotte *Observer.*

The most powerful journal in the State, this last is immensely conservative, and its policy has always been one uncompromising Southern apology. But this time it not only dispensed with apologetics, it even led the charge upon the fact. Carrying a series of sharp editorials, all pointing more or less definitely toward the truth, it crowned its efforts by printing an editorial article, written by LeGette Blythe, an able member of the staff, which unequivocally proclaimed, first, that it is the "good people" of Franklin county who are to blame for the Louisburg affair; secondly, that these "good people" are exactly of a piece in their attitude with the "good people" of North Carolina and the South generally; and thirdly, that it is high time to face the facts and act upon them.

I have no illusions. Knowing the tremendous compulsives back of the will to lynching in high and low, I think it is going to be a long time yet before the practice is effectually stamped out in the South. Nevertheless, here is plainly a sound beginning at last. Here is unmistakable evidence of a rising tendency—in North Carolina at least—to lay aside the old ferocious Southern sensitiveness and stubborn blindness, and confront the issue. And so here is ground for solid hope.

5

SOUTHLAND TURNS TO BOOKS WITH FULL VIGOR

(Book-page article, Charlotte *News*,
February 9, 1936)

The goodly crop of Southern writers energized by the taunts of Mencken, Cash thought, were still too restricted in subject matter. In wondering, near the end of this article, why no Southerner had yet written a good novel of the Old South or of the New South, Cash was really proposing himself as candidate. He projected an Old South novel in his Guggenheim-fellowship application of 1936, and in 1940 he proposed writing a novel about the New South (the fellowship was granted in 1941).

*F*rom being virtually sterile so far as the production of anything that could rationally be called a literature was concerned, the south has passed in the last two decades to an almost frenzied activity in the field. Today it is grinding out new books faster than any other equal portion of the United States, and a new writer bounces on the scene at least once in every thirty seconds or so. Indeed, in view of the fully geometrical rate at which these new writers are multiplying, and in view of the fact that every freshman of my acquaintance who is making "A's" on his college themes confides in me that he intends to junk the old man's furniture business and pursue a literary career, I estimate that in another ten years at least three-quarters of the (more or less) literate southern population under fifty will be engaged in the production of beautiful letters.

All of which, and though it naturally generates some gloom in me anent the prospects for my own bread and butter (are the damn-yankees going to be able to buy all these books?)—though it sometimes moves me to wish a little that my countrymen did not insist on doing everything they do in quite such a large and extravagant fashion—is no doubt sound ground for the jubilation which it has set off in all proper patriotic quarters. I have to confess, in fact, that, in my less purely personal moods, contemplation of the thing excites me in a dizzy glow faintly reminiscent of those gorgeous days along back in 1916 when I was watching the Rev. Tom Dixon's Ku Kluckers [1] do execution on uppity coons and low-down carpetbaggers, and alternately bawling hysterically and shouting my fool head off. Besides—it proves an old theory of mine. As long ago as my collitch days, I was arguing that Henry Mencken had taken, with his "Sahara of the Bozart," the one certain way to really get the south at the practice of literature in a big way—that whatever its native reluctance, it would never in this world lie under such dirty Yankee words as that. And was I right or was I right?

None the less—. For all my quiet genuine pleasure in seeing the old country thus turn in the wholesale to activities which have always appealed to my private prejudices as desirable and important, I must in my unfortunate and de-

---

[1] The reference is to the notoriously racist motion picture *The Birth of a Nation*, first shown in 1915. Historians credit it with having helped to influence the birth of the modern Ku Klux Klan in that year and with stimulating race riots in the North and Midwest for a decade.

structive way, report that the scene does not yet seem to me to offer justification for complete and unadulterated jubilation—that, for all its gratifying features, it is still open to certain critical objections of the first importance.

The principal thing I have in mind and the only one which I shall attempt to touch on here is that all this writing is already showing a tendency to fall into a few extremely rigid and very narrow patterns. Thus there is the Faulkner–Caldwell pattern—the grand prevailing one at the moment; there is the Maristan Chapman–Paul Green pattern; there is the Peterkin–Heyward pattern; and, though we have as yet had little of it, I have no doubt that there is in the making a tremendous Thomas Wolfe pattern—that in the next ten years we will be deluged with not less than fifty mighty odysseys of the lonely souls of tortured young men in the south. Set aside Cabell and Miss Glasgow (both of whom have done their work), Elizabeth Maddox Roberts, and perhaps Stribling, and there is hardly a writer—hardly a young one at least—in the south who does not fall fatally under one of these headings.

I do not mean that I object to any of these writers per se. William Faulkner is not the transcendent genius or the "angelic" writer which Arnold Bennett made him out to be. But he does write with gripping power, and his single primary theme of violence is authentically a part of the southern scene. So are Caldwell's appalling poor whites automatically a part of that scene, a big part—and the fellow is a magnificent reporter and increasingly a master of drama. If Chapman and Green are engaged in the curious enterprise of reducing the old local color stories of thirty or forty years ago to a kind of faunish realism and at the same time dressing them up in a poetic prose out of John Millington Synge—well, the result in their hands is more pleasing than not. I like Mrs. Peterkin's black men, and if Wolfe is only telling us his own story, I incline to believe that, in the last analysis, no man does more.

What I do object to is the apparent conviction of all the rising young men that there is no way to glory but along the channels marked out by these. I am getting mortally tired of seeing William Faulkner or Mrs. Peterkin multiplied by ten. I am pretty sick of detailed photographs of nigger lynching which are exactly like the other 211 I have read. I'd like to see my poor whites through some other eyes than Caldwell's—and I'd like to see the country represented as being populated by somebody besides these poor whites and the coons. Between Green and "The Playboy of the Western World," I get about all the poetical prose I can absorb. And if every man can tell only his own story, there are a million other ways to do it than through the autobiographical novel, a form already worn so threadbare that only the exceedingly great talent of Wolfe can redeem it from banality.

I think, in short, that there is no reason for the paucity of themes and the poverty of treatment which is on view. There are plainly other—and often bigger—themes lying about untouched. Thus, for one thing, there is no good story of the old south in existence—no true picture of what life in it was like. (I forgot Stark Young and "So Red the Rose"? Far from it. The story is a compound of the old sentimentality and movie melodrama, which not even its excellent writing can save from the oblivion which is already descending upon it.) For another, no one has adequately told any part of the story of the great dream of progress, now ringing slowly to its end—of the rise of mills and towns in the hill-country of the south and its repercussions in the lives of men and women.

And as for treatment—in the absence of any tradition to trammel and bind, treatment ought clearly to be almost infinitely varied.

REALISM AND ROMANCE: SOUTHERN VIEW

(Book-page article, Charlotte *News*,
October 18, 1936)

*As a critic Cash sharply differentiated between sound romanti-
cism and sentimentality, between sound realism and literary
photography. In this article he defined his categories and gave
examples that fell into each.*

Now that *Literature* has finally come upon Dixie, and
at least half the boys and gals currently in our
southern colleges no longer yearn to be governor or
to queen it over society in the old home town but to write
the great American novel or at least the great southern
novel, a question which still asserts itself now and then is
this: ought the said boys and gals, in order to do their duty
by God, the human race, and the Confederate dead, to make
their masterpieces realistic or ought they to make them
romantic?

But for my part, I think they might well make them
neither or either—and I think they might better make them

both. And if you suspect me of merely playing the paradoxical Smart Aleck or of warming up for the psychopathic ward, then let me hasten to say that what I'm really trying to do is to suggest that distinctions are necessary.

When we speak of a romantic novel, what is almost invariably understood is something after the manner of, say, Mr. Thomas Nelson Page—or Mr. Stark Young. And say that a novel is realistic, and what we immediately suppose is that the author has set himself down laboriously to "copy life," to give us actual people and actual scenes from his own experience with photographic exactness—with the additional proviso, of course, that all the people he has known have been unmitigated swine, and all the scenes hog-wallows—after the fashion which has more or less incorrectly been assigned to Mr. Theodore Dreiser and Mr. William Faulkner.

But I venture to think that this is grossly to abuse two perfectly good terms. Nobody ought to write a novel in the fashion of Mr. Thomas Nelson Page, nor yet in that of Mr. Stark Young. But that is not because they are in the romantic tradition—they aren't. But because they are in the sentimental tradition. The charge against them is that they are simply not true. They give us Cloud-Cuckoo land inhabited by cardboard figures, made to move and talk by a machinery taken straight out of the romance of Galahad, the rule of chivalry, and the sermons of Rev. De Witt Talmage. And they give us this, not as Cloud-Cuckoo land but as the Old South; not as cardboard figures in a fantasy but as the actual men and women of the Old South.

Sound romanticism is quite a different thing. It is in nowise equivalent to falsity. It is simply the recognition—and representation—of the fact that man is himself a romantic creature; that there is a strange aspiring and upward-reaching in him; that, condemned to death and inevitable defeat in the flesh, he can and does (and wholly apart from theological determinations) assert his spirit as immortal and incorruptible—a shining sword and a flame against which Time and the grave may not prevail; that he builds up in the little round cell where he dwells his inexplicable images of Beauty and of Glory, and most wistfully serves them in justification of himself before destiny. Serves them imperfectly, in stumbling and frequent apostasy? Oh, yes—no true romanticism could ever forget that—as witness the best loved tale of modern times, that of Sidney Carton. The very essence of true romanticism, indeed, lies precisely in the contrast here.

But if nobody has any business writing a novel after the fashion of Mr. Page or Mr. Young, neither has he any business taking Dreiser or Faulkner as a model without first taking care to understand their method. And in so far as their method is that of mere photography, I think he has no business imitating it at all.

Sound realism is not photography. It can't be. For the business of the novelist, as of all artists, is with essentials. It is his function, exactly, to discover and represent the forms which, under the very terms of the case, do not lie on the surface of the phenomenal world, the forms that nature never makes overtly manifest. To that end he must be free to simplify and arrange, to add to and take away from, to break down and recombine, to turn the elements of a hundred characters, a hundred scenes, a hundred actions, into one. Shelley sums it up after this fashion:

> He will watch from sun to gloom
> The lake-reflected sun illume
> The yellow bees in the ivy bloom;
> Nor heed nor see what things they be,
> But from these create he can
> Forms more real than living man,
> Nurslings of immortality.

Nor does a sound realism mean an exclusive eye for the appalling and the revolting. On the contrary, it is simply the perception and the rendering of man's life as a whole: the refusal to blink any part of it. It may concern itself with running sores and sewers, on the ground that these also exist. But it will hardly imply that these are all. It will recognize that dungheaps and syphilis and dogwood in April and starving babies and the snow that fell last year and the Man on the Cross are all integrally and equally real. It will recognize specifically that man is a romantic creature, and take account of his eternal encounter with destiny, of his infinitely pathetic and his infinitely proud aspiring.

Still, granting that there is, after all, perfectly good room for both a sound romanticism and a sound realism—that these boys and gals who are coming along can go either way in safety—you doubt that they can well go both ways, that the two can be combined in a single author and a single book? I point you to Joseph Conrad's magnificent "Lord Jim," and his scarcely less magnificent "Victory." Here are two of the finest romantic novels ever written in the world. And here also, and precisely, are two of the most perfect and surefooted examples of realism which have appeared on this marvelously wheeling ball.

OLD KARL'S IDEALISM

(Charlotte *News*, February 14, 1937)

As a liberal with his feet on the ground, Cash was too cannily analytical to be beguiled by the siren song of the then-fashionable Popular Front. His concern in this article is not with the conspiratorial nature of the Communist International but with what he considers the soft-headedness of Marxism itself.

This past week I have had my nose in the pages of old Karl Marx again, and as usual I emerge from them feeling vastly sardonic.

I am always amused and exasperated by those people who grow red in the face and shout out denunciations when they hear old Karl mentioned, for most of them quite obviously have never read him. As a matter of fact, there is almost nothing in the old boy to infuriate anybody with a shadow of goodwill in him; there is only a lot of descriptive stuff which every reader above the level of a halfwit will immediately recognize as being at least mainly true, plus an enormous amount of the most seductive and fetching idealizing of the human race ever heard of in the world since Francis of Assisi passed to his reward.

That is what is the matter with the book. That is what was the matter with old Karl. So far from having horns, and for all the fact that there was a streak of deadly hate in him, he was one of the two or three most naive idealists who have lived on this planet. The communism he preached and prophesied is no wicked nightmare but one of the loveliest dreams ever conjured up by the brain of man—and that when measured by the ethical system which Western man prevailingly professes. For the essence of that communist resides precisely in the slogan: "From each according to his capacity, to each according to his need." And if I can read it all, that comes to exactly the same thing as the Golden Rule.

The whole trouble with the dream is that it is too lovely. It assumes that the human race is capable of a high degree of rationality and disinterested cooperation, that men will of their own accord give over their lusts to exploit and rule one another, and take to living together in genuine brotherly harmony. For that, of course, is precisely what old Karl does assume. There was to be a dictatorship of the proletariat, certainly, but only for long enough to abolish the foundations of the old order of society. The underdog was to be made the upper dog, and having been made the upper dog, he was to use his power just long enough to make sure that the old upper dogs did not once more get into the saddle, and having done that he was voluntarily to abandon that power, and enter on equal terms with all men upon the era of voluntary and intelligent cooperation.

Merely to state the proposition is to reduce it to a manifest absurdity. There never has been a dictatorship of the proletariat .in the world; what Russia has had has been simply the dictatorship of Lenin and Trotsky, and since of Stalin, with the proletariat having exactly nothing to do with it. And for my part, I cannot imagine how an actual dictatorship of the proletariat could ever anywhere be brought about. But in any case, this much I am willing to bet my head on: if the proletariat ever actually got its hand on a dictatorship, ever actually got to be the upper dog, it would never voluntarily let go till the last lone cow was home in the barn and Gabriel was trumpeting open the pearly gates. The notion that it would is simply a child of Jean Jacques Rousseau's dogma that man is, in his primitive shape, an inherently noble animal, and that therefore the masses, being closer to the primitive, can be trusted to be more noble in conduct than their masters.

That is pure nonsense, of course. The fact is that the closer we get to the primitive the less noble the human creature becomes, on the average. For humanity is not inherently noble. And what is more—but hold! I am speaking of "humanity" and "the human race" quite as though I belonged to another and superior species. Alas, I shall have to climb down. I shall have to report that, after long and hopeful inspection of myself, I am bound to plead guilty—to confess woefully that all I have said and all that I shall hereinafter say applies to me, too.

What I was going on to say, though, was that humanity is not only not noble inherently but also not in any other fashion—that it is noble neither in its primitive shape nor in its most developed shape. Not by and large. Not habitually and continuously. It has its moments, no doubt. At least certain individuals do. And perhaps there is even occasionally an individual who is predominantly noble, though I frankly doubt it.

But for the body of us most of the time: we are not intelligent. We see only to the end of our noses—to the tiny limit of the immediate personal benefit we have in view. We are ruled by ego. We are out to get ours, and damn the hindmost. And we are quite incapable of extended voluntary cooperation.

I am blaming none of us. I have a notion that we are inevitably what we are because of everything that has gone before us from the first day of the world. It seems likely that, in view of our late Neanderthal cousin, we have done fairly well with the mere forty thousand years or so since he flourished. Even if the Cro-Magnon brother had a bigger brain than we have, we can still argue on our side that he probably ate his fellows and that we don't.

All the same, I think we'll do well to keep the facts in the case well in view. They'll save us from succumbing to the seductions of old Karl's vision, with the reflection that, at our present rate of progress, it will be at least another forty thousand years or so before any such thing as actual communism has any chance of succeeding. And on the other hand, they ought to save us from getting so senselessly mad when his name is mentioned—from such heaping up of stupid epithets on a man who (for all the fact that his doctrine, like all doctrines that do not fit the facts of our nature, is raising no end of hell) hardly deserves them.

8

AWAY IN
A MANGER

(Charlotte *News*, December 24, 1937)

Overexposed to fundamentalist faith in his youth, Cash thereafter had small use for conventional churchgoing religion. People who gave him up as an unbeliever, however, were mistaken in their man, for Cash always kept a Bible by his side and read Ecclesiastes with a fine appreciation of that worldly-wise Preacher whom the Hebrews called Koheleth. To Cash religion meant an experience of awe, and this Christmas editorial is typical of his emotionally moving writing, admittedly unorthodox, on religious lines.

*A*s *we like* to think of it, it was very quiet and still in that simple place on that morning. Only the babe, red-faced as all the new-born are red-faced, with his tiny fists pressed to his mouth, sleeping in the stone manger. Only the mother—she was afterward to be called the Mother of God and the Mother of Sorrows and the Star of the Sea and many other fine and lovely names—sleeping on the straw with no other glory about her as yet save the pale beatitude that lies upon the face of all women who sleep after giving birth. Only the man who stood as father to the child, keeping watch. That and no more, save the cocks hailing in the lonely day, a donkey stamping now and then in a near-by stall, the hurried, sounding footfall of a traveler belated in these busy times of tax-gathering, and the soft rustle of the breathing of the sleeping pair.

These three alone in the pensive morning with the mystery of birth, and the mystery of life which is contained in birth, and the mystery of death which is foreshadowed in birth. So we like to think of them. And so, indeed, did the old primitive painters of Italy and Belgium sometimes like to represent them when the influence of the Byzantine splendor and the cult of earthly kingship were not too much upon them.

There are many facets to the spirit of this day, to be certain, as the tradition has come down to us through the centuries. And one of the best of them is that which Shakespeare meant when he recorded that,

> *At Christmas I no more desire a rose*
> *Than wish a snow in May's new-fangled mirth . . .*

What he meant, of course, was all those things we know best in the pages of Washington Irving—the creature delight of sitting warm and snug by the fire while Winter reigns outside, the heavy-laden tables, the fruits of the gracious and abundant earth gathered before us, the bright-faced, breathless gabble of children, the generous laughter ringing through the house, the gentle goodfellowship. And very fine and precious things they all are, we think. We do exceedingly well, we people of the European heritage, to make this the jovial, joyous day we do make it, with St. Nicholas as the symbol of it all.

But over and behind all that, though not in conflict with it, is something else—that this of all days is the day which is dedicated to the great simplicities which are the great mysteries. The whole story of Jesus is in some sense the story of man's passage through those simplicities which so exceed understanding that all men become as one before them. This is the day, then, for the humble heart and the contemplative mind—for the renewal of the sense of how strange and how marvelous and how splendid is this common way we go.

And so, it is as we have painted them that we like to think of them, these holy three, alone in the stillness of that morn, the Christmas morn.

9

GETTING
MR. GANNETT

(Charlotte *News*, March 30, 1938)

*As one of the few editorials for which Cash was given a by-line,
this one fully attests his libertarian concern. The Reorganization
Bill so violently opposed by the anti-New Deal publisher Frank E.
Gannett (he foresaw a Roosevelt dictatorship) was simply an act
to reorganize the Executive Department, a long-overdue reform.
For Gannett's ideas Cash had small use; for Gannett's rights Cash
had an eloquent defense.*

*M*r. Frank Gannett, publisher of the Gannett
chain of newspapers, is hopping mad these
days. And for once I think he has excellent
cause. Mr. Gannett is not one of my heroes. I think, as a
working newspaperman, that large chains of newspapers,
such as his, are unhealthy and dangerous. Moreover, it seems
to me that Mr. Gannett's attitude toward the President of
the United States is generally arbitrary and rabid. If he has
ever found a single good thing in the whole body of things
Franklin Roosevelt has done, I am not aware of it. On the
contrary, he inveighs against every move as a diabolical
scheme to destroy democracy, deprive us of our historical

liberties, and hand us straightway over to communism or fascism.

But in one of the many excited communications with which he regularly favors this office, Mr. Gannett asks a question:

> How would you feel tonight if two agents of the Government walked into your office or home, threatened you with jail, and ordered you to appear in your nation's capital tomorrow morning at ten o'clock with all your correspondence, letters, records, checks, books of accounts, all written records of every kind that you possess, for examination by inquisitors?

To which I am bound to respond that I'd be hopping mad, too.

The thing to which Mr. Gannett refers did not, as I understand it, happen to him in his capacity as a newspaper publisher. Merely, the Senate Lobby Committee (the so-called Black Committee) subpoenaed him in his capacity as president of his own outfit set up to fight the President's reorganization bill which was passed by the Senate Monday—the outfit he has named The National Committee to Uphold Constitutional Government. I don't like that name. I believe it is an appeal under false colors. And I don't believe the reorganization bill involves any Constitutional issue.

Nevertheless, the Constitution guarantees Mr. Gannett, along with all the rest of us, certain rights, to wit:

1—The freedom of speech.

2—The right of petition.

3—Freedom from searches and seizures of his person or papers save upon a warrant charging him with a crime against the laws, said warrant to issue only upon probable cause, and to specify the papers to be seized.

And in this case, there is no warrant. There is no charge that Mr. Gannett has committed a crime against the laws of the United States. There is no probable cause. There is no specification of the papers to be seized. There is only a blanket subpoena issued by this Senate committee in the hope of finding something with which to smear him, and failing that, still to make it so hot and unpleasant for him that other men will be deterred from following the course he has followed. In short, there is nothing but a manifest attempt by the Senate of the United States to do, by the use of subpoena, what it is forbidden to do directly. And, of course, the Senate has no right to do that.

If Mr. Gannett appeals to passion and prejudice with the name he tags on his organization, the right to appeal to passion and prejudice is inevitably a part of the right of free speech. But what he says is untrue? That is only a matter of opinion. He undoubtedly believes it is true. But even if he didn't—the right to peddle about what one knows to be untrue is also an inevitable part of the right of free speech. But Mr. Gannett has been stirring up people all over the country to deluge Congress with telegrams protesting the reorganization bill? That is an essential part both of the right to free speech and the right to circulate a petition. It is no violation of the law, furnishes no probable cause, and could not serve as the basis of a search and seizure warrant.

Mr. Gannett is strictly within his rights, therefore, when he refuses to obey the subpoena. And I trust that, if the Senate is foolish enough to attempt to force him, he will win in the courts. For such methods plainly have no place in America.

10

RUM, ROMANISM
AND REBELLION;
or, RIDE FOR A
LEARNED MAN

(Book-page article, Charlotte *News*,
June 12, 1938)

As W. J. Eulenspiegel, Cash attempted one of his rare experiments at humor as he parodied a novel of the Agrarian school, portraying himself as "Mr. Casshe, the villain of the piece." As W. J. Eulenspiegel he was the male counterpart of Tillie Eulenspiegel, a pseudonym adopted by his fellow book-page contributor Mary Ross Northrop. Mary and Jack had met for the first time only a month before, but already he had announced to her that they would be married.

Mr. John Jacob Neanderthal has written a book and seems to think he has discovered something. Well, he should've ast me. I knew about it all the time.

Mr. Neanderthal is admittedly the first citizen of North Stumptown Landing, South Carolina, where the brackish waters of the Pee Dee basin daily back up to his cabin door.

Tidewater literature inevitably carries a burden of mould and mildew, but despite the hoary precept Mr. Neanderthal so delightedly presents to an indifferent world, some of the salt tang of the marshes has crept into his book, "The Conflict of Present Day Atavistic Agrarianism With the Neo-Sapphic Outlook of Populist Survivors in Ante-Bellum Areas of the Deep South."

The great truism this cape-jessamine Jason seems to regard as his personal Golden Fleece snatched from the slavering jaws of limbo by his own strong-arm perception, is simply this—that young love and mellow moonlight will conquer all in spite of hell, high water, and the miasmic magnolia-cum-friedcatfish economy that has suffocated the South more than half a century. Now did you ever?

Well, anyway, Sally Lou, the girl-wife, and Jim John, the boy-husband, are presented with a skill which proves Mr. Neanderthal has something on the ball. We see Sally Lou in all her stark languescence, the petal soft skin, the great dreamy eyes, and we feel a poignant ache in our hearts at those calluses this pearl among fishwives got from standing around barefooted on hot wharves, waiting for the shrimp boats to come in.

It was there on the dock that Sally Lou first met Mr. Casshe, the villain of the piece, a college man if there ever was one. He wore a crew sweater bearing the varsity letter he had won for debating. Sally Lou hadn't much book learning and it was hard for her to make out what the letters were, but she thought they were I.C.S. He dealt in shrimp futures.

And now here comes the exciting part. Really, I like to died along about here. I know it's silly of me and I always swear I'll never do it again, but I turned over to the back of the book to see how it was going to end, it got so good.

Well, it seems that Jim John was the best shrimp fisher at the Landing. He would go out into the dawn empty-handed, and come back into the sunset with such a catch he had to have pockets sewed onto the sails to take care of the overflow. It was awful when he had to take a reef, because a lot of mad shrimp would fall down on him and bite him, but he stood it for the sake of the little lady at home.

But soon he began to notice something amiss. To make a long story short (and why not), Casshe had been telling Sally Lou that the sea would get Jim John eventually, and if she wanted to keep him for herself she'd better take him upstate and go back to the land. Casshe had told her about the benevolent Agrarian Group, formed way off there in Nashville for the purpose of getting everybody back to the land, and who (whom?) had for years been chartering relief trains to bring inland thousands of shanty-boaters, barge dwellers, showboat companies, river gamblers, and others who made their living upon the treacherous deeps.

"Honey, we got to git us a plow instid o' this hyere trawler," Sally Lou moaned. And I moaned right along with her, because I knew all along that what this Casshe wanted was Jim John's boat, which he had discovered was coated with some stuff Jim John had invented to attract shrimp, and that he didn't give an old broken singletree whether the two lovers got back to the land or not. All he wanted was to insure the futures of a lot of steady shrimp.

Now, when I review a book I never give away the plot, so let's just say that everything comes out all right in the end. You've had enough to get the idea.

But have you got it?

Well, nobody can say I'm not paternal to my little readers, so here it is.

The obvious conclusion to be drawn from what some people may consider this kindergarten exposition on an old, old theory, is that the Agrarian crowd are urging all these people to go back to the land so they can take over all marine industry for themselves. And furthermore, all other industry as well. When the entire industrial division of mankind has taken to farming, the Agrarians will get the business and finance gravy. Unless, as I suspect, they are but tools in the hire of Wall Street! Or—Moscow? Who knows—perhaps both.

11

THE SOUTH
HIDES ITS EYES

(Book-page article, Charlotte *News*,
October 2, 1938)

*Cash had the utmost scorn for the kind of Southern "leader" who,
on hearing the South termed the nation's "Number One Economic
Problem," did nothing positive, but cried out instead that he and
his region had been insulted. In this article Cash named names:
Senator Olin D. Johnston (South Carolina Democrat) the kind of
New Dealer who strove to shout "nigger" louder than any com-
peting politician; and anti-New Deal Senators Josiah W. Bailey
(North Carolina Democrat) and Walter F. George (Georgia
Democrat).*

*T*wo of the gloomiest things about the South that I
know are the reaction to the report of the National
Emergency Council that the South is the nation's
"Number One Economic Problem," and the fact that I can
nowhere descry any political or economic leadership which
seems in case to deal with the matter realistically.

Before me, as I write, lies the report of a speech by a
gentleman wherein he adverts to the report and sets himself
down as believing that it is not true. Not true! That report

was based entirely on the findings of Dr. Howard Odum's "Southern Regions of the United States," and the United States Census Reports, and behind it lie many years of systematic examination and tabulation of facts by a corps of workers trained in gathering just such data. There is not a single statement in the report which is not backed by an enormous amount of material which has been checked over and over for errors. And all that material adds up the fact that, by every measure known to sociologists, the South shows a vast and accelerating lag—that, under all the indices of civilization, the region, which is potentially one of the richest on earth, is increasingly backward as against the rest of the nation.

To say that you don't believe it is true is precisely as rational as though you had said that you do not believe it is true that the earth is round, simply because you had never taken the trouble to examine the evidence.

The gentleman whom I quote is not, however, very important, and if he were the only one it would not matter. But alas, he is only echoing a general chorus. Over in Tennessee a gentleman who represents the Southern States Industrial Council was so infuriated by the report that he wrote directly to the National Emergency Council denouncing it for having "insulted" the South! His organization, as I understand it, exists for the purpose of getting factories to come South, and I suppose he was partly actuated by fear that the report might scare some of them away. But to say that a recitation of statistics and facts is an insult—whew!

Nor does it at all stop with him. The Richmond Times-Dispatch, the Norfolk papers, The Montgomery Advertiser, the Atlanta papers, The Raleigh News and Observer, The Charlotte News, The Greensboro News, The Chattanooga News, and a few others did, indeed, accept the report as authoritative and concern themselves only with what might be done about it. But if the papers I see are representative—

and I see a great many of them—the reaction of the greater part of the Southern press was most remarkably like that of the gentleman I have just cited. "What! Have we then nothing to be celebrated for?"—Such was the general tenor.

And when we turn from the newspapers to the politicians—oh, yes, there were politicians in the South who greeted the report with open arms and from the housetops loudly proclaimed their belief in it. But who were they? Why, simply the Olin Johnstons. Men who have hitched themselves to the New Deal wagon for political purposes and who loudly applaud anything the New Deal does, not because they have looked into or understand or give two hoots about the merits of the case, but simply because it promises to be a good vote-getting device. Men whom the South quite naturally distrusts.

But the overwhelming majority of Southern politicians rejected it out of hand. Josiah William Bailey came down to North Carolina and made a speech to the Young Democrats at Raleigh in which he denounced it by innuendo all the way through, and made appeal to all the old bloody shirt themes to rouse up sentiment against it. George of Georgia did much the same thing. And so all along the line. Indeed, many of them actually gave their clientele to understand that the thing is somehow a menace to White Supremacy in Dixie.

It is a prospect which is baffling. These men are the ablest men in politics in the South. And yet, faced with a factual report, they refuse to consider and recognize it—perhaps even to look into the evidence upon which it is based, but simply decree that it is not so and have recourse to nonsense about "Sherman's Second March."

Obscurantism has always been the greatest curse under which the South has had to labor. There are understandable historical reasons why it should have developed a vast defensive-complex during the slavery–Civil War–Reconstruction battle, why it should have insisted for many years that it had absolutely nothing wrong with it but was in fact the nearest thing to paradise on earth. But that sort of thing is too utterly dangerous now for any man with any intelligence or sense of responsibility to indulge in. The South faces pressing problems—the problem of how to use the resources so as to increase its wealth, without merely giving it away as under the idiotic Mississippi Plan—the problem of what to do with the tenant farmers and croppers who in ever-increasing numbers are being thrown out of employment and onto the relief rolls by the machine and the decline of the cotton economy—the problem of a decent living for its Negroes and its white slum-dwellers, who presently pile up such an appalling disease and crime bill for Dixie precisely because it does not afford them that decent living.

And not to face them, to go on yelling that everything is lovely and that all we need is to be let alone, is simply to invite disaster. Any man who does it ought to be retired from public life as certainly as the Olin Johnstons.

12

WHAT IS
A LIBERAL?

(Book-page article, Charlotte *News*,
November 6, 1938)

Cash's idea of liberalism was not the acceptance of crackpot re-
form panaceas, not the simplistic personal liberty of John Stuart
Mill, not the wide-open laissez-faire *"liberalism" identified with*
Adam Smith, but an open-minded acceptance of whatever useful
elements they offered as filtered through an intelligent skepticism.

*I*t seems to me that the good old word, liberal, is in imminent danger of getting to mean nothing at all. For it
is being bandied about as an equivalent of "good," and
made to mean whatever the speaker or writer wants it to
mean.

Thus the President of the United States says it means
anybody who is hospitable to new ways of tackling old
problems. And under that definition proceeds blithely to
apply it to Mr. Sheridan Downey, Democratic candidate for
a California seat in the Senate of the Congress of the United
States—who got the nomination by campaigning for the
"Ham and Eggs" scheme of "$30 every Thursday." But, of
course, Mr. Downey is not liberal. He is either a pretty

unpleasant sort of demagogue who is playing on the ignorance of the unfortunate or he is a crackpot on his own
account.

On the other hand, if you'll listen to Dorothy Thompson
and Co., a liberal in our time is still exactly what he was in
the nineteenth century—a person who believes in complete
civil liberty and the economic and political philosophy of
Adam Smith and John Stuart Mill. But that is nonsense, too.
The plain fact is that the economic philosophy of Adam
Smith and the governmental philosophy of Mill have not
worked out as they themselves confidently predicted they
would. We have not got everybody comfortable and well-
fed. Competition has not kept down the appearance of aggregations of economic power that are as formidable and as
perilous to actual democracy as any aggregations of political
power that ever existed or that exist now. Instead, we have
got millions of people who haven't bread to eat—and grand
dukes of wealth, who are often definitely anti-social in their
conduct. And nobody who is in favor of merely letting things
stand still or who imagines that our ills can be cured by a
few slight "reforms" can rightly be called a liberal.

Yet I do not believe it is impossible to define the word
satisfactorily in general terms. Certainly, a liberal is in favor
of the rights of free speech, free assembly, etc., which the
New Deal shows itself pretty indifferent to sometimes, as in
the case of its continuance to play ball with Hague of Jersey
City, and as in the case of the Senator from Indiana who
wants to gag the newspapers.[1] On the other hand, a liberal
is just as certainly hospitable to new ways of solving old

---

[1] Cash referred to Senator Sherman Minton (Indiana Democrat),
who was to end his public career on the U. S. Supreme Court. In 1938
Senator Minton introduced a bill making it a felony punishable by two
years in jail and a fine of $1,000 to $10,000 to publish a "known un-
truth." The guilty publication would be suspended from the mails for
six months. After taking vigorous editorial condemnation for sponsoring
such a bill, Minton dropped it.

problems, and does not believe that they can be solved in terms of philosophies that have already blown up. Merely, he insists that these new ways of solving the problems shall be such as are compatible with the preservation of civil liberty and with sincerity and intelligence. So far as that goes, the liberal has always had a strong bias in favor of the underdog, and that bias will naturally be stronger these days. But the true liberal has always been a man intelligent enough to know that the underdog's cause is not to be saved by schemes which are impossible of fulfillment, like the Downey scheme. And he has always been sincere and intelligent enough to insist that any program put forward for the benefit of the underdog shall be capable of adding up logically to that end.

That is the chief criticism of the New Deal. I do not believe any genuine liberal can fail to be wholeheartedly for its announced objectives. I do not believe, either, that it can be denied that it has gone a long way toward the realization of those objectives in many respects. Nevertheless, some of its schemes are obviously at odds with other of its schemes, and often it is manifestly both insincere and unintelligent. Under those circumstances, the true liberal will certainly be the man who remembers that skepticism is, after all, the very essence of the spirit of the liberal tradition.

Ah, well, perhaps I do not define it, after all. And even if I do, perhaps the liberal is only a quixotic soul who is doomed in the modern world. Maybe there is no way out which really faces and attempts to solve modern problems, and which at the same time can be reconciled with the liberties whose names at least we have so long revered. But it is what we have to hope and strive for—or make up our minds to surrender to totalitarianism.

13

HIS SISTER KNEW
TOM WOLFE WELL

(Feature article, Charlotte *News*, July 30, 1939)

*Shortly before this interview with the sister of Thomas Wolfe,
Cash had visited his fiancée, who was then working in Asheville,
and they both made a pilgrimage to Wolfe's grave in Riverside
Cemetery. Cash had at first envied Wolfe his success, so striking
by comparison with his own obscurity, but eventually came to a
just appreciation of Wolfe's stature. Wolfe's early death seems to
have shaken Cash, who was well aware that the two of them had
been born in the same year, 1900, Wolfe on October 3 and Cash
on May 2.*

Sitting in the lobby of the Selwyn Hotel, Mrs. Ralph
Wheaton, of 48 Spruce Street, Asheville, told me
about the death of Thomas Wolfe.

Mrs. Wheaton is Tom Wolfe's sister Mabel, older than
the novelist by ten years. You will remember her if you have
read "Look Homeward, Angel" and "Of Time and the River."
Mabel Wheaton looks remarkably like her brother even for a
sister. There is a certain softening of the lines in these Wolfe
faces, a distribution of the bony structure, a flattening of
round surfaces, which strongly suggests the Indians of the

Southwest or the peasant types of Central Europe—or Brittany or Provence. I have seen brown-faced women about Arles, where all the strains of the North and the Mediterranean have met and merged, who reminded me a great deal of Mrs. Wheaton—of Thomas Wolfe. Contemplation and force: these are the qualities in those faces that immediately impress you. The brown eyes look at you with a penetrating directness, give you the impression of extraordinary concentration. And there is something else there, too—a feeling of profound kindness and understanding, an eager will to like and be liked, the absence of the mean little hostility and suspicion, the will to impress, with which most of us encounter strangers.

There was a time back in October, 1929, when life was not pleasant in Asheville for the Wolfes, including Mabel Wheaton. "Look Homeward, Angel" had just been published and the town was buzzing with the outrage of little people who had not yet learned that they had been projected into something at least resembling immortality, who retaliated by pointing scornfully to the things Wolfe had revealed about his own family—none of which came to anything but the admission that they were human. But Mabel Wheaton wrote her brother a letter asserting her absolute faith in his intention, her understanding of what he was about. He replied by telegram—for he himself was already troubled by what he knew the inevitable reaction would be, as he afterward revealed in "The Story of a Novel," and besides he was a fellow of impulsive generosity, quick to respond to any warm gesture with another in kind.

"No novel," that telegram said in effect, "should ever be judged by line and detail but only as a whole. And when you look at it that way, you will see that I have painted all of you, all the Wolfes and all of Asheville, as a great people." Looking at Mabel Wheaton, you know what he meant.

She has had her share of the ups and downs which make

PART II: *A Reader*

up our passage under the sun. In her girlhood, she was a singer in vaudeville for a while. Then she married Ralph Wheaton, whom Asheville still calls a Yankee though he left Ohio 30 years ago. Ralph sold cash registers, made a lot of money. They lived in Grove Park in those days, the Wheatons —were the rich kin of the Wolfes. Then Ralph got caught in the boom spirit which struck Asheville in the Twenties, and which Tom Wolfe has described in "Boom Town" and various chapters of "Of Time and the River"—lost his money. His health gave out about that time, too, and the cash register company dismissed him. (You can read the story of the Wheaton's cash register days in a story "The Company" which Tom Wolfe wrote and Mike Gold published in the New Masses.) After that, the Wheatons moved to Washington, where Mabel ran a rooming house for several years. Tom Wolfe, home from Guggenheim fellowship days in Europe, and writing "Of Time and the River" in a Brooklyn lodging house, used to come down to Washington to see them when he got too lonely, which was pretty often. Lately the Wheatons have been living in Florida. One evening Mrs. Wheaton went out to a neighborhood movie, an automobile struck her and broke her leg. She walks on crutches now, her leg in a cast, her foot bare and swollen. At present they are in Asheville. When Mabel Wheaton is well they will go back to Washington, where she will run a book shop.

But if Mabel Wheaton by ordinary [standards] looks remarkably like Tom Wolfe, she almost becomes Tom Wolfe over again when she talks—she talks a great deal—and especially when she talks of her brother. The words come with the same torrential rush that you find in his books, and there is a feeling of image piling upon image so rapidly that the tongue is unable to keep up with the brain. The effect is a little incoherent at first, but it all turns out in the end to have its pattern.

She reaches back into the past to dig up a picture of Tom

Wolfe as a great lumbering boy with his sleeves halfway up
to his elbows, Tom Wolfe debating in the graduating exer-
cises at the North State Fitting School in Asheville, her pride
in him as she stood outside the hall and heard Wolfe charging through the crowd to her shouting, "my voice won for
me!" He had had the foghorn voice which was his in manhood since he was eleven years old. Tom Wolfe, handed a
check for $10,000 by the man from Harper's, turning away
to stare out the window of the Chelsea Hotel with tears in
his eyes—pouring out his joy in a letter to her that at last
somebody had had faith enough in him to give him more
money than he had ever seen before, for a book he had not
yet written. Oh, he would justify that if it tore the heart out
of him. He would write the finest novel he could write—he'd
show 'em. Never in his life was he ever to quite get it through
his head that he had already arrived. Occasionally his pride
rose up and asserted itself, but for the most of the time he
remained a humble and wistful boy.

All that, and a thousand things more, as Mabel Wheaton
tells you about the death of her brother. She was with Tom
Wolfe in his last days.

He had gone out there to Seattle, to the West, to escape—
from what he did not quite know, from all the oppressions of
all living. "You can't go home," he had written her from New
York on the eve of the journey—on that theme had been
writing "The Web and the Rock." And now he had been ill
for weeks in the Providence Hospital at Seattle. His brother,
Fred, who runs the Bluebird Ice Cream Co. in Spartanburg,
was out there. But the ice cream business needed Fred, and
Tom needed to be looked after during his convalescence
from pneumonia. So Mabel Wheaton closed up her rooming
house, sent Ralph off to his people in Florida, and went to
Seattle.

Tom Wolfe had fallen off—50 pounds. When she got him
up from the hospital bed and dressed him, she had to fasten

up the slack in his waistband with two safety pins in the back of his pants. But it made him look better. He was handsome now. He put his hands in front of his belly. "I can do without that for good," he grinned. And sickness had done something for his skin. The Viennese Jewish doctor from Vienna came in and showed them some X-rays. The pneumonia shadow which had been big as a hat once was down to the size of a dollar now. Yes, Tom Wolfe could go. There were some other X-rays, but that was just a matter of form. It was all right now. Tom Wolfe sat on the edge of his bed and grinned at his sister. "Everything's going to be all right now, isn't it, Mabel?" She said, "Of course, Tom."

But first she must go out and rent the best apartment in the best hotel in town. She demurred on the score of economy, but he would not hear. "I've got it now," he said. "We never have had it, but we're going to have it now." And then she must buy food according to his loving specifications. Huge steaks, loin lamb chops, French bread, Roquefort cheese, he'd tell her how to make a real salad, so much olive oil, so much vinegar, so much pepper, so much salt. "We've never had it, but we're going to have it now."

When they helped him into the automobile, he climbed into the back seat, lay back among his bags. He cocked his hat on the back of his head. "Well, we're out!" he boomed, grinning.

But at the apartment he felt weak, had to go to bed. And then, while Mabel Wheaton was busy with the preparation of the food he had wanted, there came a telegram—from Dr. Watts of the Providence Hospital staff, who was away at Bellingham. They had developed and examined those X-rays. "Abscess or tumor of the brain."

On the phone she talked to Dr. George W. Swift, the celebrated Western neurologist. "So Watts has taken to diagnosing the brain!" he growled and came over. "Tom," said the doctor, a tall and handsome fellow, who was himself to die within five months, "I've read your books. You are a great fellow." Tom said, "I know you, Doctor. You're a great fellow yourself."

"Tom, would you like for me to examine you?"

"Sure," said Tom, grinning. He knew nothing of the telegram. "But I'm all right. I want to get out of here in a few days and go down to Palo Alto." He had some friends down there, Dr. Russell Lee and his wife, Dorothy.

Swift tested Tom's reflexes. "Um, pretty good," he said. Then he went over and looked out the window at the dark waters of Puget Sound.

"Tom," he said, fingering his face, "where is your mother?"

Wolfe slowly froze. "Why—why, she's in Asheville, North Carolina. But I don't want to go back home yet, Doctor. I've got to go to Palo Alto."

"Oh, no, you haven't, Tom. You're a very sick man. And you've got to go back East to the Johns Hopkins and the finest brain man there is—now, tonight. They come to me from all over the West to work on their brains, but they don't like me sometimes."

Tom grinned weakly. "That's when you fail, eh, Doctor."

So that night the journey began. Tom sat on the edge of the bed in the drawing room and grinned. "Everything's going to be all right, isn't it, Mabel."

"Of course," she said, "it's going to be all right, Tom."

Day and night the train rolled Eastward across the continent. Whistling through the mighty mountains and over the great plains, past millions of incurious faces. He had written much about trains. Their whistling as she climbed up from the south and east through the hills of old Catawba, and shouted away westward along the French Broad, of the dream of the power and the glory which stirred in a boy as he listened, and the dream of the far splendid places to which they hurried. Of trains sweeping down through the vast reach of the American land, trains in France, Germany, Russia, England, Italy. But he heard and knew little of their passage now. For most of the time the nurse kept him asleep. Once or twice he awakened, grinned at his sister. "Everything's going to be all right, isn't it, Mabel?"

"Of course, Tom," she said.

At Chicago, Tom's mother joined them.

In Baltimore, Dr. Walter Dandy shook his head. One chance in twenty, he reckoned. Mabel Wheaton a little resented that. She thought he was merely trying to increase the miraculousness of the cure. Of course, everything was going to be all right. Tom Wolfe could not die now. He had too many books still to be written.

"Tom," said Dr. Dandy, "I want to cut a little hole in the back of your head, a little wee hole like that. Do you mind?"

Tom grinned. "Of course not, Doctor. Go ahead."

But a moment after he fell to talking of what a fine hotel they had got into.

But Mabel Wheaton knew that Tom Wolfe would die, the evening after the operation when she attempted to go into his room. She had a premonition, had come to reassure herself. The nurse shooed her firmly away, closed the door. But she had glimpsed his face. And now she fled down the long corridors of the Hopkins, through the streets to the rooming house where Fred and his mother were staying. The mother was out. Fred she found kneeling.

"Come quick," she panted, "Tom is dying!"

"Mabel!" said Fred, "you've been sounding Tom's requiem for two days. Tom's all right. You better kneel down here with me and pray."

But her vehemence at length infected him with alarm also, and together they hurried back to the hospital. Tom Wolfe had been dead five minutes when they arrived.

Mabel took him, still warm, into her arms, kissed him again and again, turned his head with the self-torture of grief to look at the incision made by the knife. The brother, beside himself, implored the doctor to do something. "Bring him back, for ten minutes, five minutes, one minute! I want to talk to him!"

"You do not understand," Mabel told him. "Tom is dead."

So Thomas Wolfe died. Afterward part of him did come home again. Once more the great train climbed up through the old hills of Catawba, and passed on westward along the French Broad, leaving another mound behind in the Asheville cemetery.

14

A FANATIC MENACES CIVILIZATION

(Editorial, Charlotte *News*, September 1, 1939)

In reading this editorial in the context of Cash's mounting distress over the menace of Hitlerism, one detects the editorialist's virtual sense of relief that the issue has at last been joined. Whatever or whoever created Hitler is not the issue. "Even though John Jones himself inoculated his dog with the virus of hydrophobia, the dog is still mad and must be dealt with as mad dogs are dealt with."

*T*he myth built up by many people that Adolf Hitler was essentially a shrewd bluffer, who, with clairvoyant power, knew instinctively just how far he could safely go, and who had no intention of going a whit further—that myth is blown to pieces. We know now, what should have been apparent from the very tone of "Mein Kampf"—that the man is a fanatical hysteric who identifies himself with God, who believes that he is resistless, and who meant all along to have all his way even though it involved a world war and the deaths of millions on millions.

Gone, too, is the myth that, however hysterical Hitler himself was, the German people at large remained sane and reasonable. Where are those generals who, as it was said, were going, when it was clear that war impended, to step in and control him as they once controlled the Kaiser? And where are those common people who did not want war and who were going to rise up and make it plain to Hitler that they would not have war?

Those generals are this morning directing the rape of Poland—the systematic murder of women and children in Warsaw—the systematic killing off of Polish soldiers. And those common people are shrieking in the streets "Heil Hitler!" and "Sieg Heil!" and "We want to see our Fuehrer!"

The Western World faces now what it should have realized long ago—that Naziism is no civilized philosophy made a little grotesque by a few wild aberrations, but a system invented by a gang of criminals for the deliberate purpose of taking a whole nation back into barbarism, and using it as an instrument to carry barbarism over the whole earth. Germany now is as strictly a barbarian horde as was that which Genghis and his sons and grandsons fetched out of the Great Gobi and over all Asia and far into Europe. Its purpose is naked and ruthless conquest by the sword—conquest which spares neither woman nor child. And, for brutality, the man who heads it makes Genghis, Tamerlane, Attila, Genseric, Theodoric—any of the old barbarian conquerors—look pale by comparison. To gratify his ambition, they say, Tamerlane at Bagdad raised a pyramid of a hundred thousand skulls. To gratify his, Adolf Hitler proposes to raise one of many millions of skulls.

But the good man made an honest effort for peace with his sixteen points, and was turned down? There will not be many people left to believe anything so foolish. Plebiscite? There were to be plebiscites in Czechoslovakia. An international commission to have charge of the plebiscites? There was an international commission which was to have charge of the plebiscites in Czechoslovakia. What a plebiscite means in his language we know well, from the cases of the Saar, Austria, Czechland. They mean the importation of the Gestapo and thousands of thugs in brown shirts—the systematic terrorization of the population into staying away from the polls or voting for Hitlerism.

But still he did have a just claim when he demanded "self-determination" for Danzig, with its German population? Did he, with his legions lording it over Czechland and Slovakia? Did he, when in the same breath he demanded the Corridor, which is predominantly inhabited by Poles? Did he, when Danzig controls two-thirds of Poland's Baltic trade, and to give it to him meant that Poland became his economic and so his political prisoner?

In point of fact, Danzig and the Corridor have little to do with the real question at issue here. Hitler wanted these merely by way of strangling Poland to death and establishing his tyranny—the worst that man has known since the Dark Ages—as he has established it over Austria and Czechoslovakia. And he wanted that merely to the end of preparing himself eventually to establish it over all Europe and the Western world, as you may read in his own "Mein Kampf" and in Mr. Rauschning's "The Revolution of Nihilism."

In the last war, there was a lot of talk about civilization being at stake. Much of it, at least, was hooey. But at length the slogan has come true. The thing that is at issue now is precisely whether or not we shall all be Nazified, whether we shall return into barbarism, or whether civilization shall survive—whether men shall retain some dignity as men or revert to blood-drinking beasts. Perhaps it was the mistakes of the Treaty of Versailles which set the thing off. Perhaps it is something inherent in the German philosophy which has been taken and magnified by the Nazi criminals. It makes no difference. Even though John Jones himself inoculated his dog with the virus of hydrophobia, the dog is still mad and must be dealt with as mad dogs are dealt with.

Adolf Hitler yesterday told the Reichstag that he had donned his uniform never to take it off save in victory or in death. It may safely be said that that was rhetoric. The record shows that the man is a coward and is not likely to risk his precious hide before bullets. None the less, he spoke with perfect correctness. He will either win or he and all his gang will hang or beat the hangman to the draw by blasting out their own brains. More, his people have donned their uniforms for the same fatal test. Either they will win or Germany will vanish from the company of the nations. For the Western World is passing into uniform, and none of them will ever be doffed until either Nazism is dead or civilization is done for.

15

BOOK REVIEW OF FRANCIS GRISWOLD'S *A SEA ISLAND LADY*

(*North Georgia Review,* Spring 1940)

Cash frankly avoided other new books about the South while he was completing The Mind of the South, *but now his work was nearly finished and he did want to accommodate Lillian Smith and Paula Snelling, editors of the little magazine that had published excerpts from* Mind *in 1936. He did not prize Griswold's overgrown novel any more than he did that of Margaret Mitchell, but Miss Mitchell was later to admire* Mind *and to entertain, in Atlanta, its author and his wife.*

*T*he one sure way to the best-seller lists these days seems to be to write a Mack Truck novel. I remember a time back in the Aurignacian 'Twenties when publishers and critics were unanimously warning arrived and would-be writers that the public of the machine age had grown much too impatient to read a book of more than 250 pages, and that the best system was probably to hold it under 200. The earlier fate of *Look Homeward, Angel* appeared to bear that out. But then came *Anthony Adverse.* And now the publishers seem almost to believe that the public won't read anything unless it runs at least, 1,292 pages. And the public bears them out; at any rate to the point of insuring that each new Mack Truck sets its author up to a Cadillac V-16, four houses, a power boat, and an annuity for the rest of his long days.

All of which is by way of saying that it seems to me that Francis Griswold would have written a much better book if he had forgotten *Gone With the Wind* when he was turning out *A Sea Island Lady*.

I have no quarrel with long novels; on the contrary, I have a decided weakness for them. But *Tom Jones* and *The Peasants* and *War and Peace* and *The Brothers Karamazov* and, to a lesser extent, *A la Recherche du Temps Perdu* and *Jean Christophe* and *Look Homeward, Angel* and *Of Time and the River* are long novels because the vastness of their design requires it—because to set forth the absolutely germane or the at least pertinent it is necessary to use up so much white space, the laws of physics being what they are. But I do not think that the same is true of *A Sea Island Lady* any more than it is true of *Anthony Adverse* or *Gone With the Wind*.

That is not to say that the book is without merit. Mr. Griswold's prose is often pedestrian and a little inept, but it is always smooth and sometimes it attains a considerable distinction. And the descriptions of the sea islands about Beaufort, S. C., and of Beaufort itself are exceedingly well done. It is one of the ironies of the novel that Mr. Griswold is full of nostalgia for the beauties and the slow and languorous way of old Beaufort, mildly indignant about the ravages of Progress in the place—and that the excellence of his description is sure to bring down an influx of tourists upon the town and so speed the ravages of Progress.

The whole background of the novel, both physical and social, is indeed a big theme. And in some respects Mr. Griswold has done a good job of it. A Yankee himself, he has had the discretion to make the protagonist of the tale, Emily, a Yankee come South to play "missionary" to the black men freed by the Civil War. Such "missionaries" had a lot to do with the bitterness of feeling engendered in the South by Reconstruction, and one can easily understand why when looking at the Rev. Atwood Moffet, who has married Emily and fetched her down for the holy work, and Mrs. Sager.

The chapters dealing with this period are the best in the book, and it had better have ended with them. Mr. Griswold, who has lived much at and around Beaufort, has absorbed the stories native to the section thoroughly and has a better grasp of southern psychology in the time than most northerners have ever managed to attain. Sometimes he is guilty of the fault of a good many Yankees, that of leaning too far to the southern side, once their sympathies have been enlisted for it. And throughout the only ones among his principal characters who really come to life are those from above the Potomac River. Atwell's progress into scoundrelism and his taking up with a former Negro slave of the Fenwicks is made convincing enough. So are the adventures of Emily, within certain limits. But Stephen Fenwick, whom Emily eventually marries, is still very largely a shadowy ghost from the legend of the Old South and Thomas Nelson Page, despite Mr. Griswold's best efforts to lend him individual character. The only fully convincing southern whites in the book are Stephen's incredible old aunts—incredible, that is, in any other land than Dixie—and they are the sort of stock characters no one could miss.

The last half of the book seems to me simply dull and unnecessary. Mr. Griswold has followed the same formula throughout that Margaret Mitchell followed in *Gone With the Wind*. That is to say, he has collected all the appalling and dramatic things which ever happened to anybody in the Beaufort district, has added a generous portion of others from his imagination, and then has had them all happen to a single woman in a single lifetime. It is, of course, a dubious method, under any view of the case. But he succeeds in making it plausible so long as the theory is confined to the last days of the Civil War, Reconstruction, and the poverty-haunted decades that followed. But, after that, it becomes just a bore. You yawn, or you laugh as the incidents pile up intolerably, but you are neither moved nor edified.

Ultimately, Emily, no weakling, is not a character powerful enough to bear the building of a novel of 964 large and close-packed pages on her shoulders. And a good part of that length is explained by detail which has no real relation to the story. What Emily thought, what she did in the garden, what she read in the newspaper, this and that, most tiresomely.

Like *The Tides of Malvern*, this new novel by Mr. Griswold fails to quite come off. Of the two, I think, in fact, that the first was the better.

And like *Gone With the Wind*, *A Sea Island Lady* is another epic of Reconstruction which is less than an epic. The Civil War and the years which followed it undoubtedly offer the most dramatic and powerful material available to the American novelist, and above all to the southern novelist. And someday we shall probably get a really great novel out of it. But we haven't had it yet.

16

AT A TOMB

(Editorial, Charlotte *News*, July 1, 1940)

A news photo of Hitler, his hat on his head, "paying homage" at Napoleon's tomb at the fall of France in June 1940, inspired this editorial comparison of the two conquerors to the infinite disadvantage of "the little rat-like man." At that time Hitler vainly tried a gesture of goodwill to the French, sending back the remains of Napoleon's son to rest near those of his father. Internal evidence in this editorial strongly points to Cash's once having visited the Invalides in Paris, thus resenting all the more the baleful presence there of Hitler.

*U*nder the dome of the Invalides, in his tomb of green and red marble, brought from Scandinavia, the great man slept as he had slept since they bore him there from the lonely and barren rock in the South Atlantic upon which he died.

And in that shadowed and shining place the rat-like quality of the little man who leaned on the balustrade above and looked down upon him was accentuated and heightened. He had come there almost by stealth, the little rat-like man, in fear that there might be a Frenchman left to remember France, in fear that the sword of Jeanne and Charles Martel—that sword foretold by Merlin—might stir for a moment from the evil spell that held it.

It was a silent and empty place now. There had been no crippled guard to cry *"Votre chapeau, m'sieu"* to heedless tourists at the door, nor any tourist, but only a gray green creature upon whose face was the mark of the Beast of the Apocalypse, servilely presenting arms.

But the great man slept on. In his time, he had been the master of all Europe, save only England, too. At his command kings had arisen and other kings had fallen. And over all the teeming millions of the great continent he had held the power of destiny.

For him there were things to be said. He had never taken the gorilla for his model. He had not dreamed of destroying the culture of other peoples, of wiping away the values of three thousand years and replacing them with those of a tribe of naked barbarians on the steppes of Mongolia. He had not dreamed of raising up a slave society, to toil humbly for the glory of a myth called The Master Race. He had been brave. He had not warred on women and children. He had not called himself The First Soldier and skulked safely out of the range of the guns, but had been found wherever the battle most raged, in his special dress and on his special mount, so that all men might know him for the man he was. He had not sneaked into the cities he had taken, surrounded by steel and hosts of brutal guards with orders to shoot into the crowds if any man moved, but had gone openly and in the light of day. He had been a lawgiver wise and humane enough for his people to retain his code even after they were free.

But his power had crumbled from his hands and he had died on that bleak rock standing alone in the South Atlantic, his imperial greatness reduced to two or three shabby followers and mocked by the jailers who ringed him about—a prisoner, a fat and maudlin old man mumbling over his past. And now he slept. And his glory was only a name in a book. And the planet which he had trod rolled swiftly on to its

inexplicable goal in the constellation Hercules and the time
when Paris would not be there, when the red and green
marble and the bones of his body would not be there, and his
name would be as lost as the name of the first man to dwell
in the caves southward of his resting place, on the Lot.[1]
And in the world there was nothing certain save that, after
his brief span, he slept and would sleep—and that the empires
fragile man raises are fragile things.

But the little rat-like man leaning on the balustrade with
his cap on his head was proudly smiling as he roused himself, strutted about the great room to stare at the banners
hanging from the walls—the banners which the sleeping man
had borne from towns whose names he had made like
trumpets and the rolling of drums: Ulm, Marengo, Austerlitz,
and Leipzig. Was still proudly smiling as he came out and
was saluted by the gray green creature and hurried into a
swift and armored automobile and fled away lest the sleeping
sword of Sainte Catherine de Fierbois, which had once been
raised under the citadel of Chinon, should stir again from
the fateful spell upon it.

---

[1] The Lot is a river, tributary of the Garonne, which flows through
the mountainous Auvergne region.

17

SUICIDE SURGE

(Editorial, Charlotte *News*, July 24, 1940)

One year and one week after writing this lighthearted piece about suicide, Cash was dead by his own hand. Here he takes a certain satisfaction in the fact that the Hitler-inspired Munich crisis, which brought on the "suicide surge," left his native South Carolinians with the lowest suicide rate in the nation. "They never were a people to scare easily," Cash recalls with a touch of pride.

More than twice as many persons committed suicide in the United States in 1938 as in 1920, according to figures just released by the Census Bureau.

Why that should be so the Bureau does not say, but it is easy to see that it is directly related to the difficulty of the times. In 1920 there was a slight depression but the dizzy days of the great boom were just around the corner and everybody was confidently counting on acquiring a yacht next year.

But in 1932, at the nadir of the great depression, the suicide rate was the highest on record—17.4 per 100,000 population. It fell after that until the year when Hitler really heaved up on the American horizon, 1938—the year of Munich. It was back to 15.2 per 100,000 that year.

Among the states Nevada has the highest rate—35.6 per 100,000. Maybe the mountains and the price they get for all that silver makes 'em dizzy. And as for the lowest rate, that belongs to South Carolina.

The large Negro population explains a good deal of it, of course; Negroes rarely commit suicide. But it obviously doesn't explain all of it, since other states have an even larger proportion of Negroes than South Carolina. And considering cotton prices, Cotton Ed Smith and other tribulations, all cannot be complete joy in South Carolina.

Maybe it's just that they don't pay any attention to Mr. Hitler down there. They never were a people to scare easily. Or better still, maybe they are saving up to have a poke at him. Pacifism and its resultant frustrations have not, we suspect, very much caught on in South Carolina yet.

18

MEMO: WJC TO JED — ROOSEVELT VS. WILLKIE

(Signed editorial, Charlotte *News*,
October 13, 1940)

As the only two editorialists for the Charlotte News, *Cash and J. E. Dowd (his chief and employer) held opposed views on the merits of Roosevelt vs. Willkie in the 1940 election. They dramatized their differences by publishing editorial-page memos to each other in parallel columns, Cash championing the cause of Roosevelt, and Dowd that of Willkie. As it happened, Editor Dowd's misgivings about Willkie were far greater than any that Editor Cash entertained about Roosevelt.*

Roosevelt's worst faults as President, it seems to me, are a certain vagueness of mind and indecision which sometimes amount to procrastination. The first has led him to listen to and act upon the advice of advisers who recommended things irreconcilable with one another, results in inefficiency and wastefulness, and a failure to follow through in many cases when he ought to follow through rapidly. The second fault makes him hesitate and procrastinate when he ought not to, causes him plainly to dread carrying issues to the people when he clearly ought to, and sometimes results in sudden rash decisions. His stubbornness is often a fault also, but it can be a virtue.

On the other hand, in time of crisis he seems to have the power to rise above himself and display great energy and decision. I have read all the arguments against the notion that he saved the country in 1933, but I still think he saved it— magnificently. Nor do I subscribe to the notion that he has canceled that out by wrecking it since. He has chosen his administrators badly in many instances and too much money has been spent for the results achieved. Nevertheless, I am far from sure, remembering what went on in the World War, that anybody else would have done much better—and I think they might very well have done far worse. Would the country have been better off if Hoover had been President from 1932 to 1936? Or would it be safer with Alf Landon in the saddle in these times? I don't think so.

Despite all his vagueness when it comes to detail or to doubtful matters, Roosevelt seems to me to have had a clearer notion of the general needs of our time than any other American politician. He plainly believes that the "depression" we have been going through is no ordinary "business cycle" but the result of fundamental dislocation such as that which has brought Europe to its present pass. I think that is so. He hasn't succeeded in remedying that dislocation—and it plainly must be remedied ultimately if we are to escape revolution and chaos. But I am far from certain that anybody else would have yet found the way out either.

Mr. Willkie suffers from the same vagueness of mind as Mr. Roosevelt. It is hard to make out precisely what it is he proposes, but as well as I can get at it he stands about where Woodrow Wilson stood in 1912. This is, he believes in a laissez-faire system with such government control as may be absolutely necessary. He fails to define "absolutely necessary." Laissez-faire broke down completely in the late twenties, and I doubt seriously that it can ever be made to work again in the complex world we live in. It certainly showed no power of revival in the four years of Hoover, when the rules were all made to favor it.

I recognize that there is truth in the argument that high taxes, the hostility of the Roosevelt Administration to business, the general uncertainty as to what is coming next, have operated to discourage enterprise and investment. The other side of that, however, is that business has often held to the notion that the profit margins of the 1920's represented the normal and has demanded that it be allowed to set the stage to go back to them. They weren't normal, of course, as any reader of Adam Smith knows.

The waste margin aside, I think the high taxes were inevitable. In the absence of a sweeping solution to our impasse, any Administration would, I believe, have had to follow much the same course Roosevelt has followed. It is easy to say "let 'em starve." But to practice it is to destroy the humane basis of American tradition. And I believe profoundly that it is to wade into absolute disaster. Trouble is people won't starve quietly, and what you actually get is, at best, wholesale disorder, at worst, complete revolution. Maybe a lot of them deserve to starve. Certainly a lot of them are chronic malingerers and good-for-nothings and unemployables. How much they are ultimately to blame for that I don't know. I think it might be wise to sterilize the worst of them, though the power would be dangerous. But for the present there they are. The goal of course is so far as possible to put the employable and useful among them to work. But for the rest I doubt that much can be done besides what is being done.

But it seems to me that the foreign case eclipses everything else in this campaign. And there Roosevelt seems to me to stand head and shoulders above Willkie. Mr. Willkie has yawed about pretty wildly and has not seemed to know what he did think. I suspect that he has been listening too much to Hugh Johnson, about the worst adviser on foreign policy I can imagine. He has certainly made some extremely rash promises. Roosevelt hasn't been entirely above those either. But he has the great merit in my eyes of having seen clearly what was coming up before us long before any other politician saw it. His timidity and indecision have shown up in his failure to hammer the theme home to the country and to arouse it to arm sooner. But I doubt that he could have roused it if he had tried. As it was, he was labelled warmonger every time he opened his mouth. And Congress has consistently cut down such arms appropriations as he asked. The Republicans voted solidly to cut $200,000,000 off the naval bill last Fall and the Alaskan and Guam bases were sabotaged by them. Surely, the Republicans don't get on to cast stones at Roosevelt on this score.

What is more important even is that Willkie is the candidate of the Republican Party. If he is elected a Republican House will probably be elected also. That means, for one thing, a general turnover in the vast personnel of the Government. That is, for six months after his entry into office there will be general turmoil in the capital and the jobs will be filled by men who know little about them. Or if that doesn't happen, if he defies politics and keeps the main body of the personnel on, then he will begin with a Congress bitterly antagonized by the failure of the pork barrel. I think either situation might be disastrous at the time.

Supposing, however, that the worst didn't happen. It is still true that the majority of the present Republican membership has got itself on record, far beyond Willkie, as isolationist in sentiment and as determined to have nothing to do with "Europe's war." Most of them will probably hew to that line. What is worse, the foreign affairs leadership in the Senate will be in the hands of Hiram Johnson, of Ham Fish in the House. And that could delay or block aid to

Britain whatever Mr. Willkie wanted, and certainly might block or delay our decision as to Japan or Europe dangerously long—might get us into a position where we would have to fight alone or resort to appeasement, again regardless of Mr. Willkie.

I think myself that we have got to fight. And that being so, I believe it is immensely better to fight the war away from these shores than inside them. The South remembers what war on your own territory is like. Maybe the navy can settle it if we strike hard and fast enough. Maybe not. Maybe we shall have to send armies abroad. In any case, I think it is coming. And for a war President I have a great deal of confidence in Roosevelt. For all his great faults, I think he is capable of being a great statesman before such a crisis. It is that which clinches the matter for me.

19

SEA FIGHT

(Editorial, Charlotte *News*, November 14, 1940)

This widely admired editorial is indicative of the prayerful admiration with which Cash viewed Churchill's Britain during its awful "Year Alone"—those desperate twelve months between the fall of France and Hitler's onslaught against Russia. Cash was put up for a Pulitzer Prize in 1941, and this editorial was the chief argument for it.

> *If blood be the price of Admiralty,*
> *Lord God, we ha' paid in full.*[1]

*S*he was just a fat merchantman of 14,000 tons, crawling while the swift ships of war ran. In the days of peace, the men on the swift ships smiled contemptuously upon her as they passed, scorned her crew in port as a lesser breed. Her name was reminiscent of a butler in a novel by Mr. Wodehouse.

But in the *Jervis Bay* the British navy had today a new name to stand by that of the *Ajax* and the destroyers which went storming to destruction in Narvik Bay—the newest in the long line of gallant ships since the *Great Harry*, with the *Victory* at their head. And one more pressing reason to

---

[1] Rudyard Kipling: *The Song of the Dead, II*, from *A Song of the English*.

tighten its belt and vow that the Nazi pocket battleship, now loose in the Atlantic, should not be long in paying in full.

Her sides were tissue paper for the eleven-inch guns of the Nazi. Her guns were, relatively speaking, pop-guns. She was the turtle to the Nazi's fox.

There was no illusion aboard her. The men remembered well the fate of her sister ship, the *Rawalpindi,* expected that it was certain death they confronted as they raised the British cheer. It would be her business to engross the Nazi until the convoy of 38 freighters could get clear away. And once away it would be the business of those freighters to steam hard for England, not to look back or remember the fate of the men of the *Jervis Bay.*

Wherefore, she laid down her smoke screen to cover the convoy and steamed for the Nazi, her pop-guns roaring. It was a sunny afternoon and on the bright sea the Nazi was not long in finding the range. His terrific salvos turned her poor sides into sieves. He smashed her steering gear and she wallowed helplessly in the sea's insensate grasp. He tore away the arm of her commander, Captain Fogarty Fegan (the saga-men of Iceland and the Great Red Kings of Ireland would have known that name), and still she roared defiance. He shot away her ensign, and a new one was lashed to the masthead as fast as men could climb. The afterbridge was gone now and the wounded captain was staggering to the main bridge, great shells were exploding below the water line and she was on fire—a rapidly sinking hulk. But until the very last moment before it was necessary to abandon ship or go down with her, her guns kept on firing coldly and methodically. Not until the survivors of the battle were in the lifeboats did the Nazi draw off to chase his real prey—the merchantmen of the convoy. And not even then until he had first vented his brutal spite by shelling the lifeboats with shrapnel. Then she went down, her ensign still flying, Captain Fogarty Fegan aboard, in a great cloud of hissing steam.

Not quite fully had she succeeded in her appointed work. For the Nazi was swift in his pursuit of the convoy. But by Tuesday afternoon 28 of the 38 ships had come safely to port in England, and there was another which would come a little later.[2] He was a Swede. If it was binding upon British freighters to make for England, regardless, it was not binding on him. And he had seen what stirred the heritage in him from his Viking ancestors. Nazi or no Nazi, back he went to pick up 65 of the survivors and carry them safely home.

Three hundred and fifty-two years ago, men of a tough and nameless merchant and fishing sailor breed met the might of Spain in the Channel and established the basis of England's sea greatness. The breed survives unchanged.

---

[2] Note: Since this was written the British Admiralty has announced that six more ships have arrived safely, leaving the Nazi's bag at only three.—W.J.C.

20

IN ECSTASY—
HYMN DONE IN
IMITATION OF THE
DITHYRAMBIC
MANNER

(Editorial, Charlotte *News*, November 18, 1940)

The origin of this satiric piece, as recalled by Cash's newspaper mates, is as follows: On the Monday morning following an upset football victory by North Carolina over Duke, the Charlotte Observer's editorial page bore a gaudy panegyric in honor of the lowly Tar Heels who had overcome the vaunted power of the Blue Devils. Cash could not have cared less, but he winced at such a to-do over a football game when Hitler dominated the European continent and the very fate of the West hung in the balance. Although the editor of the rival Observer was anything but an isolationist, Cash was minded to puncture him anyhow. That editor, a native South Carolinian like Cash, was Julian S. Miller, whose Observer staff was encouraged to call him "Doctor" by virtue of the honorary LL.D. conferred upon him by his alma mater, Erskine College. Miller had enrolled at little Erskine in Due West, South Carolina, after only one year at Chapel Hill— and he used that year to justify his hot partisanship for the football Tar Heels. Cash whipped up this "dithyrambic" reply to

Miller, full of classical allusions, quite spontaneously and without stopping to check references.

*A*h, me, masters, the Greeks at Thermopylae and Koritza just weren't in it. And Fogarty Fegan, of the *Jervis Bay*, was a mere piker.

There they were, you see, the intrepid little band of Ray Wolf's Spartans, the Six Hundred at Balaklava, Achilles all alone before Troy, Richard's men encompassed by the men of Saladin, the cadets at New Market, Pickett at Gettysburg, and Lady Godiva in the streets of Coventry.

And in front of them, not only the serried host of the Persians, not only the Moslem, not only the damnyankee and Peeping Tom, not only great Hector and the Czar's might, but the restless power of (old) Rome's legions, Lord Hitler's Blitzkrieg, and also the assembled potency of Olympus itself.

Aphrodite born of the sea foam—well, maybe not Aphrodite, either, but anyhow the Titans resistless and Mars and old Saturn and Neptune, plus a couple of Nazi pocket battleships, and Vulcan and Mercury of the winged heels and all the demi-gods and heroes, Hercules and Ajax of the mighty shoulders and Sisyphus (not Sissy-puss, silly!) and Icarus and what have you, plus maybe old Silenus and a plentiful helping of gnomes out of Walt Disney. And at their head shining Apollo himself, revered from pole to pole and throughout the starry universe.

But were they downhearted, that little Spartan band which hadn't a look-in? No! And no, two more times. Theirs not to reason why, theirs but to do and die. They piled Pelion on Ossa and Ossa on Olympus, and then struggled up those rocky and bleeding slopes, panting and whooping. With all guns blazing they steamed in, the *Bonhomme Richard* and the *Jervis Bay* rolled into one. They piled into the black ships and went sashaying around the Mediterranean on the course of old Odysseus.

With the steady blaze of their brilliance, they outdazzled Apollo. And they littered the bloody field with the slain enemy.

And all that, mind you, within the short space of less than two hours. Ring out, oh bells, ring out. And be still in your graves, oh you Lacedaemonians and you men of the *Victory!* Rise up again, oh, Homer and Tennyson. Now arriveth the greatest victory, the most deathless deed, of all times. For countless ages men will cheer and sob aloud to hear. Weep, Devils (3), and sing, Tar Heels (6).

21

EASTER

(Editorial, Charlotte *News*, April 12, 1941)

For this, the last Easter of his life, Cash wrote this unusual edi-
torial tribute to "the everlasting return and the eternal resurrec-
tion." His references to the pagan origins of Easter could not have
appealed to fundamentalist readers in the Charlotte area, but by
this time Cash's prestige as author of The Mind of the South
seemed to entitle him to a certain toleration.

It is perhaps the oldest and the loveliest of man's ceremonial and holy observances—the everlasting return and
the eternal resurrection. It was incalculably ancient when
the first of the Beni Israel left their Bedouin brothers behind
in the desert. And the name we know it by is that of an old
Norse pagan goddess. And that *pagan* means at last nothing
but *country*. *Peasant* is from the same root. Wise with hoary
wisdom was the old Church when it took over the festival
and bound it in with the new story of the greatest Resurrection.

It is the story of the cycle of the earth and of the impen-
etrable mystery of life upon that earth. First there is the
dying of the harvest, and crucifixion of the golden Summer
upon the shining and glorious cross of the falling days. And
afterward the entombment in the sad and dark vault of

brown Winter. And then again the stirring and the bursting of the bands, the breaking of the shell of the silent and weeping tomb and the trumpet voice rich with the promise of the golden Summer's return, "He is Risen!"

The story of the fecund and teeming and mysterious earth, unutterably terrible and unutterably beautiful. And of man—earthbound and terrible and bloody and aspiring man, with his fateful dream within him. The fragile leaf and the white bud and the new-born babe. And the great triumphant chorus and the brooding sadness which sees in the bud the shriveling of the rose, beyond the coming Summer the return again of Death.

But always and forever there is the Resurrection.

22

BOOK REVIEW OF
HUGH S. JOHNSON'S
HELL-BENT FOR WAR

(Charlotte *News*, April 16, 1941)

In this gloves-off treatment, Cash displayed the urgent frustration he experienced after the fall of France when his pro-British editorials appeared month in and month out on the same page with the syndicated isolationism of General Hugh S. "Ironpants" Johnson. Moreover, Cash clearly saw at the time what historians have since ratified by consensus—that "no man could have re-armed the nation between 1932 and 1940." As a refutation of isolationism, this review is a perfect period piece in the pre-World War II Great Debate.

*G*eneral Hugh S. Johnson, otherwise Ironpants, has re-
hashed some of his recent columns into a little book
of 155 pages under the title of "Hell-bent for War." It
is published by Bobbs-Merrill at $1.50 in case you are inter-
ested in hearing it all over again. The General, as everyone
knows, is a bitter-end isolationist. Isolationism is the philosophy which has it that what happens in the world outside our
own borders is not the slightest concern of ours, and that we
have no responsibilities in the world scheme. All we need to
do, it holds, is to pull our borders in around us and let the

world go hang. It is the philosophy sold to the country at the end of the last war by Borah, Reed, Lodge, Hiram Johnson & Co., partly out of provincialism, partly out of partisan and personal spite toward Mr. Wilson.

It called and still calls itself hard-boiled, but it is in fact the most unrealistic philosophy which ever duped a people. For at one and the same time it told the world to go jump in the lake, enacted politics which were sure to wreck the world and make it our deadly enemy, and—disarmed.

Ironpants, of course, maintains that he didn't want to disarm. On the contrary, he says, he has continually preached rearmament and blames Mr. Roosevelt for our present state.

As a former Army officer he probably didn't, in fact, want to disarm. But he coolly overlooks the fact that the way isolationism was sold to the country was by representing to the people that we were not in danger of any attack, had never been, and weren't going to be. The claim that the German menace was a pure myth was the bedrock upon which isolationism was ultimately based. And the American people consented to disarm precisely because they had been persuaded that isolationism in itself was quite sufficient protection. All we had to do was to stay at home, mind our own business, and there would be no trouble.

The charge that Mr. Roosevelt is responsible for the present disarmed state of the country is a vicious distortion of the facts. The psychology of the country was such that no man could have re-armed the nation between 1932 and 1940. Mr. Roosevelt's constant attempts to increase naval appropriations were hamstrung by both Republicans and Democrats. And whenever he sought to arouse the nation to the rising danger of Hitlerism, as at Chicago in 1937, Ironpants led the nation in roaring "warmonger!" The President was simply an excitable hysteric—so Ironpants argued. And so the people thought, quite reasonably, "since there is no danger, why arm?"

Isolationism has now brought us to the most dangerous pass in our history. But Ironpants has no intention of admitting it, since that would be to confess that General Hugh S. Johnson has been wrong—an unthinkable thing in the Ironpants code. And so he goes roaring up and down the land that there is no real danger to us, and convincing many millions—perhaps will go on convincing them until it is everlastingly and fatally too late.

Ironpants now asserts that he favors all aid to Britain which will not "cripple" our own defense. That really means exactly no aid. For the record of his column shows that he has uniformly inveighed against every move to aid Britain, from the first sale of arms right on down to the Lend-Lease Bill.

The General is more candid when it comes to question of letting Britain fall or aiding her. He says flatly that he thinks we will not be seriously hurt by the fall of Britain. And he sneers loudly at the idea that the Monroe Doctrine has rested partly on British sea power. One thing is clear: either the late great Captain A. T. Mahan didn't know what he was talking about or Ironpants doesn't. For ourselves we prefer to go along with Mahan. Ironpants, after all, trained as a naval expert on a horse.

Can we live with Hitler? Emphatically yes, says the General. In face, we probably shall get rolling rich by living with him. But what about his slave labor competition? Pooh-pooh, says Ironpants, is anybody going to say that the great American system can't meet any competition? "Shame!" he cries. That is a fine appeal to chauvinism but it hasn't much sense in it. Anybody who knows anything about our record in international trade ever since the Civil War knows that we have increasingly failed to meet even the free-labor competition of other nations.

Altogether, a bad, misleading, and, in these times, even a dangerous book.

23

LETTER FROM
W. J. CASH
TO HIS FATHER

(c. May 1, 1941)

*Written shortly before Cash's departure for Mexico, this poignant
letter sets the stage for the author's hoped-for future career. The
son speaks optimistically to his father about the bright prospects
ahead for a writer who has to his credit a prestigious book and a
Guggenheim fellowship.*

DEAR DAD:

This leaves me still ten dollars behind on last month,[1] but
I've been so hard run that I couldn't lay hands on any money.
I'll get $200 for the speech in Texas, and since it is on the
direct rail route to Mexico City, it is just so much picked up.
That still doesn't solve the money question fully—of paying
my debts and getting some fairly decent clothes before I
leave here. I'll have to have dressclothes, of course, for that
speech. I hope to write some stuff I can sell this month. But
if not I can get some money from Knopf, though I prefer to
leave that alone for the present—as an ace in the hole.

I am sorry that you have felt so lonely. We had planned

---

[1] Cash was then paying $30 monthly toward his parents' upkeep
out of a weekly paycheck of $50.

to come up there this week end because we knew you would feel that way. But the opportunity developed for us to go to Chapel Hill and it is Mary's last chance to see her mother before we leave.[2] Mrs. Ross won't get here until sometime in June, after we are gone.

I know you don't like me to go off to Mexico on this Fellowship. I know also that it has some risks, and that I shall have to work in order to make myself financially safe at the end of the year. More than that, I hate to go away and leave you feeling as you do, with everybody else pretty far away from you, too. I thought about it a lot, and was sometimes tempted to turn it down. But it didn't seem to make good sense. I owe it to myself, to you and mama, to Mary, and the whole family to go ahead and try to have as good a career as I can, and to have been a Guggenheim Fellow gives you a long shove ahead—to say nothing of giving me a year free for writing and seeing what I can do toward achieving complete independence. I failed at that once before, but it was the terror of my economic condition that mainly paralyzed me. This time I'll have fair security for the year. And more than that, I now have reputation enough to make it easier for me to get a job if I need and want one. To ask for a job as one who is unknown, broke and down and out, who hasn't had a job for several years,[3] and to ask for one as a Guggenheim Fellow with a solid record as an editorial writer and as the author of a book which has made a great reputation—these are very different things. And I don't think you need to worry on that score. There wasn't any prospect of advancement here and not much of more money than the

---

[2] On Saturday, May 3, 1941, Mr. and Mrs. W. J. Cash were at Chapel Hill, where he addressed a banquet of the N. C. Scholastic Press Institute. Mary Cash's widowed mother, Mrs. Joseph Russell Ross, was then employed as housemother in a Chapel Hill fraternity house.

[3] Cash refers here to his situation on joining the staff of the Charlotte *News* on October 18, 1937.

shabby salary I have been paid. So I thought it best to make the decision and go ahead.

If war breaks out we shall probably leave Mexico and come back to the United States, and that seems very likely. However, if I could get a job as a correspondent I might stay down there awhile, though I might send Mary back. That all remains to be seen, however. We will have round trip tickets, so we can be sure of getting away at any time we want to. And in any emergency, I can always fly into Charlotte in about fifteen hours for little more than rail fare. I don't like flying in general, but it is no more dangerous than the trains or ships and a darn sight less dangerous than an automobile.

Tell Mama not to imagine things about earthquakes. Mexico City has slight shocks practically every day, but the heavy stone walls are built for it. The reason for these shocks is that the city used to be an island—a marsh, rather. And the ground is still soggy and shifts about easily. But this same sogginess keeps the city from suffering from the genuine earthquakes which sometimes rock other parts of Mexico. The city has never had a serious earthquake since Cortez entered it in 1521. And she must not imagine, either, that it is wild country. It is in fact a city of nearly a million and a half people, modern in its sanitation and as well policed as any city of the United States. There are sometimes riots at election times but we have them, too—not to mention our labor riots. All you have to do to be safe is to stay out of the crowded districts at election time.

Mary's mother is related to Mrs. Josephus Daniels, who is Ambassador down there, and Jonathan Daniels, son of Josephus, is my good friend, and so we will be well looked out for down there. Incidentally, Jonathan Daniels, Thomas Wolfe, Paul Green, and myself are the only four North Carolinians who ever won a Guggenheim Fellowship in the field of literature.

We'll have to leave here Saturday morning, May 31, to

be in Austin on June 2 when I am to make the speech at the University. I had promised Bill Dowd to stay here until the end of that day, and he had made his arrangements accordingly. If I possibly can we'll leave here Wednesday and come up to Shelby until Friday night. If not we'll come the Sunday before and again on Thursday afternoon. I feel bad that I can't stay longer, I wanted to, but things have me crowded so that I can't.

We see you next Sunday.

Love to Mama,

Love,

WILBUR

And thanks for remembering my birthday.[4] I don't particularly mind them anymore.

---

[4] Cash's forty-first birthday, May 2, 1941.

24

BOOK REVIEW OF WILLIAM ALEXANDER PERCY'S *LANTERNS ON THE LEVEE*

(Charlotte *News*, May 10, 1941)

In this, the last book review Cash wrote, he lashed back at an unnamed reviewer who had severely attacked Cash's own The Mind of the South. *That man was the late Richmond C. Beatty of Vanderbilt University, whose attack had appeared in the Nashville* Banner *of February 26, 1941, and was a rare discordant note in the almost unanimous chorus of praise for Cash's book. Percy's* Lanterns on the Levee *was issued by Cash's own publisher, Alfred A. Knopf, and Cash's review was intended to show that neither author had needed, as Beatty had insinuated, "a shrewd eye for the lucrative northeastern market."*

Not long ago I read the most ill-natured book review it has been my fortune to read. It was written by a young man who grades English A at Vanderbilt University, and who belongs to the Agrarian group which loudly professes to be made up of Southern aristocrats.

I mention it here because it charged, among other things,

that the author of the book had pandered to the Yankee, and that in fact no Southern author could get a book published who did not so pander.

The claim was idiotic on its face. The fact was, as every schoolboy knew, that Southern glorifiers had found publishers in the North from long before the Civil War on down. And the particular publisher in question was Alfred A. Knopf, who had published every shade of opinion he disagreed with, including that of Fascists who wanted to assassinate all Jews and liberals—and Mr. Knopf was both Jewish and liberal.

But if Mr. Knopf and the other Yankee publishers had conspired to make a donkey of the fellow, they could not better have gone about it than by having Mr. Knopf publish William Alexander Percy's "Lanterns on the Levee" (348 pp. $3) hard on the heels of the review.

Percy is that exceedingly rare thing, a surviving authentic Southern aristocrat, as distinguished from pretenders to the title.

I think it is instructive that there is no ill-nature in him save on one point. He is urbane, sensitive, gentle, candid, wise, and witty. And above all, kind—save in a single respect which is understandable when you look into his history.

Born on a Mississippi plantation and now poet-laureate of his state, Percy has it in him to smile at the lordly legend of his ancestry. The first Percy was an adventurer who myth said had been a pirate—the disinherited son of the mighty Percys of Northumberland—but all that is certainly known about him is that he landed in Mississippi with many slaves and that he was a bigamist. Other Percy ancestors lived in a log house after the Civil War, and are plainly French-derived bourgeois. But you had better not suppose that William Alexander Percy is not filled with a mighty pride in his heritage. I suspect that, at bottom, he likes to believe that he is in fact the scion of the great Dukes of Northumberland, that Hotspur was his kinsman. And nobody can rightly blame him. In any case, he is profoundly convinced that he comes down from the salt of the earth. And with reason. The Percys were very much somebody in Mississippi from the beginning. And justly. They had courage, great pride, integrity, decency, intelligence above their neighbors.

Percy, as a genuine aristocrat, does not feel it necessary to assert his patent by deriding democracy, as so many pseudo-aristocrats-and-intellectuals now do. On the contrary, he believes that it is on the whole the most rational way of adjusting man to man. Merely, he laments its decay, believing that its one hope is to be led by its men of superior capacity and decency—its men capable of disinterestedness. And who, with a grain of sense, doesn't agree?

But Percy has his blind spot, as I have already suggested. It is profoundly moving to hear him talk of the Negro. There is in him no trace of that hatred and spleen toward the black man which has always disgraced so many Southern whites. His attitude is that of the very best men of the South—by no means co-extensive with the planter class—from the beginning.

Yet Percy hates and excoriates the poor-whites. One understands why, and even sympathizes, when one knows that, as a young man, he took active part in the campaigns of his father against J. K. Vardaman for the United States Senate— saw the skulking poor-whites gather under the torchlights, heard their gross insults to his good and able father, felt his hand tighten on the pistol-butt as violence against his father seemed inevitable. For a shrinking, sensitive man the experience was searing, and it is not wonderful that he has not forgotten.

I can understand, indeed, exactly how he feels when he almost plumps for the proposition that men who are not handy with their fists ought to be allowed the use of the pistol. I have myself sometimes felt exactly the same way. Yet he fails to see that his philosophy adds up at last to pre-

cisely the same philosophy of violence which he so resents
and despises in the poor whites.

But what Percy fails to see goes beyond that. The Southern poor-white is a debased creature, yes, but who would not
be debased after a century of despair. Where Percy is blindest
of all is not seeing that though his father and his friends were
good men after their kind, they were not wise enough to
grasp the fact that the world they had built served themselves
exclusively—to be more exact, themselves and the Cotton
Snobs who had always made up the majority of their class.
There was a time when the common whites had followed the
Percys and their kind with fanatical devotion. And if in the
end they turned away from them, for all their great merits
and rightful claims to leadership, to follow after the dema-
gogues, it was because they (the Percys) had failed. Because,
given the resources of the Southern world, they had not succeeded in leading the way to an adequate life. Had not even
had the vision to see such a life.

But perhaps I am too absolute. I have the feeling that in
the last analysis Percy himself is always essentially kind.
Simply, as an aristocrat he feels bound to give lip service to a
cruel philosophy which grew up to hide and rationalize the
failure of the Southern master class actually to lead in the
crucial times. Thus, in the beginning he dogmatically asserts
that Mississippi is made up of three classes, aristocrats, Negroes, and poor-whites—in that order. But later on a school
master of his reminds him to except the yeoman farmers—
probably the best people the South has ever produced in any
numbers, and its chief hope today.

And in his last chapter a graveyard moves him to reflect
that the essential difference between himself and the town
thief and the town baggage resides in the accident of birth
and environment. That is not the philosophy of a man who is
either intolerant or cruel at heart, who lacks understanding

of the fact that human life is mainly grotesque and always infinitely pitiful.

On the whole, an excellent and admirable man, this William Alexander Percy. And his book is a fine one, the merits of which ought not to be obscured by any ideological disputes. The passages which concern his childhood and the struggles of a sensitive young man to adjust himself to the world are as good as any American novelist has produced. Sometimes the style is a little marred by over-coyness. But in general the book is beautifully written.

25

THE SOUTH IN
A CHANGING WORLD

(Commencement Address, University of Texas,
June 2, 1941)

*The manuscript of this last speech has not survived, but the
speech was recorded, as delivered, on a set of old 78-r.p.m. phonograph records. The account here is from the stenographic tran-
script taken from that recording, which is the only one known of
Cash's voice, and has now been preserved through a tape recording made by the Southern Historical Collection, Chapel Hill,
North Carolina. The subject matter, for the most part a brief
restatement of the author's thesis in* The Mind of the South, *
avoids the pessimistic conclusion of the book and ends on a much
more hopeful note.*

*D*istinguished guests, *ladies and gentlemen, the graduating class, and the audience in general: Not long
ago I read a very fine novel by Marcus Goodrich
called *Delilah*, the story of a destroyer at sea in the Philippine
Islands just on the eve of the last war. The thing, I found the
whole book very moving and interesting, but the thing that
moved me most in the book was a short incidental section
on the defense of the Alamo. Now I suppose that the subject

of the Alamo is a fairly hackneyed one to Texans by now, but I am sure that it is not one to which they do not respond in their private hearts, at least, with a feeling that it's a very proud thing to be a Texan. I can imagine that heroic defense of plain men on the American frontier twenty-five hundred years from now nerving the hearts and arms of Texans as surely as the memory of Marathon and Thermopylae has lately nerved the heart and arm of the unhappy Greeks in their heroic defense of their homeland.

But I do not speak of the Alamo merely to pay tribute to Texas and Texans, but to emphasize of course that it is the primary tradition of Texas and so is in some ultimate sense also the tradition of the whole South. The people who came to—the people who settled Texas—came from all of the states in the Union, of course, as it existed at that time. They also came from many foreign lands, and I have no desire at all to detract from the credit of any of them; but ultimately, Texans were mainly drawn from the stock of the older Southern states, and the tradition of Texas is therefore the tradition of the older South, a tradition that was already formed and was different from the prevailing American tradition in a great many respects at the time these people began to arrive in Texas.

I emphasize tradition here because tradition is very important in the world in which we live at present, the world in which the Class of 1941 will be going forth. Totalitarianism is apparently sweeping over the world. It certainly swept over Europe and is at the present threatening the United States. Well, there are people who tell you that it's an irresistible wave, men and women in the United States who say that the only rational thing for us to do is to give up quietly, that we are seeing the decay and death of an order of civilization. Well, for my part I shall not believe that till I see it proved. I shall remember the history of the Alamo and of my country, and believe that it will survive.

When that is said, however, it is necessary to fix in mind very firmly that the world into which we are going is certainly going to be a very different one from the world which we have known in the recent past, the world in which the Class of 1941 will live, which will shape its lives and destinies and also the life and destiny of the United States, of the South, and of Texas. That being the case, and since tradition is everywhere under attack, since the whole tradition of the Western world is under attack, and our tradition in the South of course is ultimately just a part of that tradition of the Western world, I think it is very necessary that we should try not only to approach the problems of the times that are coming with good will, but also with as intelligent as possible an understanding of what our tradition is.

Now, as I say the whole tradition of the Western world is actually involved. Well, the limitations of time don't allow me to go into all of that here this evening. What I am concerned with is the tradition of the South with Texas bound into that tradition as an integral part of it.

Well, what then is our Southern tradition? The best way to answer that I believe is to remember who we were and are, what we were at our origins. The answer to that is that we were a plain people in general in our origins. John Bright used to like to talk about the poor proud homes of England. Well, if you add the poor proud homes of Scotland and Ireland and France and Germany, perhaps, Spain now and then, why you would probably have just about where most of us came from.

Of course there's the tradition of the Southern aristocrat. We've all heard of them all our lives and a great many of us even now and then claim to be descended from them. Well, who were they? The answer is that we created to a certain extent our own aristocrats. The people in Virginia and lower South Carolina, the people around New Orleans, up the

Mississippi Valley to some extent, were there a long while before the mass of immigrants got into this country and they had time enough, some of them, to grow into aristocrats, but to start with they were undoubtedly mainly simple people of the same sort as the rest of us. The greatest planter in Norfolk, for example, the Norfolk area, was Adam Thoroughgood, and he came into the colony as an indentured servant. Another famous family up there which I need not name here, the founder of the family [1] paid his passage across the sea as a ship's carpenter.

Well, I instance these cases merely by way of insisting on the primary simplicity of our origins. A few of the people who came to this country, of course, actually did belong to families of considerable rank in England, Scotland, Ireland—anyhow, in Europe. But that was the exception and not the rule.

I ask your leave to question how a notion of aristocracy got so widely established in the South. In part I think it's explained by the rapid acquisition of land and slaves by a great many people who had been poor and plain up until after the invention of the cotton gin. The plantation system, of course, was carried over the South by cotton, and the growing of cotton became profitable on a wide scale only after the invention of the gin. Well, these people who had acquired land and slaves naturally imitated the wealthier people of Virginia and South Carolina, in particular, sometimes Louisiana, New Orleans.

But there is more to it than that, I think. We come now to what seems to me to be one of the most important things to understand about the South, that it has been from the

---

[1] The reference is to William Randolph (c. 1651–1711). According to an oral tradition, which historians have been unable either to prove or disprove, the patriarch of the great Randolphs arrived in Virginia shouldering a broadaxe with which he proceeded to carve out a fortune in land.

invention of the—from the beginning of the fight over slavery, a society on the defensive. It was on the defensive because it had a guilt complex about slavery. The South was settled not only by Christian people—but mainly by Protestants and they brought over with them the great dislike of slavery which has always distinguished Calvinism.

In the early days of the Abolition movement the antislavery cause actually won more support in the South than it did anywhere else in the American colonies, the American nation. But the South had a self-interest in slavery and didn't want to give it up. Now you notice that I say the *South* had a self-interest in slavery and not merely the slave owners. The introduction of Negro slavery over the South generally had brought in the notion of racial superiority. And though slavery involved a great deal of hardship—economic hardship—and disadvantage for white people who did not own slaves, it was always pretty well balanced out by that feeling of racial superiority plus a more or less conscious protection from the danger of competition, economic competition, which the Negro if he were freed would bring on.

So we find that reading a book like Hinton Helper's *Impending Crisis of the South,* written in 1856, I believe, or '57,[2] we find that the masses of the white men were quite often even more determined not to let the Negro escape from slavery than the plantation owners—owners of slaves. That brings us back to aristocracy. You see, for the South to paint itself as an aristocratic society was to say that it was a superior society, and it set up this doctrine that it was an aristocratic society undoubtedly as an answer to the Yankee's and the North's moral superiority over slavery.

And so we have in the Old South a society arising from originally plain, proud, poor people, and the growth of the plantation and typically the cotton plantation. Some of them

---

[2] The correct date is 1857.

by the time of the Civil War were genuinely aristocrats. Others were on the way to being such. But the great majority, even of the ruling orders, were not aristocrats. Yet the claim to such rank was virtually coexistent with ruling orders and often reached down below them, because the Old South was in the last analysis a society which stood on the defensive.

Torn between two powerful impulses—moral disapproval of slavery on the one hand and powerful self-interest, economic self-interest, on the other—the South had begun to retreat into unreality, to romanticize and sentimentalize itself and its peculiar institution. That tendency to unreality, to romanticism and sentimentality was its most striking trait, I think. It extended through the whole of Southern life and impressed every part including religion and morality. By the time the Civil War came on the best brains of the South were preoccupying themselves with such futile projects as trying to prove by the Bible that God had ordained the Negro to be the slave of the white man, and while the ruling—while the official ruling Southern moral code was that of Puritanism, the conduct of many of those who professed that code was often anything else but puritanical.

Mind you, I am not accusing the Old South of hypocrisy. Hypocrisy is a coolly calculated, conscious thing, and the South was not consciously engaged in double dealing. Merely it was responding to a situation it found impossible to face, precisely as any other people would have responded, by retreating toward unreality.

But of course the Old South had other qualities besides this one I name of unreality and tendencies to romanticism and sentimentality. Many of them cannot be mentioned here because of the limitations of time, but one of them deserves special notice. I mean the characteristic of extreme individualism. This quality had extremely deep roots. The effect of the survival of the tradition of the frontier is obvious and

I shall not labor it here. But it also has to be noted that most Southern white men retained some sort of land, eventually to be absorbed naturally by the plantation. But lands that were good for the growing of corn for food and for a little cotton for clothing were pretty well universally possessed by Southern white men. And that is to say, of course, that they retained their independence, and independence is naturally the soil in which you get extreme individualism.

With that background we come to the great disaster of the Civil War and Reconstruction. The march of the Old South toward an aristocracy was ended, toward a plantation aristocracy was ended. So was slavery. But for the old proud sore defensiveness in attitude which we had before the War, we now had added, we now had a much more developed sort of thing, the sensitiveness of a defeated people. If slavery was gone, in the North well-meaning and not so well-meaning men were demanding that the Negro should suddenly acquire not only equal rights with white men, but often even superior rights. To that the South responded as any other people would have responded, given the same tradition and the same environment. Often that response was violent and brutal. And so much was to be expected from them, from men with a long tradition of the frontier behind them. The South had always been violent. It was violent before the Civil War. Lynching and the duel both flourished there as it flourished nowhere else in America. But let us understand in saying that that we are simply trying to understand something, not to pass moral judgment. Faced with the same problem, given the same environment and background, the North would have responded very much as we did in the South. The violence, of course, is incidental. What I want to emphasize most is that the South's tendency to reality—to unreality, to romanticism, to sentimentality, was enormously reinforced by the Civil War and Reconstruction.

If the movement toward the plantation aristocracy was ended, if even the people who had already achieved aristocracy were more or less being extinguished, yet in this period the South was of such a notion of aristocracy in the Old South with far greater vigor than ever before, again as an obvious defense mechanism against the Yankees. The idealization and sentimentalization of the past is of course a normal enough thing for defeated peoples, and so is this defensiveness in general. Ireland is a good example, and our Southern literature of the Thomas Nelson Page era with Marse Chans and squires, has its parallel in the literature of any of those nations which have been defeated, Ireland or Poland, name them as you please. In itself the idealization of the Old South as a country full of dueling gentlemen and ladies in farthingales might not be important. What is important is that the tendency to unreality which is summed up in this attitude extended to all fields of thought and so had the greatest consequences.

Patriotism to the ideas of the South had always been an integral part of Southern defensiveness. Probably it had more to do with the South's pugnacity before the Yankee than slavery itself. But now it was enormously expanded. Everything that was Southern became sacrosanct, immune to criticism, an object for pride. Everything that was not Southern became anathema, at least suspect. The result of that was that before long these people who had always had land before the Civil War, who had had their independence, found themselves being sold out and reduced to the status of sharecroppers, white tenants, in order to make a living. Of course on the terms that were available, and those terms were fixed by the Negro's competition. But not even the white man's status of white tenant and sharecropper made him safe from the competition of the Negro. Numbers were so great till it soon became apparent that we were going to

have open conflict, and that is fundamentally the reason
that the South turned to industrialism.

I say that this is fundamentally the reason. I understand
of course that the desire of the early entrepreneurs for profit
played a very great part in the industrialization, the rise of
industrialization, of the South in the 1880's to 1900 and
afterward. But there certainly was also this patriotic motive
of providing a sanctuary for the masses of white men. The
organization of new cotton mills, factories of any sort in the
South, in those early years was often a communal project.
In fact, as late as the war period, the early 1920's, that was
still true to some extent. And the man who built a cotton
mill, who organized it and led the enterprise, was looked
upon as very definitely a community benefactor. And he was,
of course. He felt that himself, and the people granted him
that it was a great public benefaction. But as time went on
it was no longer necessary to make the sacrifices which had
been made in the beginning. Low wages and long hours,
child labor probably, were necessary, at least semi-necessary,
conditions for the early growth of industrialism in the South,
because it had little capital, and the extent to which Northern capital was willing to aid has been greatly exaggerated.

It had positively to lift itself by its own bootstraps and
to do that, for one thing, they made very cheap products
also. To make enough profit on the processing of cheap
cotton goods it was necessary to have low wages, long hours,
and so on. But time passed and it was no longer so necessary.
With this attitude you see that old unreality, the desire to
believe what you like to believe, coming back in there. The
man who built a cotton mill still thought himself to be a
public benefactor whether or not he was actually doing
anything but pursuing his own personal ends. And the attitude of the people remained.

That is the explanation, I think, of the enormous hostility

that has been shown in the South toward the labor union idea. It was somehow an attack on what we call progress, and so an attack against the integrity of the South, the South's right to defend itself in the world.

Now this has been a deliberately critical speech. I haven't tried to cover the whole history of the development of the South. You can't do that in one volume, as I found out. It would take a dozen. But what I have tried to do is to suggest some of the main lines of our development and some of the things that it seems to me most important for us to know to take into account this very great rich land of this Southern country of ours. Texas alone, I believe, has greater resources than all of Europe. Certainly the South is the richest comparable area in the world. Yet we face now a need for renewed sacrifices. As the country moves into the national defense program and we prepare to try to resist totalitarianism, we are going to have to make up our minds there are hardships; but I see no reason at all why we should make up our minds to more hardships, more sacrifices than are necessary under the circumstances.

And it is for that reason that I made this critical speech in which I point out what seems to me to be the vice of unreality, of romanticism, excessive romanticism and excessive sentimentality. I have no desire to attempt to stamp sentiment out of the world. We have had too much of that recently in Europe. But sentimentality is a false sentiment which exists for the purpose of hiding something, for dodging something, and it is a very dangerous vice in the South now. As far as individualism goes, why it can be a great virtue, just as the pride that goes with it can be a great virtue, but it can also be very dangerous if it isn't kept in check by the realization that man after all is a social creature and that none of us has the right to stand outside the social organism.

Thank you.

26

REPORT
FROM MEXICO

(Unpublished manuscript, June 1941)

Cash arrived in Mexico sick and never fully recovered thereafter. In this free-lance effort Cash refers to the Fifth Column element in Mexico, but he calmly cites the views of two opposing observers he had met in a pensión where he and Mrs. Cash stayed during their first week in the country. The man who wrote this piece was quite obviously not himself when he perished under the terrible delusion that the Nazis were hunting him down personally.

*M*exico, D.F., it strikes me as a newcomer, is probably the earth's noisiest city per square inch. All night it roars with the most ominous roar I have ever heard—a roar that still is a long menacing growl away out on the Calle Rio de la Plata where I live, and which is somehow like those somber clouds which hang over Chapultepec, visible from my window.

The growl is punctuated and made complete in its effect by the almost constant shrilling of the lonely policemen's whistles, whose eerie sound must certainly date from the Aztec period. It is overfanciful to say that, awakening suddenly, one can imagine uneasily that old Popocatepetl has stirred at last from his long slumber and is pouring fire and doom down upon the town, or that Huitzilopochtli, the ancient war god, is again on his throne in the great oppressive pile on the Zocalo,[1] with the priests tearing out the smoking hearts of 70,000 captives in his honor. But, to the North American mind, Mexico is an overfanciful city.

By day downtown, one is driven often to seek comparative sanctuary in the Alameda [2] with its muffling screen of old trees.

The explanation seems simple. The Mexican obviously delights in noise with childlike joy. With excuse or without he sounds his horn at least once every thirty seconds. And if he hasn't a horn, he makes up for the lack by the use of his powerful, if most usually tubercular, lungs. Nearly everything on wheels, indeed, does have a horn—buses and streetcars as well as automobiles. And no piddling, half-hearted horns but mighty deep-throated ones, fit to serve battle fleets in the fog.

Contrary to the popular opinion in the United States—to my own, until I came here—the city swarms with automobiles, nearly all of United States make and nearly all relatively new. I have seen fewer jalopies here than anywhere I have been in the last five years. Moreover, the cars run generally to the more expensive makes. The taximen stick largely to the cheaper three, but with private owners Buick seems most popular, with the larger Packards and Cadillacs visible in great numbers. The Mexican, I hear, still holds to the notion that a long black automobile is the best symbol of rank and power, and promptly buys one the moment he can.

Downtown there are a few traffic lights, but for the rest the cars dash about on their own at breakneck speeds. The

---

[1] The principal square of Mexico City.
[2] The city's downtown public park.

drivers are the most skillful I have seen—else the whole automobile population would at once be dead. For the pedestrian, crossing a street is an enterprise to be undertaken only after extreme unction. But the little Indians glide nonchalantly among the speeding machines with cat-foot agility, remaining miraculously unhurt.

More wonderful than the noise and the traffic is the building activity. I have never seen anything like it. Even in Florida in the 1920's the effect was less spectacular, since it was spread over a greater territory. One gets the impression that every other street is being torn up to be rebuilt. And downtown the city gives exactly the effect which I imagine is made by a city which has been heavily bombed and is in process of reconstruction.

The unfinished gridiron building at Juarez and Reforma, with its front knifed away and its walls cracked and seamed (apparently no effort has yet been made to restore it) by the earthquake of last April, adds verisimilitude to the effect. And for block after block the scene is unbrokenly one of old town houses coming down and huge new skyscrapers going up—no flimsy, goods-box skyscrapers like those of much of the American hinterland, but massive and impressive structures, most usually in the pyramid style so often seen in New York, though the influence here seems to be that of Mexico's past.

Nor is it only the downtown district. From my window I can see a dozen apartment houses rising, all in the modern functional manner of which Mexico has become the chief exponent. I can walk fifty feet around the corner and see a dozen more. And throughout the whole so-called "river area" of the city (stretching along the west side of the Paseo de la Reforma from, roughly, the neighborhood opposite the American Embassy to the Heights of Chapultepec), much the same thing is going forward, as also in the Colonia de Valle, the fashionable Heights of Chapultepec, etc.

Perhaps the government employment programs have something to do with all this building activity. But the main occasion for it, I am told, is that the former owners of the *haciendas* have finally about given up hope of getting their government-confiscated lands restored and are pouring into the city to invest their liquid funds in real estate holdings, at once to insure their incomes and in the hope of avoiding further confiscation.

About politics I am much too new here to risk any opinion. I can report, however, that in a single day I have had two diametrically opposed assurances.

One came from a man in the employ of the United States, who for many years has regularly traveled over all Mexico. There is no doubt at all, he told me, that Mexico is solidly lined up in support of the United States foreign policy, and that not only the government but the great majority of the people will back Washington to the hilt if war comes. The Indians out in the country, he admitted, are concerned only with their own affairs and don't much care about the war one way or the other, when they know about it—which isn't often. And the towns swarm with Nazi and Communist agents. But these, he said, have now been decisively defeated and are reduced to gnawing their nails in rage, while the great body of the people who are concerned with political matters are lined up behind the government.

The other assurance came from a studious young woman from the western United States who has been down here for two years and who is an intimate of a number of Mexican journalists of decided anti-Nazi sympathies. According to her report, the Good Neighbor policy has been successful only in superficial ways. Even in the government, she alleged, only the foreign minister and the education minister are really wholehearted in their commitments to Washington. Furthermore, she said, the government is far from really enjoying the support of a majority of the people, won the last election [3] only by fraud and force, and the nation is actually divided about fifty-fifty between pro-Americans and pro-Nazis. After all, they say (according to her), it is the Gringo and the British who have done everything evil to us in the past. Sure, probably the only reason the German didn't do it was that he had no chance. Even so . . .

I offer these opinions entirely without prejudice, having, as I say, formed none of my own.

Viewpoint: A friend of ours, another U.S. employee, just missed trouble the other evening. Invited out to make a night of it by two young Mexican officers, he had regretfully to decline because of a previous engagement. The two officers went on anyway, and in the course of their celebration got into a fight with the police, were finally jailed after a long battle when the cops' whistles brought reinforcements to their aid. Next day, when the judge began to lecture the officers, still somewhat in their cups, on their duty toward the civil authority, they attacked him also. Now, of course, they are in trouble up to their necks. A captain in the army shook his head sadly when he talked to our friend about it. It was, he avowed with choler, a disgrace to the army. Yes, a burning disgrace. Any army officer should know that the way to deal with cops was to sock them quick and hard and then get away fast before they had time to bring up aid.

---

[3] That of 1940, in which Manuel Avila Camacho defeated Juan Andreu Almazán.

INDEX

i

Index

Index

Index

A Note About the Author

JOSEPH L. MORRISON, a native of New York City, became a Phi Beta Kappa graduate of the University of North Carolina not long before Pearl Harbor. Postwar, he received his M.A. in history from Columbia University and his Ph.D. in history from Duke University. Since his return from World War II military service he has been teaching at the University of North Carolina at Chapel Hill, where he is now a professor in the School of Journalism. His last previously published book is *Josephus Daniels: The Small-d Democrat* (1966). Dr. Morrison has also written articles for *American Heritage, Virginia Quarterly Review, Journalism Quarterly,* and other publications.

A Note On the Type

The text of this book is set in Caledonia, a typeface designed by W(illiam) A(ddison) Dwiggins for the Mergenthaler Linotype Company in 1939. Dwiggins chose to call his new typeface Caledonia, the Roman name for Scotland, because it was inspired by the Scotch types cast about 1833 by Alexander Wilson & Son, Glasgow type founders. However, there is a calligraphic quality about this face that is totally lacking in the Wilson types. Dwiggins referred to an even earlier typeface for this "liveliness of action"—one cut around 1790 by William Martin for the printer William Bulmer. Caledonia has more weight than the Martin letters, and the bottom finishing strokes (serifs) of the letters are cut straight across, without brackets, to make sharp angles with the upright stems, thus giving a "modern face" appearance.

W. A. Dwiggins (1880–1956) was born in Martinsville, Ohio, and studied art in Chicago. In 1904 he moved to Hingham, Massachusetts, where he built a solid reputation as a designer of advertisements and as a calligrapher. He began an association with the Mergenthaler Linotype Company in 1929, and over the next twenty-seven years designed a number of book types for that firm. Of especial interest are the Metro series, Electra, Caledonia, Eldorado, and Falcon. In 1930, Dwiggins first became interested in marionettes, and through the years he made many important contributions to the art of puppetry and the design of marionettes.

Composed, printed, and bound by American Book-Stratford Press, Inc., New York, N.Y. Typography and binding design by ANITA KARL.